AMERICAN CULINARY ART

AMERICAN CULINARY ART

By
AUGUST FORSTER

COACHWHIP PUBLICATIONS
Greenville, Ohio

American Culinary Art, by August Forster
© 2018 Coachwhip Publications

First published 1951; 1958 edition reprinted.
No claims made on public domain material.
Cover image: Knives © JamesJames2541

CoachwhipBooks.com

ISBN 1-61646-451-8
ISBN-13 978-1-61646-451-6

I dedicate this Book
to my wife
FRIEDA FORSTER
who was so helpful
in its making.

August Forster

Preface

The purpose of culinary art is fine presentation of food, a subject on which emphasis is very much needed today. It is my intention to reveal some techniques in vegetable carving for which I have become known. I wish to present these to young and old with the assurance that they also can learn these methods, providing they are willing and interested enough to practice a few hours a day for two or three weeks.

We all like nice things, whether they are made to wear or to eat. The compliments derived from carefully practiced culinary art are very satisfying. Commercial use of this art will mean increased profits of many times the price of this book.

Vegetable carving and platter decoration are part of this art. As you practice, you will want to do more each day. It is fascinating work, and this book will start you with simple items and lead to more intricate ones. As you progress and become accomplished in this art, you will find yourself in great demand and may become a professional culinary expert on food presentation.

There is no limit to what you can do with food and platter decoration. New creative thoughts will come even as you are engaged in a simple design.

A book of this type has never before been published, yet, information on this subject is in demand throughout the country. Artist's drawings have been used in most cases instead of photographs as the latter do not show finished products exactly enough for demonstration and teaching.

I have experienced many happy, harmonious, and profitable hours as a cook in my youth, and, later, as a Chef, and I attribute all this to my knowledge of this art. This book, then, makes available to all who have the earnest desire to learn, the theory and practice of American culinary art.

AUGUST FORSTER

Contents

	Pages
Tools and Equipment for Vegetable Carving	12-15
Hors d'Oeuvres, Canapes, and Sandwiches	16-40
Platter Decoration	41-49
How to Carve Meats and Fish	50-61
How to Prepare and Decorate Ham	62-73
How to Prepare and Decorate Chicken	74-81
How to Prepare and Decorate Fish and Lobster	82-87
How to Serve Pheasant	88-91
How to Make Rice Socles	92-102
Butter Service	103-107
Decorating with Vegetables	108-129
Flower Carving	130-143
Figure Carving	144-157
Potato Baskets	158-163
Fruit Carving	164-183
Napkin Folding	184-197
Table Setting	198-205
Cocoa and Chocolate Painting	206-213
Working with Gum Paste	214-216
Sugar Icing	217-218
Decorating with Sugar	218-229
Wax Work	231-237
Sculpture Work	238-243
Clay Designs	244-248
Candle Molds	249-253

AMERICAN CULINARY ART

Tools and Equipment for Vegetable Carving

The tools and equipment used for vegetable carving vary according to the efficiency of the individual. The little French paring knife will do the trick at the beginning. On the opposite page are pictures of tools and equipment needed. Following are their names and descriptions.

No. 1. Small jar of fruit coloring in paste form. You also can get this in liquid form. This is obtainable at any large restaurant or bakers' supply house.

No. 2. Small French paring knife with three-inch blade and very pointed. This is the most essential tool.

No. 3. Also a French knife with an eight-inch blade. It is used for cutting larger vegetables in shapes or proper forms.

No. 4. A Parisian spoon or scoop, used to cut round balls of vegetable or fruit. It is obtainable in any cutlery store.

No. 5. A grooved pantry knife, used to cut vegetables or fruits in fancy ways instead of merely slicing.

No. 6. Instrument made of wood and steel called the Gauferet potato slicer, used for slicing potatoes.

No. 7. Common potato peeler.

No. 8. Sheet-metal tube full of round cutters of various sizes, used to cut round objects or half-moon shapes. They are imported from Europe It is called a column cutter, but is seldom obtainable, 12 different sizes.

No. 9. Tin box full of tools of various designs. This also is imported, but a good tool and die maker often can make them from the pictures.

No. 10. Common scissors.

No. 11. Egg slicer.

No. 12. Carving tools, obtainable in any art store, and used for cutting grooves, etc.

Nos. 13 and 14. Tin boxes of large round cutters. One is plain, the other zigzag. Each contains 12 sizes, used for cutting round or half-round objects.

No. 15. Glass with brushes, used for coloring, and a ruler.

No. 16. Butter curler. Insert into hot water and pull along top of butter forming round butter curls to be served on the table.

No. 17. Shoestring machine. Insert potato in teeth and turn handle to form a string three to five feet long. These are the real shoestring potatoes.

No. 18. We use wire of various thicknesses to attach to the leaves we carve, especially when they are to be put into a vase.

No. 19. Wire used for basket form.

No. 20. Wire used for handles of baskets and vases.

No. 21. Reinforcement wire for carvings when needed, for large pieces.

No. 22. Shows how leaves can be attached to thin wire and placed in vases or bouquets.

15

Hors d'Oeuvre, Canapes, and Sandwiches

It is the intention of the writer to give you a selection from which to get ideas. Since hors d'oeuvres are a combination of cold dishes, there are no specified rules to follow. Your own combination might be as good as any of these. The important thing is to have them presented properly and artistically.

Hors d'oeuvres and canapes are well liked by the American people. I have given you 48 dishes from which to choose to give you an idea of the variety possible. After you have made them several times, you will find them easy to make. Many of the ingredients are found in cans. The other items are salt, pepper, vinegar, oil, and mayonnaise. It is important, of course, to know how much of each item to use and the proper seasoning. Serve food for hors d'oeuvres as plainly as possible. Canapes, on the other hand, must be well decorated.

Serving sandwiches should also have your attention. It is important that you arrange them artistically. I have presented here some ideas along this line, including ways to serve them on round, square, or long platters. Remember, always use a green garnish.

Bread and Rolls for Sandwiches

In making sandwiches and canapes, we must be aware of the differences in breads and select them carefully. It is not correct to use the same bread for the entire party. Select your own combinations of breads. There are many to choose from, so I am giving you eleven different kinds, and, also, hard and soft rolls.

It is wise to have bread made in advance for large parties, and made in large pullman or sandwich loaves. This enables you to cut lengthwise slices. Always cover sandwiches with a moist cloth to prevent drying out. Do not toast bread until it becomes too dry. The crusts which are trimmed can be saved for bread crumbs.

1. White Bread
2. Pullman-Bread or Sandwich Bread
3. French Bread
4. Bran Bread
5. Raisin Bread
6. Vienna Bread
7. Whole Wheat Bread
8. Rye Bread
9. Potato Bread
10. Boston Brown Bread
11. Pumpernickel Bread
12. Dinner Rolls
    Parker House Rolls
    Round and Long Buns

Principal Breads and Rolls used for Appetizers and Sandwiches.

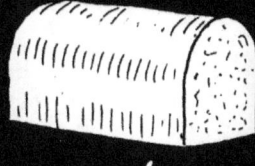
1.

2.

3.

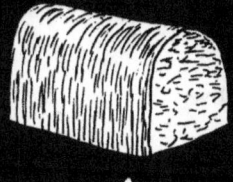
4.

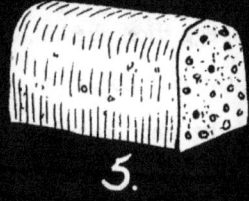
5.

6.

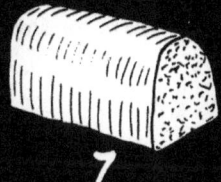
7.

8.

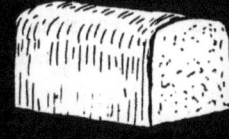
9.

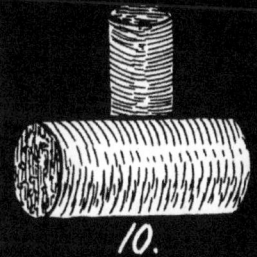
10.

Rolls.
Dinner-Rolls.
Parker House Rolls.
Buns
Round and Long
12.

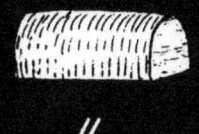
11.

Garnishes for Sandwiches and Cold Meats

No. 1. Gherkin, olive, radish, lettuce leaf, parsley.

No. 2. Radish, parsley, olives.

No. 3. Radishes, parsley.

No. 4. Gherkin, green and black olives, parsley.

No. 5. Half pickle, tomato slice, radish, parsley.

No. 6. Sliced tomato, olive, radish, parsley.

No. 7. Sliced cucumbers, green onion, olive, radish, pickle.

No. 8. Celery, radish, hot pepper, green olives.

No. 9. Three tomato slices, egg slice, gherkin, olives.

No. 10. Two tomato slices, two cucumber slices, radish, olive.

No. 11. Potato salad, sliced egg, gherkin, olives.

No. 12. Stuffed eggs, beets, radish, pickle, vinaigrette sauce.

No. 13. Asparagus, tomatoes, eggs, pimento, olives, pickles, parsley.

No. 14. For fish: two lemon slices, sliced radishes, tartare sauce, two fan-shaped gherkins, parsley.

No. 15. For steak: French fried potatoes, grilled onions, cole-slaw, tomatoes, olives, radish, green onions, pickles.

Garnishings for Sandwiches and Cold Meats.

1. 2. 3.
4. 5. 6.
7. 8. 9.
10. 11. 12.
13. 14. 15.

Sandwiches, Open and Closed

There is a great demand for sandwiches, but many people offer little variety. So, I am going to give you different designs from which you can select those you prefer. Remember, a tea sandwich is different from a sandwich made for a large party.

No. 1. Shows a plain sandwich cut from corner to corner and placed on a plate as in No. 2. If the sandwich is cut along the dotted line, it makes a finger sandwich.

No. 2. This is the general arrangement of a sandwich.

No. 3. Rye bread sandwich cut in half and the halves placed next to each other.

No. 4. This sandwich is cut from corner to corner and trimmed as shown by dotted lines. It can be arranged as shown in Nos. 5 and 6.

No. 7. Bread or toast can be cut with forms in round shapes, stars, or hearts, as shown in Nos. 8 and 9.

No. 10. Cut bread in half-moons with a round cutter and arrange as shown in No. 11.

No. 12. Hard or soft, long or round rolls are used for sandwiches.

No. 13. Triangular slices are popular and attractive.

No. 14. Long pullman bread is thinly sliced and buttered, then covered with sandwich spread. This is rolled up and placed in wax paper to hold shape. Keep in cooler for several hours, and then slice in oblong slices.

No. 15. French or Vienna bread sandwiches are made with thick slices of buttered bread, and meat, chicken, or cheese on top. This is especially recommended for bar service.

Open and Closed Sandwiches

1.
2.
3.
4.
5.
6.
7.
8.
9.
10.
11.
12.
13.
14.
15.

Canapes

No. 1. PEANUT BUTTER. Slice of white or raisin bread is toasted and peanut butter spread over it. Decorate with butter cream or Philadelphia cream cheese along the sides. Lettuce leaves are placed on each side with three black olives on one and two large walnuts on the other. Put another large piece of walnut meat on top.

No. 2. HAM. One slice of any bread toasted and buttered. Cover with a cut of boiled ham. Make a border of thinly sliced radishes and place on each side. Place lettuce leaves on each side and a slice of tomato. A pickle slice cut in a fan is on top of the tomato slice. Opposite the tomato, place one green and one black olive. Ham canapes also can be made of raw, smoked, or Virginia ham.

No. 3. SALAMI. Toast a slice of white bread and butter it well. Place a thin slice of salami or summer sausage on every inch. Place half of a black or green olive in each corner of the canape. Set four lettuce leaves at corners. Cut a hard-boiled egg in quarters and place in corners. Two small gherkins, cut fan shape, can be placed on each side of the egg. In the middle, place almond stuffed olives on opposite sides.

No. 4. SLICED CHICKEN. Chicken canapes are made on buttered toast. Use white meat only, sliced thin and placed artistically on the toast. Use two lettuce leaves, one with three radishes, the other with two green onions. At top side, put two green and two black olives with a single whole gherkin.

No. 5. ROAST BEEF. Place a medium rare slice of center cut roast beef on a piece of buttered toast. Cut in half two green gherkins and form into fan shapes. Place one in each corner on top of canape. Place a lettuce leaf on each side. On one side place four or five asparagus tips with red pimento strips over them. On the other side, place German potato salad with fine chopped parsley.

No. 6. LIVER SAUSAGE. Toast and butter bread. Spread liver sausage on and decorate by making star-shape designs in each corner. These are made of large black olives. Cut a leaf out of hard-boiled egg whites. When you have made the design, cut in half and use one-half of the olive and one-half of the egg white to build a star. In between, you can place a stuffed green olive slice. Place two lettuce leaves on the sides. One has a tomato slice, the other a radish and two green olives.

No. 7. BEEF TONGUE. Place thin slices of boiled smoked beef tongue on buttered toast. Place lettuce leaves on sides, one with two tomato quarters, and the other with a green olive, a black olive, a radish, and two gherkins cut in half and in fan shapes.

No. 8. Roast Tenderloin. Place slices of medium roast tenderloin on buttered toast with a little horseradish. Place lettuce leaves on sides, one with two green olives and a radish, the other with carrot salad cut in matches. On the other sides, place artichoke bottoms filled with pea salad.

No. 9. Roast Sirloin. Roast sirloin may require two slices of well-buttered toast. Lettuce leaves on the sides contain string bean salad and four slices of tomato, two half gherkins, and four black olives.

No. 10. Assorted Cheeses. Cut cheeses in decorative styles. Butter toast and put a bit of German mustard with a little horseradish juice on it. Cheeses may be served in any assortment. Serve stuffed celery on the lettuce leaf and, on the opposite side, stuffed olives with pimento cheese.

No. 11. Melted Cheese. Melted cheese canapes usually are served hot. Butter toast and place cheese on top. Place under broiler or into oven and slowly melt. When melted, place two strips of broiled bacon on it. Serve extra slices of toast with it. You can add olives and radishes.

No. 12. Plain Cheese. They can be made on buttered toast from American cheese, Roquefort cheese, cream cheese, or any other cheese, such as Swiss cheese.

No. 13. Chicken Liver. Cut raw chicken liver in half and sautee in butter with a little pepper and bay leaves for five minutes. Press through a fine sieve. Mix with soft butter, to an amount 1/3 of the liver. Add seasoning to taste together with a little Madeira wine. Spread this thickly over the toast. On the border put butter cream, and in the middle, a double star of green pepper and red pimento. At the sides, place two leaves of fresh lettuce with a thick slice of tomato on each together with stuffed olive slices and hard-boiled egg quarters.

No. 14. Asparagus Vinaigrette Canape. Buttered toast is cut lengthwise. Cooked and cooled asparagus is placed on top with two slices of pimento. Lettuce leaves on each side have fine chopped hard-boiled eggwhites on one, and on the other a thick slice of fresh tomato and a quarter of hard-boiled egg. In the middle, place egg yolks, fine chopped parsley and capers. Serve plain French dressing in a separate dish.

No. 15. Tartar Steak. This steak is ground beef tenderloin seasoned with salt and pepper, fine chopped onions, paprika, and raw egg mixed into the steak. Served raw as a steak, it has a raw egg yolk in the middle. Serve on toast with lettuce leaves on each side. One has two olives stuffed with anchovy, and a gherkin cut in fan shape. The other has a few slices of tomato, fine chopped onions, capers, paprika, and chopped parsley. On the extra slice of canape, place anchovy fillets cross ways. On the side, place hard-boiled egg quarters.

No. 16. CAVIAR. Sprinkle lemon juice over well-buttered toast. Spread caviar thickly on toast. Make a decorative border of butter cream on each side. Lettuce leaves on sides have fine chopped onion, capers, egg yolks, parsley, and an egg quarter on one; Russian salad, two fan-shaped gherkins, and two fresh lemon slices on the other.

No. 17. SARDINES. Cover buttered toast with fine sardines. Place them in alternate positions, head next to tail. Sprinkle with fine chopped onions and chopped parsley. On sides, place lettuce leaves with caper, fine chopped egg yolks, fine chopped eggwhite, and chopped parsley. On the third leaf, place thin slices tomato or cucumber, and on the fourth leaf, an egg quarter, two pickles cut in fan shape, and one green and one black olive.

No. 18. STANDING SARDINES. Place one slice of toast on the bottom. Cut another slice in half and place at each end. Sardines are placed in a pyramid shape and held together with a few onion or green pepper rings. Asparagus tips are placed on each side of the sardines, with two pimento strips over them. Garnish is as described above.

No. 19. HERRING. Cut herring lengthwise to fit toast. First, butter and spread canape with lemon juice. Two leaves of lettuce are placed on the dish, one covered with sliced marinated onions (these come in a glass container or barrel), and two slices of lemon. On the other leaf, place three olives with a fan-shaped pickle.

No. 20. SMOKED SALMON. Spread buttered toast with horseradish juice. Place thin slices of salmon on it in perfect order. When toast is covered, press slices with knife. Decorate sides with thinly sliced radish or butter cream. On one lettuce leaf, place beet salad with fan-shaped pickle, and on the other leaf, place two lemon slices with an egg quarter.

No. 21. SHRIMP SALAD. Cooked shrimp are cut into quarters and made into a salad. Place in a dish, cover with heavy mayonnaise, and then decorate. Flower leaves are made of blanched leeks. The flower is made of hard-boiled eggwhites, and the border of capers evenly spaced. On lettuce leaves on sides, place half-round toast pieces with whole shrimp set in mayonnaise and uncovered. At each end, place gherkin cut in fan shape.

No. 22. ANCHOVY. Place fillets of anchovy at an angle on buttered toast. Make a border of buttered cream on top. Roll anchovy around finger and place along sides as shown in picture, filling anchovy ring with caper. On one of the lettuce leaves, place a lemon quarter, a tomato quarter, and two gherkin slices.

On the other leaf, place one-half hard-boiled egg stuffed with small chopped onions, vinaigrette dressing, and gherkin cut in fan shape.

No. 23. LOBSTER CANAPE. Butter toast and spread with a little horseradish mustard. Make a salad from sliced lobster meat. Let meat stand for an hour in vinegar, oil, salt and pepper, then place in order on toast. In each corner of the canape, place a lobster claw sprinkled with a little fresh fine chopped parsley. At each side of the toast, is a thick slice of hard-boiled egg. At ends, place lettuce leaves. In one, place the lobster head with two pickles cut in fan shapes. On the other lettuce leaf, place a thick round slice of tomato, with capers on top and two lemon slices on each side.

No. 24. LOBSTER SALAD CANAPE. Cut lobster into small pieces and make into a salad. Let it stand for two hours. Place salad on buttered toast and cover with heavy mayonnaise. Decorate border with butter cream. Make dice of eggwhites, using black olive for the dots. Place a lettuce leaf in each corner diagonally, and on each, put a lobster claw with a slice of hard-boiled egg and small slices of lobster claw meat. Arrange these slices around the egg, with two lobster head shells as a garnish.

No. 25. SHRIMP. Open shrimp canape is made as was the open lobster canape. Cut shrimp in half lengthwise to fit canape. Garnish with asparagus tips, hard-boiled eggs, tomato quarters, and one or two olives.

No. 26. GOOSE LIVER. This is an expensive dish, so we trim bread in fancy patterns. Cut two half-moon slices, and two angle slices. These are toasted and buttered. Place goose liver on the large slice. You can make it yourself, or buy in cans ready for use. Place pimento in each corner of this large slice. On lettuce leaves, place mushrooms, salad, stuffed olives, and fan-shaped gherkins.

No. 27. CHICKEN SALAD. Butter toast and spread with horseradish mustard. Place chicken salad on toast and cover with mayonnaise. Using a small tube, make butter cream designs on it, placing a caper in each square. Make a border of stuffed olive slices. At one end of the canape, place two quarters of hard-boiled eggs, and on the opposite side, two quarters of fresh tomato. On the lettuce leaf, place two thick slices of tomato stuffed with vegetable salad, with sliced radishes and two fan-shaped gherkins around them.

No. 28. FISH SALAD. These canapes can be made of any kind of fish salad. Remove bones from cooked fish. Fish salad is spread on buttered toast and covered with mayonnaise. It can be decorated with flowers made out of blanched leek, or green pepper skin. The flower center is made of hard-boiled egg yolks. The petals are made out of hard-boiled eggwhites or lobster claws cut in thin slices. On each lettuce leaf, place a quarter of tomato, two fan-shaped gherkins, and four stuffed olives. Also, add tomato slices, hard-boiled egg slices, and lemon slices.

No. 29. SMOKED SALMON CORNETS. Toast is buttered and spread with a little mayonnaise. Salmon cornets are thin slices of salmon wound around your finger to form a point at one end. Fill cornets with vegetable salad, so that they will hold their shapes. On each lettuce leaf, place thick slices of tomato with two hard-boiled egg quarters and two slices of lemon on the sides.

No. 30. SOMBRERO CANAPE. Butter toast, and form sombreros of almost any kind of sausage. Cut a round slice of sausage. Cut from the middle of the sausage to the rim. Take the two corners, and bend one corner to the right, and one corner to the left, crossing each other until they meet in a funnel shape. Bend the bottom of the funnel up about $\frac{1}{4}$ inch all around. Put a toothpick in both corners to hold the sombrero together. Place on the canape together with hard-boiled eggs, slices of tomatoes, and two artichoke bottoms filled with vegetable salad. A few extra cornets can be placed all around the center. Glaze several times with aspic and remove the toothpick. Sombreros will then hold their shape.

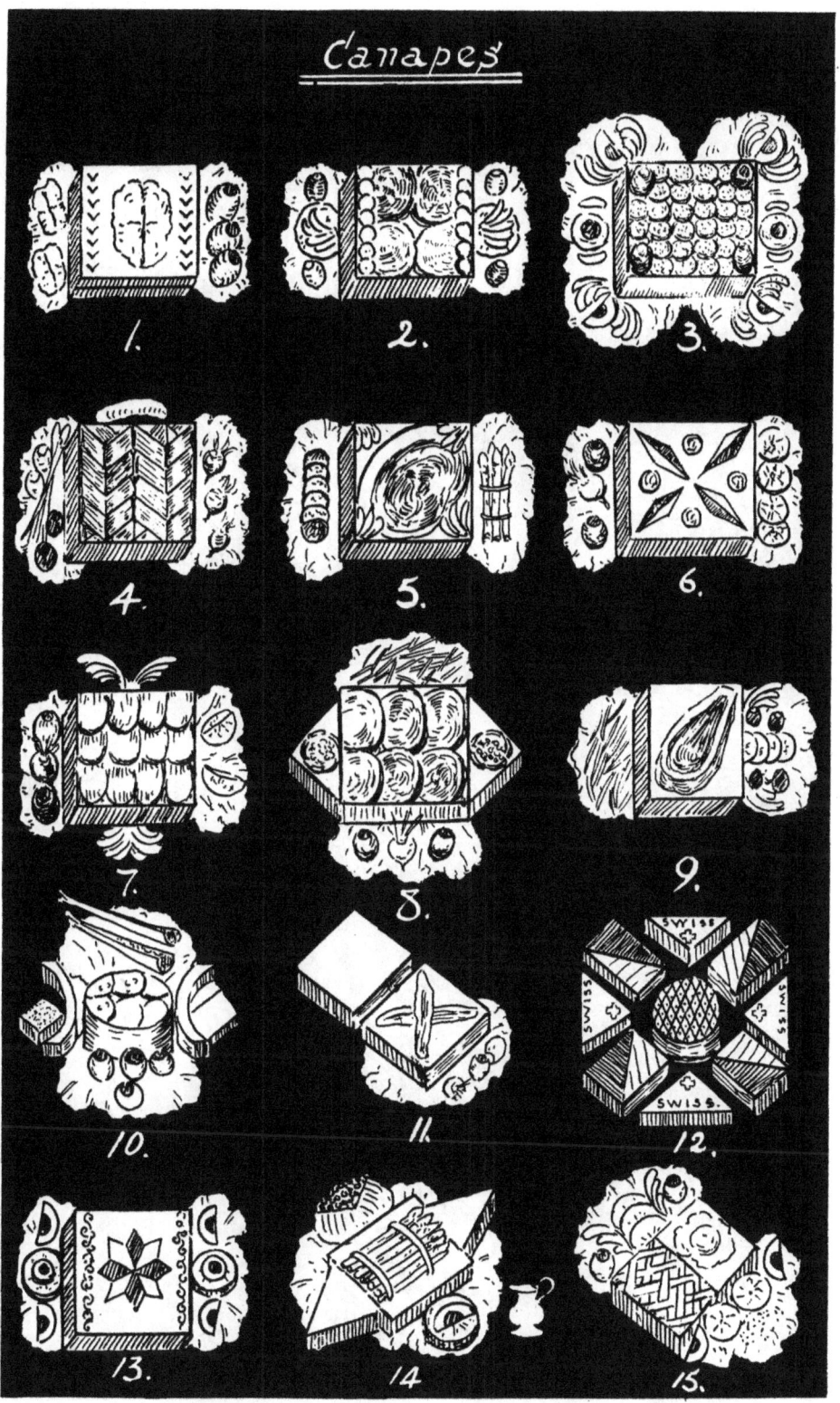

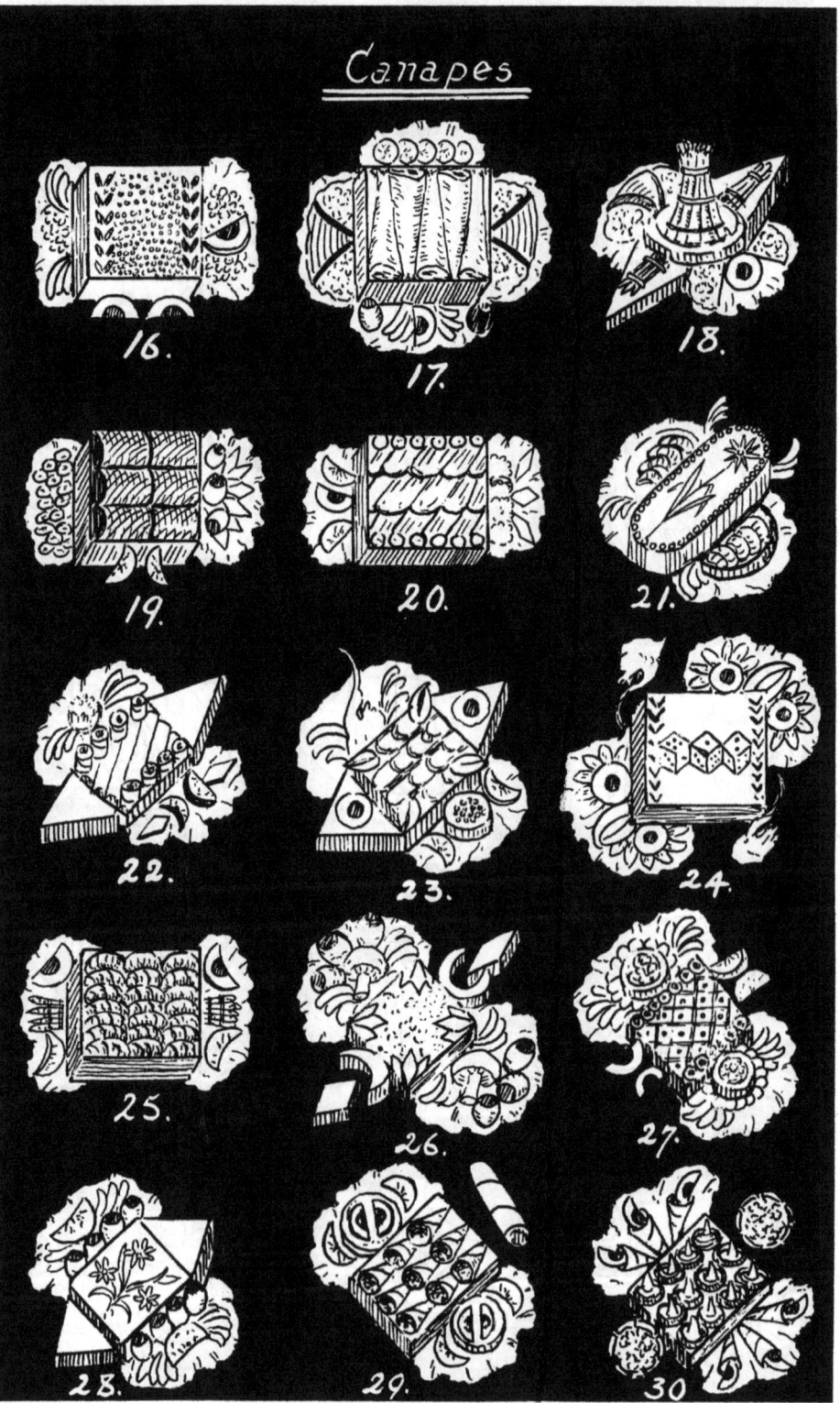

How to Create an Appetizer Platter

On a piece of paper the size of the platter, draw the design. Cut it out and place each individual design on toast or bread. Cut the bread exactly as the paper design shows.

As soon as bread pieces are cut out, lay them on platter to keep design from getting mixed. It might be advisable to have a duplicate pattern intact as a guide when assembling the design. When canapes are on the platter properly, place a moist towel over them to keep them from becoming dry and rolling up. As you cover the canapes with food, keep in mind the appetizing and attractive qualities of soft colors.

This picture shows how exactly we can fit these canapes together and with what a pleasing color combination. The middle star is made out of caviar and cream cheese. The diamond canape outside the star is Green Lobster Coral canape. The dark three-cornered canape is Red Pimento canape. The ring is made of butter and cream or cream cheese with a few black olive pieces on four sides.

The outer canapes of the ring consist of anchovies on all four points. The others are sardines, egg slices, white tuna, salmon, with a few sliced gherkins all around. Butter cream, or cream cheese, as a border should only be used for the inner ring and large star. Serve with parsley and cut lemons, a few fan shaped gherkin.

New Ideas for arranging Fancy Sandwiches

Hors d'Oeuvre

The following are descriptions of the pictured dishes.

No. 1. Goose liver rolled in salmon and asparagus tips glazed with aspic.

No. 2. Ham cornets filled with aspic and hard-boiled eggs cut in quarters.

No. 3. Sardines in oil or covered with vinaigrette sauce.

No. 4. Fried shrimp, bacon, or shelled and blanched almonds rolled in anchovys.

No. 5. Sliced tuna fish in oil or covered with vinaigrette sauce.

No. 6. Olives stuffed with blanched almonds, cream cheese, pimentos, or sardines.

No. 7. Sliced tomatoes with fine chopped onions, vinegar, and oil.

No. 8. Salami cornets filled with julienne of raw celery root salad.

No. 9. Artistic potato-salad potatoes should be cooked with jackets on a day before eating. Peel next day, and, with a round cutter, cut out uniform slices. Place on a platter with bacon or French dressing over them.

No. 10. Alaskan salmon steaks cooked in salt water, vinegar, lemon juice, and white wine. Use sufficient liquid to cover the fish. When fish is cooked, let it cool. It can be served as it is, or with mayonnaise, vinaigrette sauce, or Thousand Island dressing.

No. 11. Fresh mushrooms cut in rosettes and rubbed with lemon juice. Poach in butter, white wine, a little vinegar, oil, salt and pepper, with enough liquid to cover mushrooms. When cold, add fine chopped chives. Cooking time 15 minutes.

No. 12. Fresh asparagus cooked green. When cooked, place neatly on top of each other. Two strips of pimento with vinaigrette sauce or mayonnaise are served on the sides.

No. 13. Imported caviar served in the original container. Fine chopped hard-boiled egg yolks are strained through a sieve as are egg whites. These and fine chopped onions are each in a separate dish. A carved rose or swan should be served with it. This dish can be placed on an ice sockel, or a swan, horse, or eagle carved of ice can be placed in the center with finger sandwiches or melba toast around it.

No. 14. STRINGBEAN SALAD. Cut fresh stringbeans lengthwise in halves and cook fast in salt water. When cooked, pour off water and add ice cold water to retain the green color. If possible, add ice to beans or keep changing the water. When cold, add fine chopped onions, parsley, salt, pepper, vinegar, and oil.

No. 15. PRESSED CUCUMBER SALAD WITH SOUR CREAM. Slice peeled cucumbers very thin, sprinkle with salt and pepper. Let stand one hour, then place in a towel and press out salt water. Add chopped onions, parsley, vinegar, oil.

No. 16. LOBSTER SALAD. Cut cooked lobsters in flakes. Chop celery and onions, and season with salt, pepper, tabasco, worcestershire, mayonnaise, or vinegar and oil. Mix well and cover lobster. Decorate top with meat from the lobster claws cut into slices from which you can form flowers.

17. OPEN LOBSTER SALAD. Dice cooked lobsters. Cut celery and add to fine chopped onions, salt, pepper, tabasco sauce, worcestershire, vinegar and oil well mixed. Decorate with claws and head of the lobster.

No. 18. HALF-STUFFED COLD LOBSTER. Dice lobsters and make into a salad as described above. Cover with mayonnaise and decorate with anchovy fillets cut in half, or with olives or eggs.

No. 19. FILLET OF WINE HERRING. These come prepared in cans or jars, and in small wooden kegs.

No. 20. STUFFED TOMATO SURPRISE. Blanch and peel fresh tomatoes and trim the top slightly. Remove the inside and fill with any kind of salad—fish, meat, chicken, fruit, or seafood. Then cover with heavy mayonnaise and, using the top and stem from parsley, form as an apple.

No. 21. POACHED FILLET OF SOLE. Take raw fillet of sole and overlap in a casserole prepared with butter. Sprinkle with chopped onions, a bit of salt, and a liquid made from white wine and water in equal parts together with a little vinegar and lemon juice. This liquid must cover the fish. Poach it for 10 minutes and set aside to cool. Place fish in dish and pour liquid over. Add fresh chopped parsley. You also can use Mayonnaise and whipped cream mixed together in equal parts to pour over the fish.

No. 22. Hard-boiled egg salad arranged properly, with French dressing.

No. 23. Fresh pea salad made as was the stringbean salad.

No. 24. MARINATED CELERY. Use hearts of celery only. Make a liquid of one glass of white wine, half glass of vinegar, one glass of salad oil, one bay leaf, 2 cloves, piece of garlic, and a little salt and pepper. Cook for 10 minutes, add celery, and cook for 15 minutes. Set away to cool. Place in a dish and sprinkle with chopped parsley.

No. 25. Marinated leeks are prepared as was the celery.

No. 26. SALAMI MEXICAN HATS. Make a cut from the middle of each slice of salami and cut outward on only one side. Roll around your finger so it will form a point. When you have finished the cone, roll up the border and fasten cone with a toothpick. This is a sombrero.

No. 27. CARROT SALAD JARDINIERE. Cut carrots into 1 inch lengths the thickness of macaroni. Cook in salt water. When cold, season with salt, pepper, vinegar, oil, and fresh chopped parsley.

No. 28. ASSORTED COLD MEATS PROPPERLY ARRANGED.

No. 29. ROAST BEEF.

No. 30. ASSORTED CHEESES ON PLATTER.

No. 31. BREAST OF SLICED TURKEY, CHICKEN, OR DUCK.

No. 32. Cold decorated breast of chicken with carrot salad.

No. 33. Salmon salad covered with mayonnaise decorated with pimento, leeks, and fresh tomato peels, and truffles.

No. 34. Patty shells filled with caviar, lobster, or shrimp salad.

No. 35. HEARTS OF ARTICHOKES. These often come in cans, but you can make them yourself by boiling fresh whole artichokes and cutting out the inner portion. Place into the celery marinade, and let stand overnight.

No. 36. WHOLE ARTICHOKE VINAIGRETTE. Cut off two inches of the top and remove the fuzzy inside. Cut off bottom and rub with lemon. Tie string around artichoke to hold leaves in place. Cook in salt water until the bottom of the artichoke is cooked completely. Let cool, place on a platter, and cover with vinaigrette sauce. Serve on large lettuce leaf.

No. 37. CRAWFISH TAIL SALAD. Cook crawfish in salt water and peel. Make into salad as was the lobster salad. Serve open or covered with mayonnaise.

No. 38. SHRIMP SALAD. Made the same as lobster salad, and covered with mayonnaise and decorated with olives, leeks, and pimentos.

No. 39. STUFFED DEVILED EGGS. Cut hard-boiled eggs in half. Cut edges zig-zag to get two halves as shown here. Remove yolks and press them through a fine sieve. Add salt and pepper, a little worcestershire, a little English mustard, a little horseradish, a little soft butter, and mix well. Add to pastry bag with a star tube and refill egg halves. Place parsley all around and serve with cut lemons.

No. 40. BLUE BROOK TROUT. Kill live fresh brook trout and clean with as little handling as possible. Place on a platter and sprinkle vinegar all over.

Let stand three minutes. Make a stock of salt water, half glass of vinegar to quart of water, a lemon cut in slices, one slice of onion, fresh parsley, one stalk of celery, whole pepper, one bay leaf. Let this cook ten minutes. Slide fish into this stock, and let come to a boil. Remove from stove and cover well. Let stand for 15 minutes and fish will be cooked. This fish can now be served hot with melted butter. It also can be removed from stock and placed on a rack and covered with aspic. This is seldom decorated as you want to see the blue color of the fish. This is served cold with mayonnaise on a separate dish.

No. 41. ARTICHOKE BOTTOMS. Canned artichoke bottoms can be flaked and made into salad. Or, leave them whole and fill with salads such as pea, celery, and fish.

No. 42. ASPIC TIMBALES. Add chicken aspic to timbales which are decorated with stuffed olive slices. Aspic must be strong in flavor and perfectly clear.

No. 43. IMPORTED GOOSE LIVER. Decorate with truffles, place on a platter, and decorate border of platter with aspic. They are often served in Ice Sockels.

No. 44. LAMB TONGUES. These may be canned with remoulade sauce over them. Remoulade sauce is made as follows: add one cup of mayonnaise, 1 teaspoon full of fine chopped shallots, 1 teaspoon fine chopped parsley, 1 teaspoon fine cut chives and green peppers, 2 tablespoons full of fine chopped hard-boiled eggs mixed well with mayonnaise. You can use onions instead of shallots.

No. 45. SLICED NEW BEET SALAD.

No. 46. COLESLAW.

No. 47. LOST EGGS. Cold poached eggs are placed on a platter with the following sauce: Half mayonnaise, half whipped cream. Eggs can be decorated with truffles, olives, pimentos, tomatoes, or leeks. This is very attractive.

No. 48. Roast chicken cut into pieces.

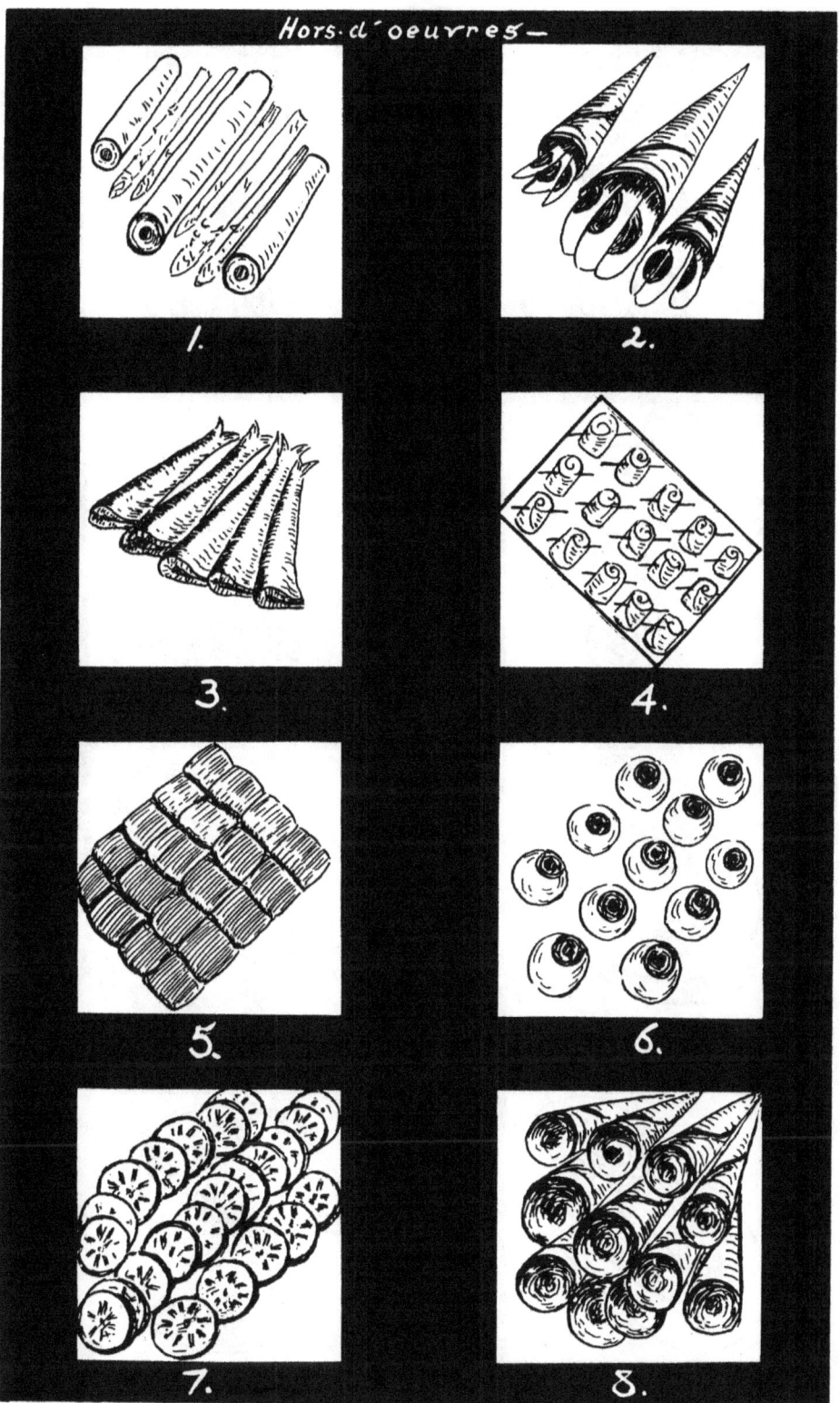

Hors d'oeuvres —

9.

10.

11.

12.

13.

14.

15.

16.

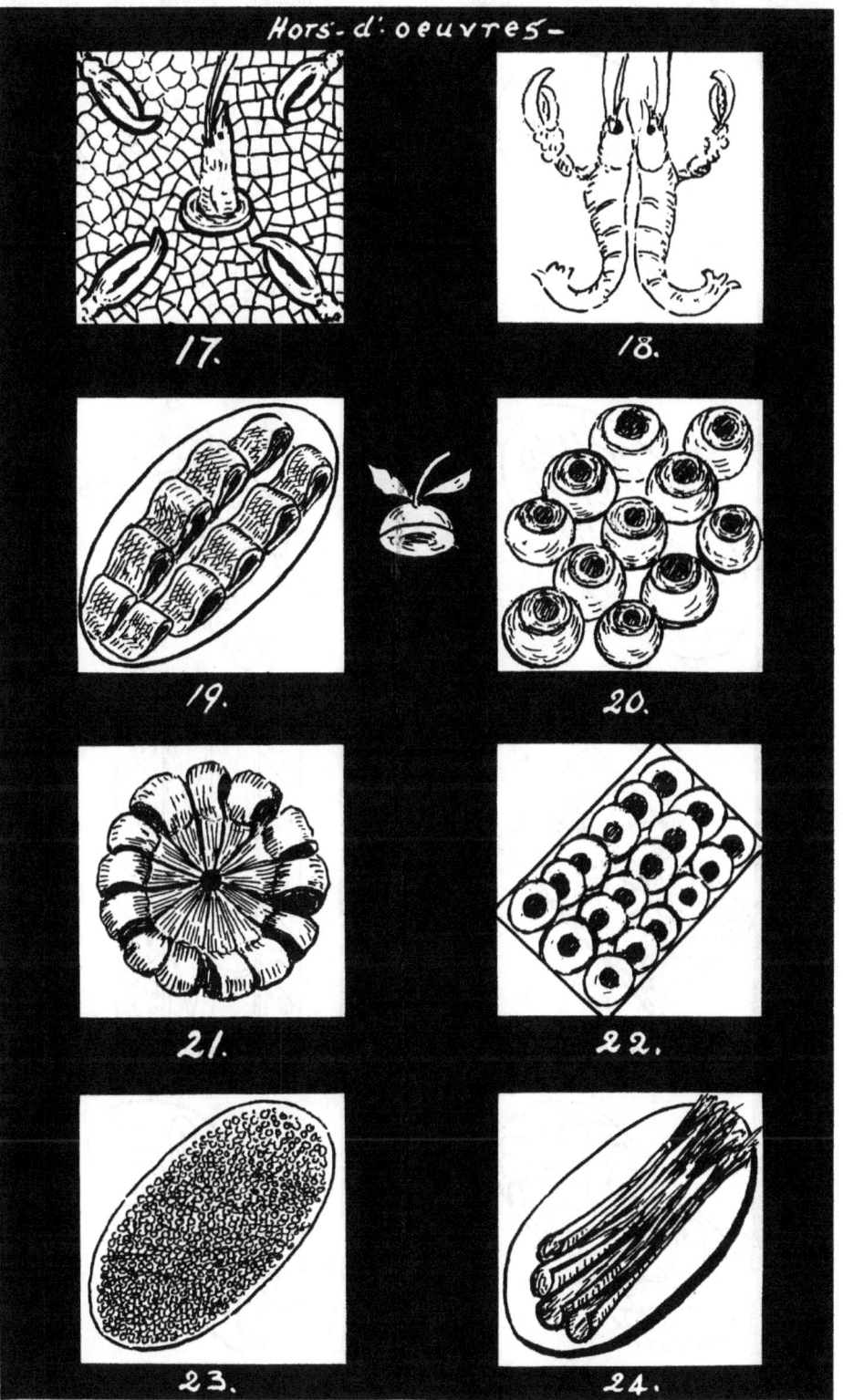

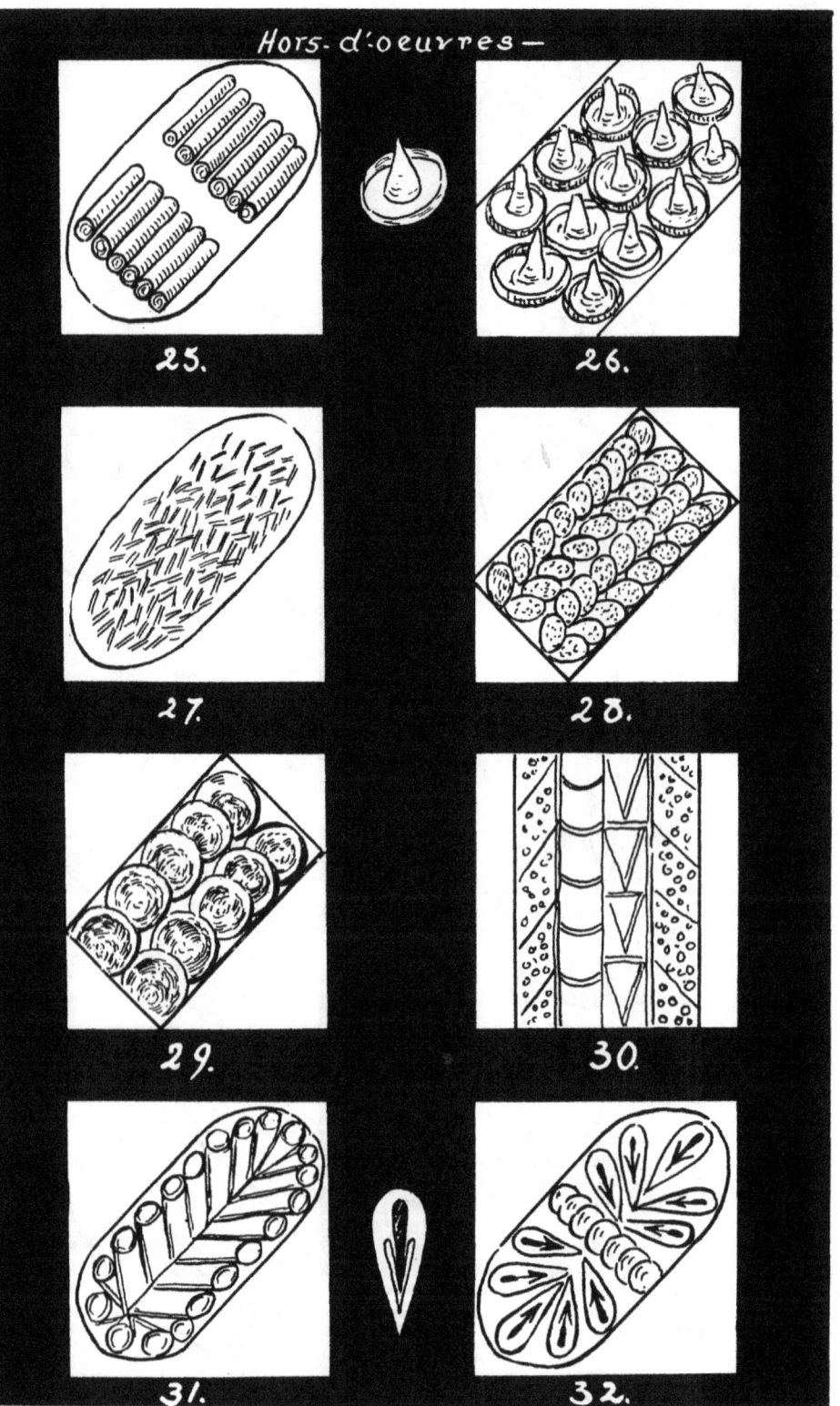

Hors-d'œuvres.

33. 34.

35. 36.

37. 38.

39. 40.

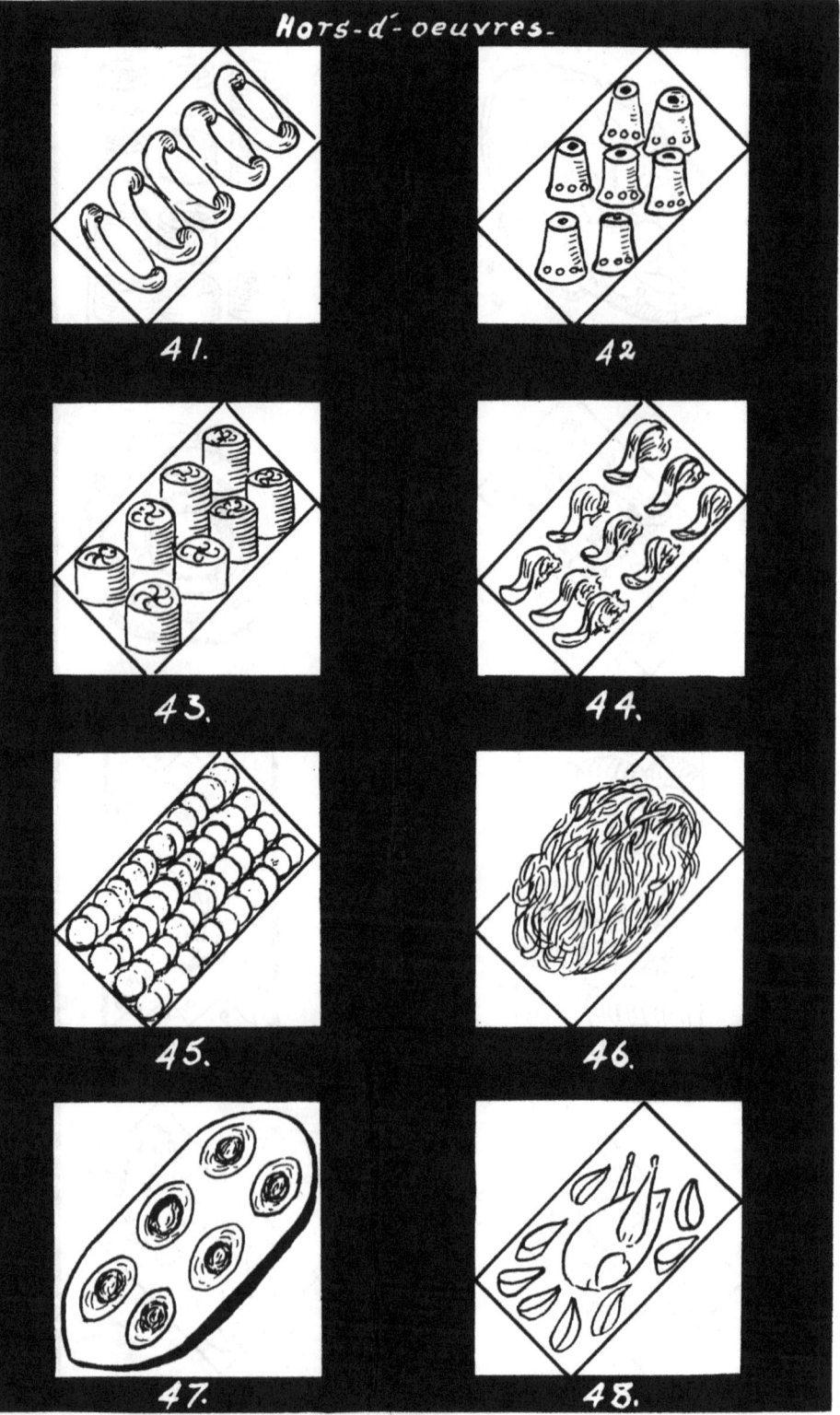

Platter Decoration

Platter decoration is an art in itself. Very few people know how to do it. There are many chefs, cooks, and housewives who are good cooks but lack the ability to serve food artistically. I think most people can follow a picture, and, therefore, I have tried to show you with pictures how to decorate a platter effectively. Some arrangements are hard and some are easy, so you can choose what you wish and with a bit of practice will accomplish what you would like to have.

Pick a porcelain, silver, or metal platter with a large border. Follow the picture in placing designs on the border correctly. Measure distances if necessary. Watch color combinations and stick to two- or three-color combinations.

A platter decoration can be stored in the ice box and used again. Water cress or parsley should be fresh just before serving.

No. 1. The star design is cut from a large green pickle or a young salted cucumber. Slice the pickle and use a star cutter. The star point can be cut in half again and replaced with points cut out of hard-boiled egg-whites. This gives you a double star effect of white and green.

No. 2. Slice green sweet pickles or sour pickles with a color combination of light and dark green. Make uniform slices, cut out with large round cutter, and lay alternately on platter.

No. 3. Cut round slices from a large green pickle or marinated fresh cucumbers. Cut these slices in diamond form. Round off one point, and you will have a leaf. Set these leaves together to form a flower.

No. 4. Use green pickles or gherkins cut in slices. Cut half slice in a fan shape.

5. Same as No. 4 but arranged differently on platter.

No. 6. Use fan-shaped pickles together with round-shaped.

No. 7. Pickles cut in half and cut in diamond shapes. Slices can be dipped in finely chopped hard-boiled eggs or finely chopped parsley.

No. 8. Cucumbers or pickles cut in half-moon shape. These can be colored and made especially attractive.

No. 9. Large pickles cut in half lengthwise with even slicing to make them uniform size.

They can be of colors sprinkled with chopped parsley, paprika, or caviar. Place diamond-shaped pickles between.

No. 10. Cut stars out of young cucumbers or large pickles.

No. 11. Half-moon and pickle slices arranged in simple design. The half-moon is made of green cucumbers; round slices are in yellow or red with chopped hard-boiled eggs or paprika over them.

No. 12. At each end of platter, place a large rose carved out of white turnips. If food served is white, color the roses. If food served is dark, keep roses naturally white. Slice cooked carrots on the side of the platter. Use the largest slices in the center and the smaller near ends.

No. 13. At each end of platter place a chrysanthemum together with three small roses and a slice of lemon on each side. In the center, place a large rose and two small ones and a slice of lemon on each side.

No. 14. Bug design is made of a green sweet pickle with mouth cut out of one end. Cut fan-shaped slices from another pickle and attach to bug with toothpicks. Use toothpicks for legs. Mark the body and the eyes with black olives. The mouth is made red with fruit coloring. On each side of the bug is a small rose in water cress. Cut red pimento in diamond shapes to form a part of a star. Place sliced cooked carrots around this. Put a bread sockel, fried until brown, in the center. Use spears with mushrooms made into roses, or small limes and lemons.

No. 15. This is self-explanatory. It represents cards and is made of white turnips sliced thin with designs made with cutters or by hand. Black can be made with black truffles which are imported in cans, or black olives. For red, use radish skins. All must be uniform in size. Use gelatin over the turnip to make the designs stick. Keep in ice box until needed.

No. 16. Leaves can be made of ham, boiled thinly-sliced chicken breast, blanched leeks, peeled fresh tomatoes, white turnips, eggplant skin, or large radishes. Between leaves use green or black olive, half of a radish, half of a grape, pimento, or a hard-boiled egg-yolk ball. This makes an attractive platter.

No. 17. Same as No. 15.

No. 18. Dice are made from white turnip. Cut squares all even in length and width. These are made with cutters. With a pencil point, press dots into turnip and insert black olives or truffles. Make the markings before impression is made.

No. 19. This design is made from thinly-sliced breast of chicken, or boiled ham, or hard-boiled egg whites and pimento, or blanched leeks and boiled carrots.

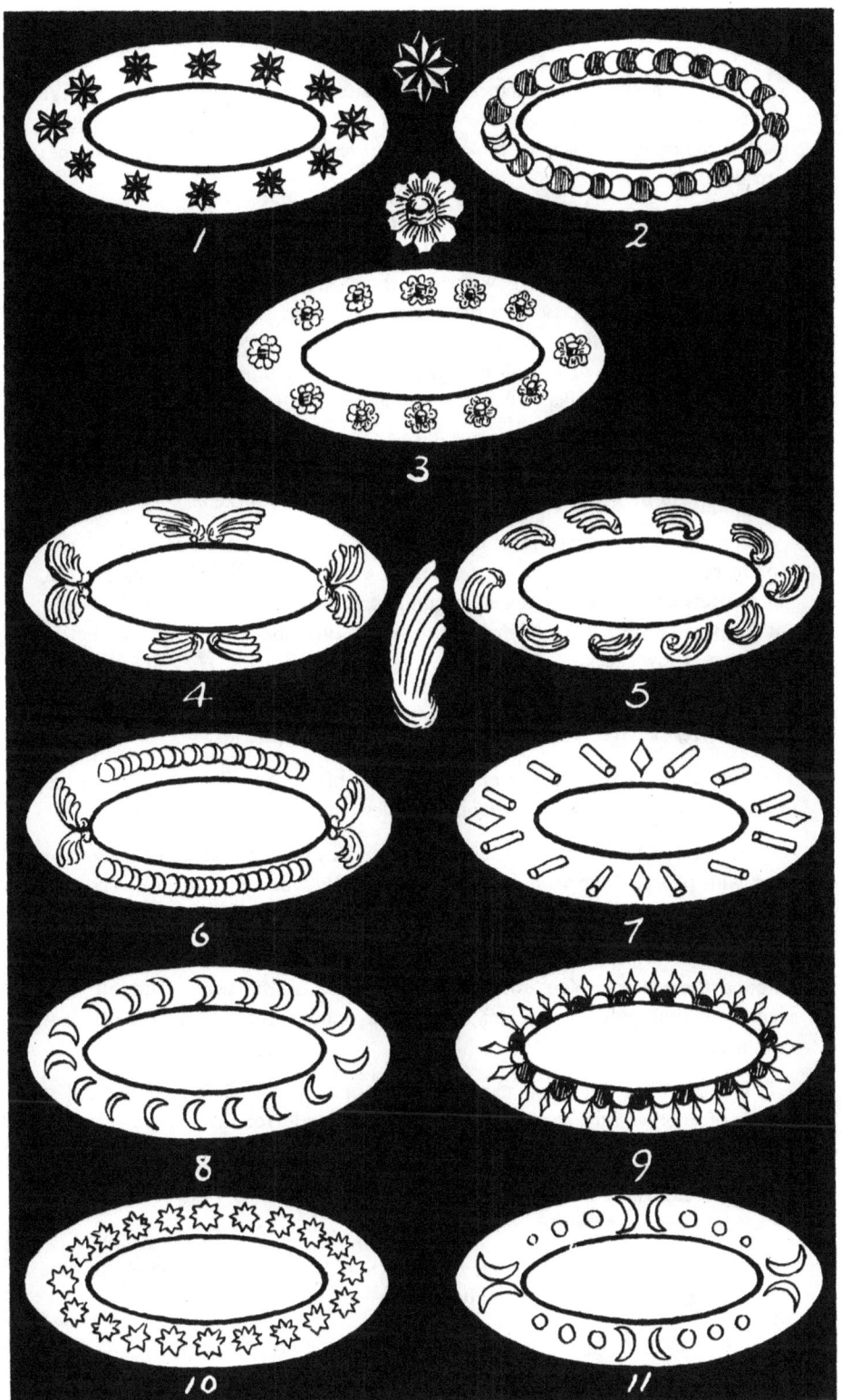

No. 20. Measure the distances on the platter so as to have exactness. Large round slices are boiled eggs. The black is truffles or black olives. The other part of the design is made of cooked carrots evenly sliced, or sliced red radishes can be used.

No. 21. Large white turnips or yellow turnips can be used. The flower can be made of tomato skin with a yellow center of hard boiled egg yolks. The tomato is emersed in boiling water for three minutes and the skin removed. The skin is cut with scissors in the form of a flower. The stem is made from blanched leeks or chives. Leaves can be made of green pepper. Between each flower is a small top of a fresh blanched tomato. The lines are made of a paste of hard-boiled egg yolks and butter using a pastry tube.

No. 22. This design can be cut out of lemon as explained in "How to Cut Lemons." It also can be made out of egg whites, cooked carrots, truffles, radishes. skin of green pepper, or thinly-cut breast of chicken.

No. 23. Shows small maraschino cherries, chives, for stems and water cress for leaves. The cherries also can be made of blanched peeled tomatoes. Cut in quarters and place in a towel, winding it so as to form a ball. Make stems of leeks or chives. With a small brush, put a little mayonnaise on the tomato to give a yellow cheek.

No. 24. This design is made with slices of salami, bologna, summer sausage or liver sausage. It also can be made of colored jello.

No. 25. Large lemon slices with 1/3 cut off. Cover one of the three sections with paprika, one with chopped parsley, and leave the other plain.

No. 26. This cross star is made of lemon. The four sections can be colored—one with paprika, one with finely-chopped parsley, another with finely-chopped hard-boiled egg yolks. The center is an anchovy ring.

No. 27. This design consists of a lemon cut in eight parts. Place them around the platter. You can remove the inside of the lemon and fill with lemon or lime jello in different colors. Let stand overnight and cut this way the next day.

No. 28. The dog on a stand is carved of rutabaga. The second stand is made of another rutabaga. Any design can be made for the border.

No. 29. The vase is carved of rutabaga. The lily can be made of white turnip as explained in the section on turnip carving under "Lily". The lily is stuck into parsley or water cress.

No. 30. This is simple and often used in commercial kitchens. Remove half of meat and bend rind slightly.

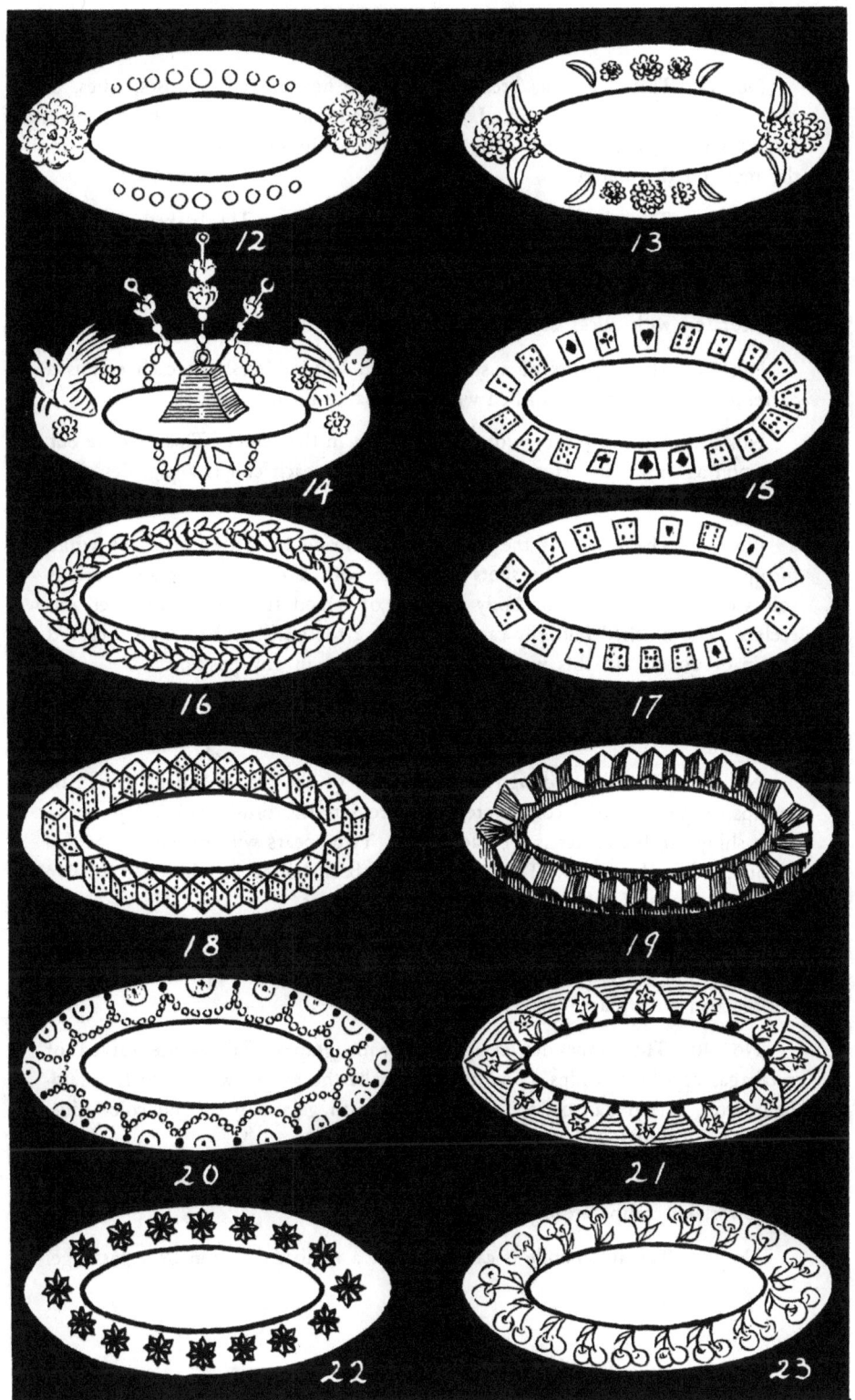

No. 31. This is a large bread sockel. The flowers can be roses, lilies, or daisies inserted into the sockel. Leaves are made of leeks. At each end, place large roses with fresh parsley. The design around the sockel shows how to place the meat on the platter.

No. 32. This shows quartered lemons or oranges. The baskets are filled with cold sauce.

No. 33. Penguins are discussed in "How to Cut Lemons." The sides can be decorated with slices of cucumbers.

No. 34. This consists of a star with two lemon slices. At each end is a barrel made of a lemon and filled with tartar sauce or mayonnaise.

No. 35. A bread sockel with an airplane is in the center. This is made out of lemon as shown in "How to Cut Lemons". At each end is a pig, described in the same section.

No. 36. The wings of the butterflies are made from thin slices of white turnips or egg whites. The spots are made with a round cutter and various colors can be inserted. The body is made of lemon rind as are the feet and feelers. The finished butterfly can be put on a toothpick and set into a carved turnip or potato. In this way it can be arranged in any position.

No. 37. The ducks are carved of rutabagas, turnips, or potatoes. They should be fastened with a paste made of flour, to stick to the platter.

No. 38. The lobster design on the border of the platter can be carved of turnips or potatoes and colored red. Before serving, brush with oil to make them shiny. In the center is a bread sockel. Two spears with two read crawfish are inserted in the sockel. The crawfish have been boiled in salt water for five minutes. Any seafood can be served on this platter.

No. 39. The swans are carved of white turnips. The bill and legs are colored yellow with fruit coloring. The eye is red, and the tips of the feathers are touched with black. This is very attractive.

No. 40. The grape design is made with grapes. Leaves are carved of rutabagas or white turnips. You also can make the grapes with a small potato-ball cutter, or Parisian cutter. Put together with gelatin paste and color blue. Leaves are colored dark brown or green.

No. 41. The wheelbarrow is carved of rutabagas. You can use any kind of flower, but tulips are especially colorful.

No. 42. The automobile is carved out of a rutabaga. It can be a passenger

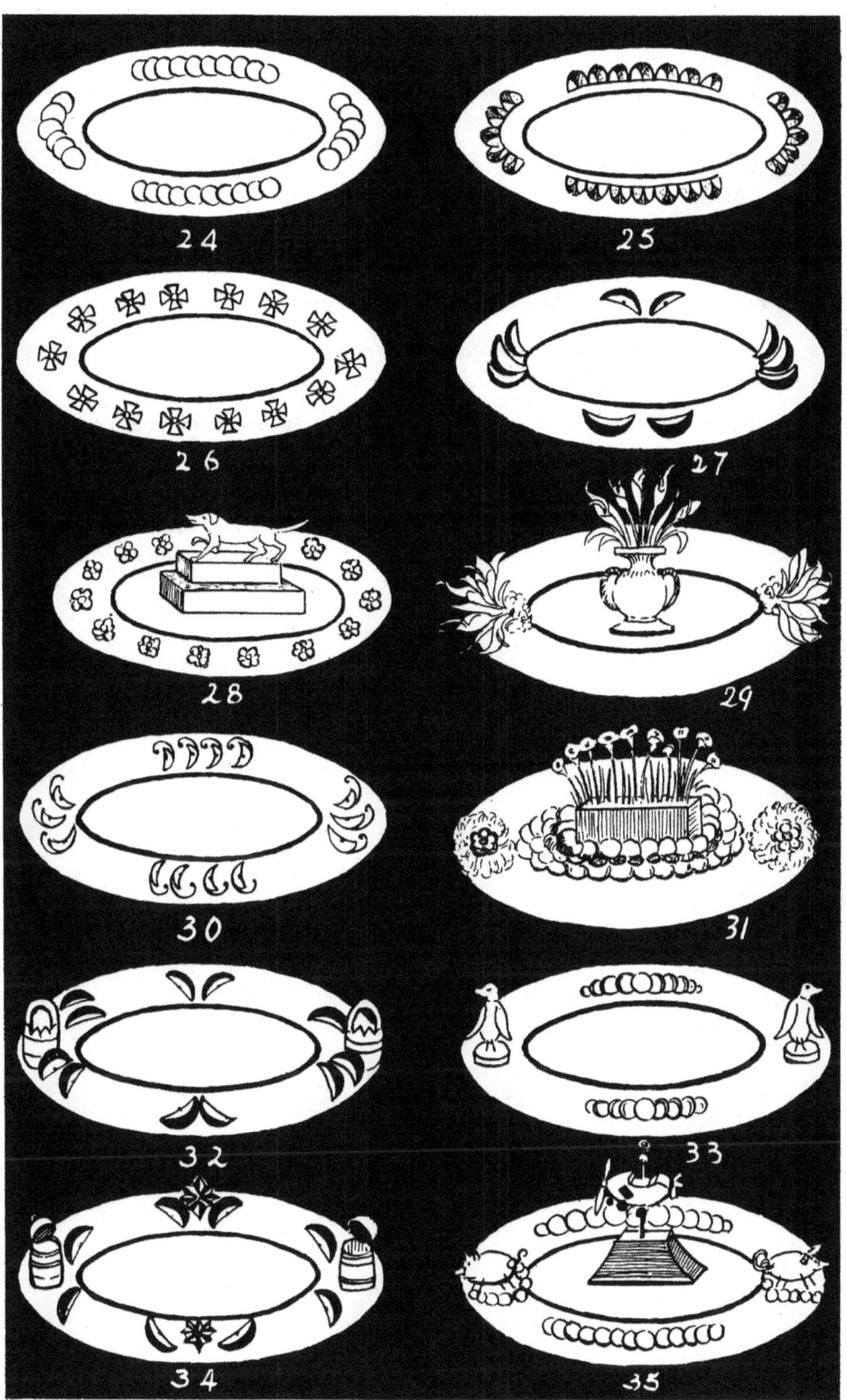

car or truck, whichever type the banquet calls for. Real flowers can be put into the back.

No. 43. The American Eagle is carved out of a rutabaga. At each end are fine American red roses. These are carved from rutabagas and colored.

No. 44. The horses are carved of rutabagas. The buckets are carved of white turnips. The horses are hard to make. You must be very careful with the slender legs and feet. The buckets can be filled with tartare sauce.

No. 45. This design can feature any type of bird. Serve with green stuff around it. This is good in serving any type of fowl.

No. 46. The deer is carved of rutabagas. The baskets are made of oranges and the slices filled with jello and placed around the border. The stand for the deer is made out of a rutabaga.

No. 47. The lion and fox design is difficult. They are carved rutabagas. They can be colored and are very attractive. Use a bit of parsley or water cress on the sides.

How to Carve Beef

A good carver requires a sharp knife, a steady hand, and erect posture before the meat.

No. 1. HOW TO CARVE BEEF
Shows how to carve the round. Always cut from the outside inward. Have plates close to you so that you can lay the meat on them without touching it.

No. 2. STANDING RIBS OF BEEF
Have a large slicing knife so you can give the knife a swing of the full length of the blade. Make a fine cut with a steady pressure.

No. 3. This shows how to pick up meat with your knife and place it on the plate all in one operation.

No. 4. ROLLED ROASTS
If roasts are hot, a fork can be used to hold the meat steady. The hand, however, can hold the meat steadier and allows you to do a better job.

No. 5. SIRLOIN STEAK
Large sirloin steaks are cut in thick slices. Handle them with the knife.

No. 6. PORTERHOUSE STEAK
It is advisable to remove the bone as you can cut them better this way.

No. 7. TONGUE
Begin cutting tongue from the small end or from the front of the tongue. Always cut at a slant.

No. 8. BEEF TENDERLOIN
Start to cut beef tenderloin from the smaller end and gradually slice on an angle towards the back or heavier part. Cut slices thin.

No. 9. POT ROAST
Large pot roasts can be cut in half. Carve the same as rolled roasts.

How to Carve Lamb and Pork

No. 1. **LEG OF LAMB**
First cut out a wedge just below the heavy bone as shown here. At dotted line, make a straight cut down along the bone. Keep slicing thin slices off exactly as shown. To make the leg stand properly for carving, trim a little off on the bottom as the shaded portion indicates here.

No. 2. Some cut the leg of lamb as though it were a ham. This is not correct, but at home you can do as you like and this is a simple way.

No. 3. Cut slices out of the big lean part as in No. 1. This is called the horseshoe slice. Serve this with one slice from the back where the meat grain runs opposite. This is the European way of cutting.

No. 4. **SADDLE**
This is the finest piece of meat and deserves great care. First remove the back or middle bone. Cut along bone on both sides to expose the bone. Now cut slices the full length of the meat. If they are too long to serve, cut them in half.

No. 5. **CROWN ROAST**
Cut down in between the ribs. As a rule, we cut one slice with the bone and one slice in between.

No. 6. **RACK**
Cut in between the bones to make one slice with each bone.

No. 7. **LAMB TONGUE**
Cut lengthwise.

No. 8. **STUFFED BREAST OF LAMB**
Slice these straight down. Do not slice the breast too thin.

No. 9. **ROLLED SHOULDER**
Slice straight down.

Pork is carved as is veal and lamb except for the ham. For this piece I have three methods:

No. 1. Hold up the ham, cut a wedge in the ham, and slice up to the bone making horseshoe-shaped slices.

No. 2. The whole horseshoe is cut out and laid on the table. Slice straight down for sandwiches and cold cuts.

No. 3. The ham is laid flat on the table and sliced. This is considered to be the correct way.

How to Carve Lamb.

1. Leg. 2. Leg. 3. Leg.

4. Saddle. 5. Crown. 6. Rack.

7. Tongue. 8. Stuffed Breast. 9. Rolled Shoulder.

How to Carve Veal

No. 1. ROAST LEG OF VEAL
Leg of veal is always boned and the natural separation falls into three major pieces of meat: the upper round, the lower round, and the nut. These pieces are tied with string to hold their shape when roasted. They are sliced as any roast.

No. 2. STUFFED BREAST OF VEAL
This is sliced the same as is breast of lamb, though the veal gives a much larger slice.

No. 3. LOIN OF VEAL
If the loin is not already boned, cut in between bones. This will require a blow with your hand on the knife. Or use a wooden hammer and hit knife to cut through the bone.

How to Carve Chicken

The whole chicken on the left is marked with dotted lines to show where leg should be cut. This part should be cut into three pieces as is half the breast. These pieces should be reassembled to form the chicken again.

When a whole chicken is broiled, merely tear it in half.

How to Carve Veal

1. Roast Leg of Veal. 2. Stuffed Breast of Veal. 3. Loin of Veal

How to Carve Pork.

How to Carve a Chicken

Whole Chicken for Broiling

How to Carve Raw and Cooked Fish

No. 1. It is not necessary to cut off the head when cutting steaks. Cut at the dotted line in the thickness you want.

No. 2. Large fish can be loosened along back bone with the entire side cut out later as seen in No. 3.

No. 3. This is usually done with raw fish.

No. 4. The fish half with bones removed can be cut into slices. This also applies to raw fish.

No. 5. If fish is well cooked, you can cut portions off with a pallet knife and place them right on your plate.

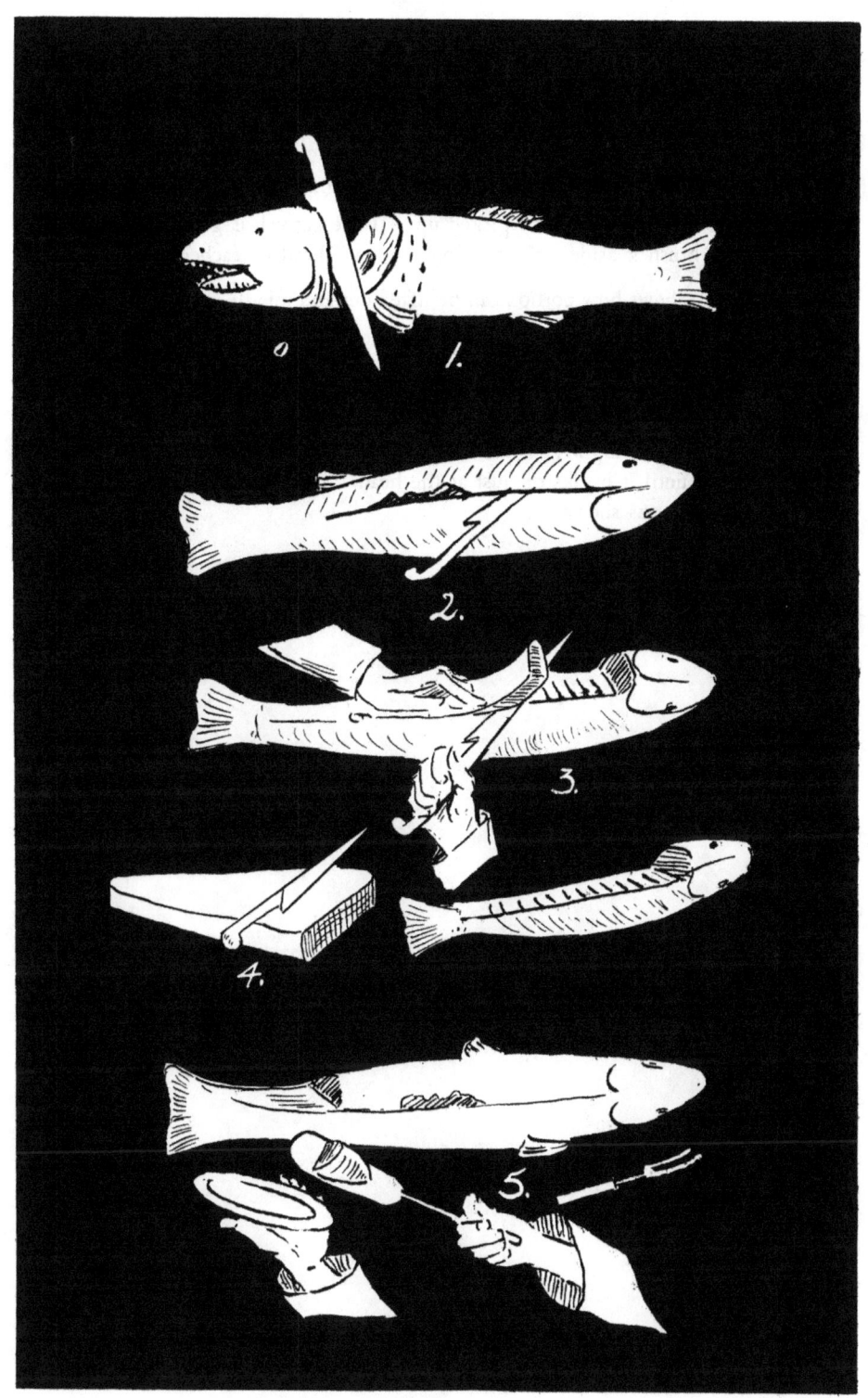

How to Carve a Decorated Fish

No. 12. Use a knife and make the first cut on the tail. Cut portions in desired sizes. When you feel the bone, turn knife from right to left, and the portion is free, ready to be picked up. If the garnish is good, serve it. If not, merely brush it aside. Keep doing this until head is reached.

No. 13. Shows how portion can be lifted out and middle bone construction.

No. 14. Shows how fish will look when fully served. Between A and B are breast bones. When this space is reached, press a bit harder on the knife and they will cut in half.

No. 15. When top half of fish is served, pick up the middle bone and bend it backwards until it breaks off just at the head. Then serve rest of the fish in the same manner as shown.

How to Carve a Cold Fish.

How to Prepare Raw Chicken

Chicken which is to be boiled and served cold requires careful attention. It must be fresh, carefully cleaned, and tied correctly so as to bring out the breast. It should be cooked slowly and cooled off in the stock overnight. The next day, the chicken is wiped off, and all loose meat is removed and covered with Supreme Sauce. This is done three times, and each time the chicken must be cooled.

The chicken can then be decorated and placed on a platter. When all the guests have finished admiring it, it can be sliced and served. My advice in decorating a chicken is that it be simple. Chicken decoration is important, as it is an important item on all buffet tables. Here are a few rules as a guide.

No. 1. When chicken is free of feathers, burn off the fine down over any flame by holding legs and head.

No. 2. Place chicken on its belly and hold the head in your left hand. With the knife in your right hand, cut the chicken neck skin lengthwise from the head down.

No. 3. Pull the skin loose from the neck, and separate the skin from the neck, cutting it by the head. Hold the skin up and cut the neck off close to the breast. The skin, then, is still on Wings can be cut off if you wish.

No. 4. The chicken skin from the neck is brought back and placed on the back between the wings. If wings remain, they are placed in position.

No. 5. To sew up a chicken properly, stick the needle through the wing, then through the skin, through the other wing, and then turn the chicken on its back.

No. 6. Now stick the needle through one chicken drum, through the whole body, and then through the other drum. At this point the chicken is very thick. Put both legs together and tie them tightly.

No. 7. A properly tied chicken, ready to be boiled, or roasted.

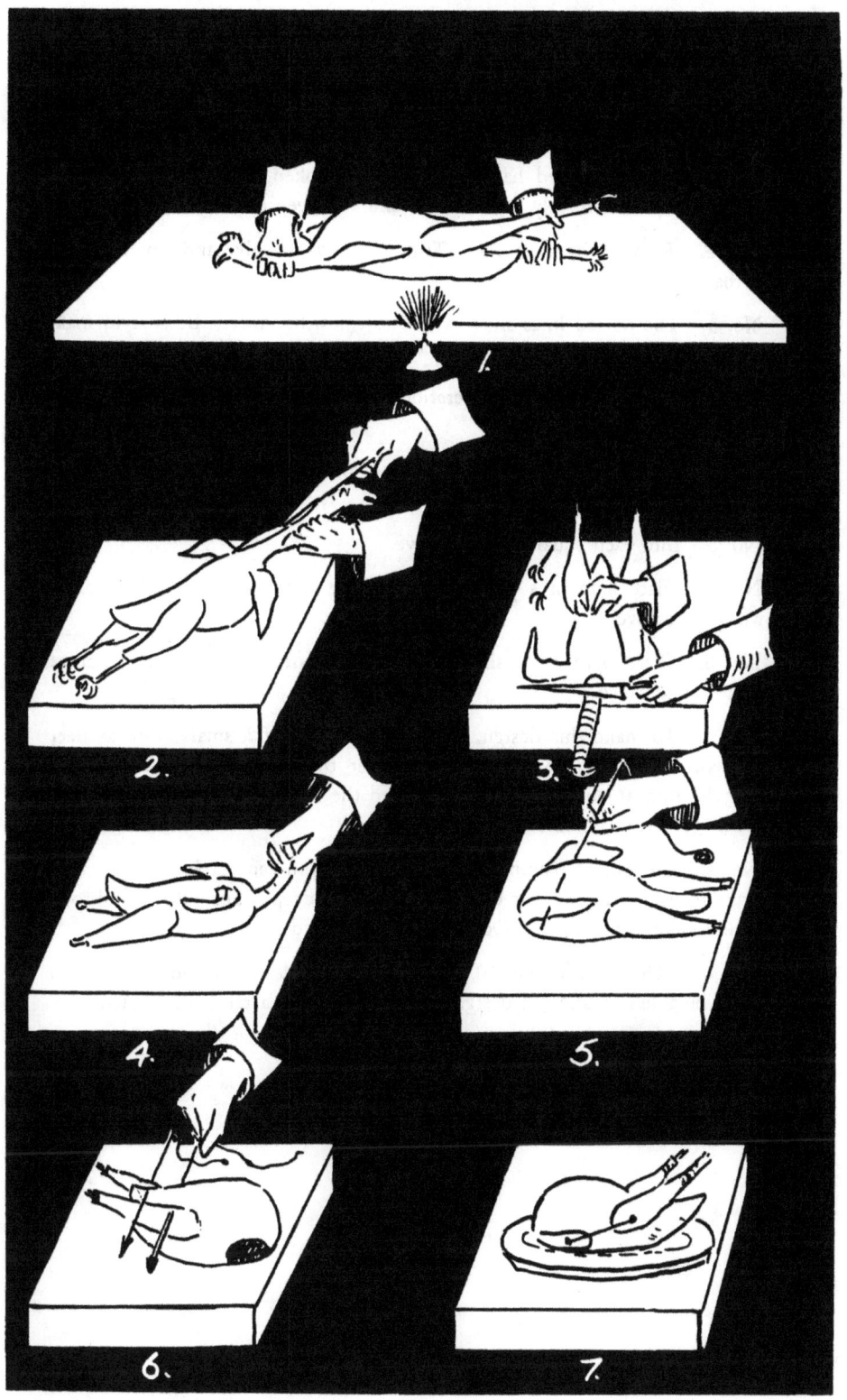

How to Prepare Baked Ham

No. 1. After a boiled ham is completely cooked, the skin is taken off. It can be hot or cold, merely begin at one end and keep pulling it off.

No. 2. Remove heaviest fat. Trim all parts evenly, and do not leave more than one inch of fat on it.

No. 3. The dotted lines show where to cut with knife. Be sure to make cuts at an angle as shown.

No. 4. Repeat same cutting operation from the opposite side, thus creating diamonds.

No. 5. Sprinkle ham with powdered brown sugar. Make sure all ham is covered, including the sides.

No. 6. Into each square place a clove.

No. 7. Place ham in a pan without adding water. Bake until a golden brown and remove.

No. 8. Place ham on a silver platter with fine candied sweet potatoes, or with orange sauce.

No. 9. To make this design, cut with the point of a small knife as deep as the skin in zig-zag shapes. Do this after the ham is cooked, and then remove the skin at one end and pull toward the zig-zag as you did in No. 1. This will give you No. 10.

No. 10. Instead of making squares as above, you can cut in a name. This is very effective. Do not cut over one-half inch deep. Sprinkle with brown sugar and bake light brown. Do not over bake, or design will be harmed.

No. 11. The same as No. 10, but with a fancy design including a wreath. You will be able to make fine designs with only a knife after a little practice.

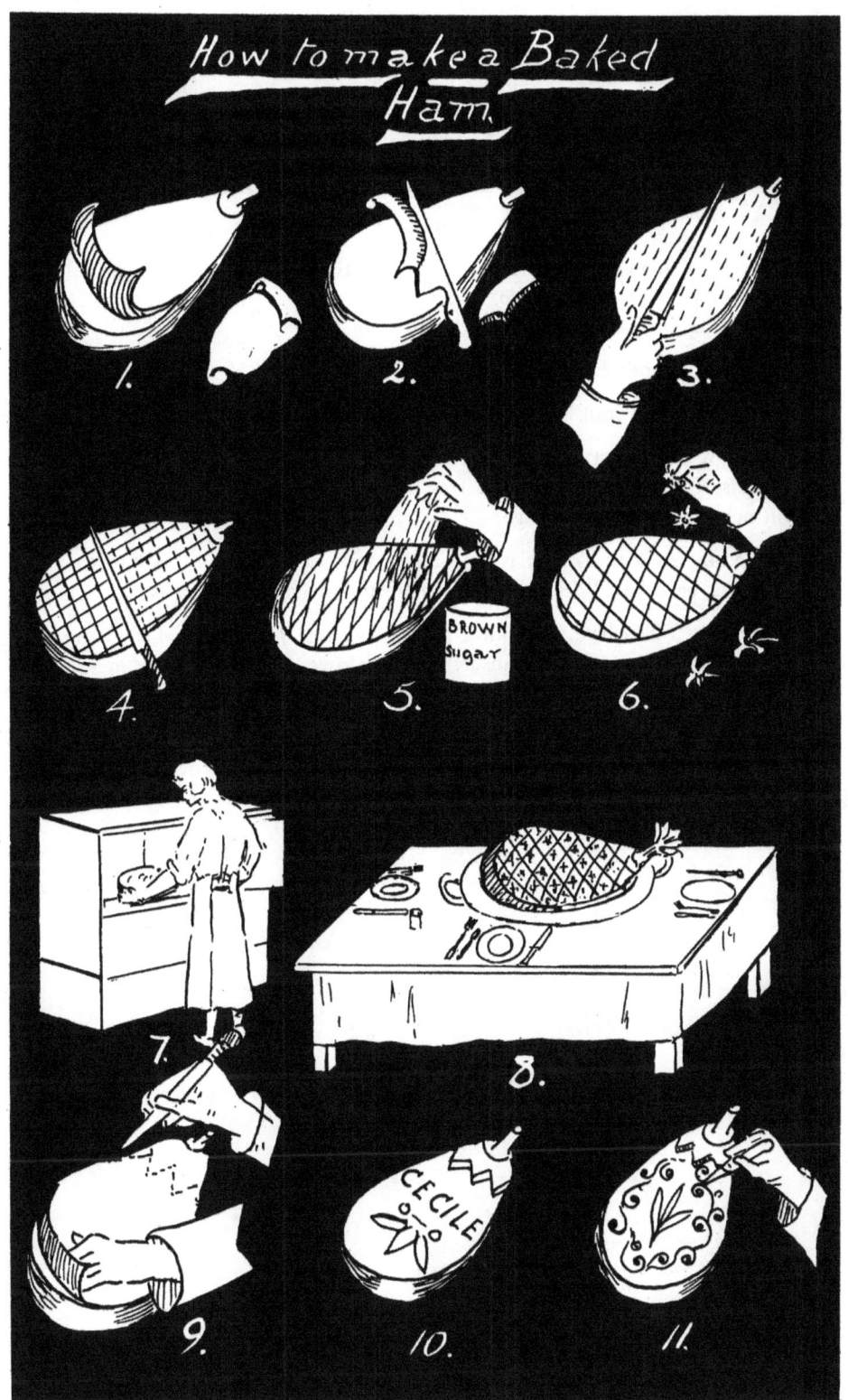

How to Prepare Fruit to Decorate Ham

Keep in mind, that all fruits, canned or fresh, should be dry and cold before dipping in aspic. Also, follow the rule of neat and exact work by having fruit pieces of uniform size.

No. 1. Canned fruit is placed on towel to dry.

No. 2. When fruit is dry, trim and place on tray.

No. 3. Dip fruit in nearly cold aspic, and place on ham with toothpick supports. When aspic is cold and fruit stays on ham, remove toothpick. This will not stand a lot of shaking.

No. 4. As soon as fruit is placed on ham, put it in the ice box to cool. This must be repeated depending on the amount of fruit you place on the ham.

No. 5. When ham is finished, place in ice box for one-half hour before glazing with aspic. This will insure a perfect covering. The glazing must be done swiftly and again the ham must be placed in the cooler for ten more minutes. Repeat this operation three times.

No. 6. Keep aspic in the cooler and warm only what you need. Place all decorated platters in the ice box until needed, but, a warning—do not leave the ice box door open.

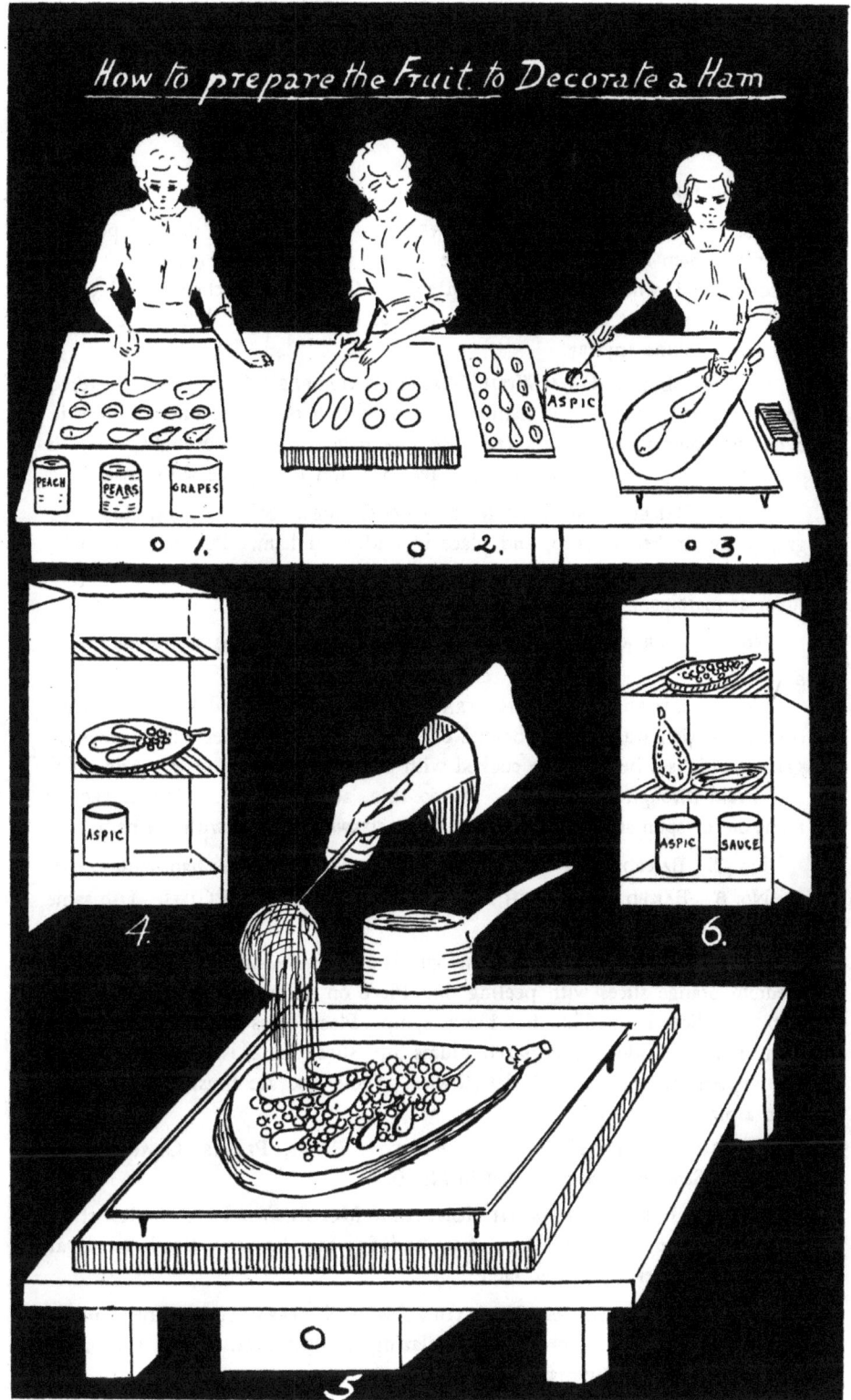

How to Decorate Baked Ham with Fruit

No. 1. Shows plain, hot or cold, sugar cured ham.

No. 2. BAKED HAM WITH PEACHES. Use half a can of drained peaches and place them in heavy syrup before placing in rotation on the ham. Place in cooler, and, when cool, glaze with aspic. Often, the peaches do not cover well with aspic, but this is of no concern, as they are covered with syrup and will have a shine anyway.

No. 3. BAKED HAM WITH GLAZED PINEAPPLE. When ham is baked and hot, place pineapple on ham and sprinkle with powdered sugar. Place in oven until pineapple slices darken. Remove ham and cool thoroughly. Brush pineapple syrup over the slices, again let cool, and then glaze with aspic.

No. 4. BAKED HAM WITH MORROCCO GRAPES. Select a good cluster of grapes, dip in heavy syrup, and place in middle of ham. Put in cooler and, when cold, glaze with aspic. Make two leaves and the little beetle out of spun sugar or marzipan. They are not hard to make.

No. 5. PEAR AND PINEAPPLE HAM. Follow instructions as for ham with grapes.

No. 6. BAKED HAM WITH STRAWBERRIES. Glaze baked ham and, when cool, place well washed strawberries on it. Brush strawberries with strawberry glaze. This is a heavy syrup cooked with a few strawberries in it. Add color and strain through a fine cloth. If too thin, add cornstarch. Leaves can be made out of spun sugar or marzipan. Serve strawberry sauce with the ham.

No. 7. BAKED HAM WITH CHERRIES. Same procedure as ham with grapes.

No. 8. BAKED HAM WITH PEACHES, PINEAPPLE, AND PLUMS. Use same procedure as ham with grapes.

No. 9. BAKED HAM WITH ORANGES, PLUMS, BANANAS, AND DATES. Slice medium orange slices with peeling on. Place on a towel and let drain until dry. Put slices in medium hot heavy syrup. Place slices in middle of baked ham. On each side, place glazed plums and sliced bananas. Border is made of stoneless dates cut in half lengthwise. These also are brushed and glazed with aspic.

No. 10. BAKED HAM WITH APRICOT, PEARS, PLUMS, GRAPES, AND PRUNES. Same procedure as that in No. 9.

No. 11. BAKED HAM WITH HONEYDEW MELON AND FIGS. Melon slices are neatly arranged in middle of ham and figs as a border. Brush on sugar glazing and cover with aspic later.

No. 12. CANTALOUPE, HONEYDEW, AND WATERMELON. The fruit is placed neatly on the ham and sugar glazing brushed over. Cover with aspic when cold. This is especially colorful.

Hams Decorated with Chaudfroid Sauce

The difference between a Chaudfroid sauce and aspic is the aspic is clear and transparent, where the Chaudfroid sauce has the look of a cream sauce.

Chaudfroid sauce is applied as is the aspic. The ham, fish, or chicken, must be well trimmed, cooled, and covered with nearly cold sauce. The sauce should be the thickness of light cream sauce. The article is placed on a wire rack so that sauce which falls can be used over. The rack, of course, must be clean.

The Chaudfroid covering is repeated three times. If sauce is too thick, two coverings are sufficient; if too thin, apply more times.

When you have finished covering the ham with Chaudfroid sauce, place ham in cooler and cover with aspic when cold. When one coating of aspic has been applied, your Chaudfroid sauce shine will last and you can begin decorating the ham, fish, or chicken. And, if you make a mistake, you can remove the design without spoiling the sauce. After you decorate the ham you give it three aspic coverings.

There are various cold sauces used for glazing in different colors. White is the most common and is made from chicken stock. Brown is made out of browned veal stock. Game is made of browned game bones. Pink is made from lobster meat and shell. Green is made out of Lobster Coral. Application of all is similar when sauces are to be used for glazing. You can combine three different Chaudfroid sauces on one piece with success.

No. 1. A cucumber.
No. 2. Cut thin slices and trim into leaves of equal size.
No. 3. Place leaves into a plate with liquid aspic.
No. 4. Use needle to pick up leaves.
No. 5. Use a round cutter to stamp out round berries from pimento.
No. 6. Place berries or cut pimento on plate with aspic.
No. 7. Place leaves and berries on ham, beginning with top.
No. 8. When half finished, put ham in cooler for 15 minutes. Take out and coat with aspic. Then quickly place ham in cooler for 15 minutes more. Finish the other half and place in cooler again.
No. 9. Repeat aspic covering as often as necessary to keep ham well covered. Three usually are enough, but if it goes to a food show, give it four or five coatings.
No. 10. When ham is cold, trim all sides and place on a silver platter.
No. 11. Shows the finished ham on a silver platter with carved vegetable roses and fresh parsley all around it.

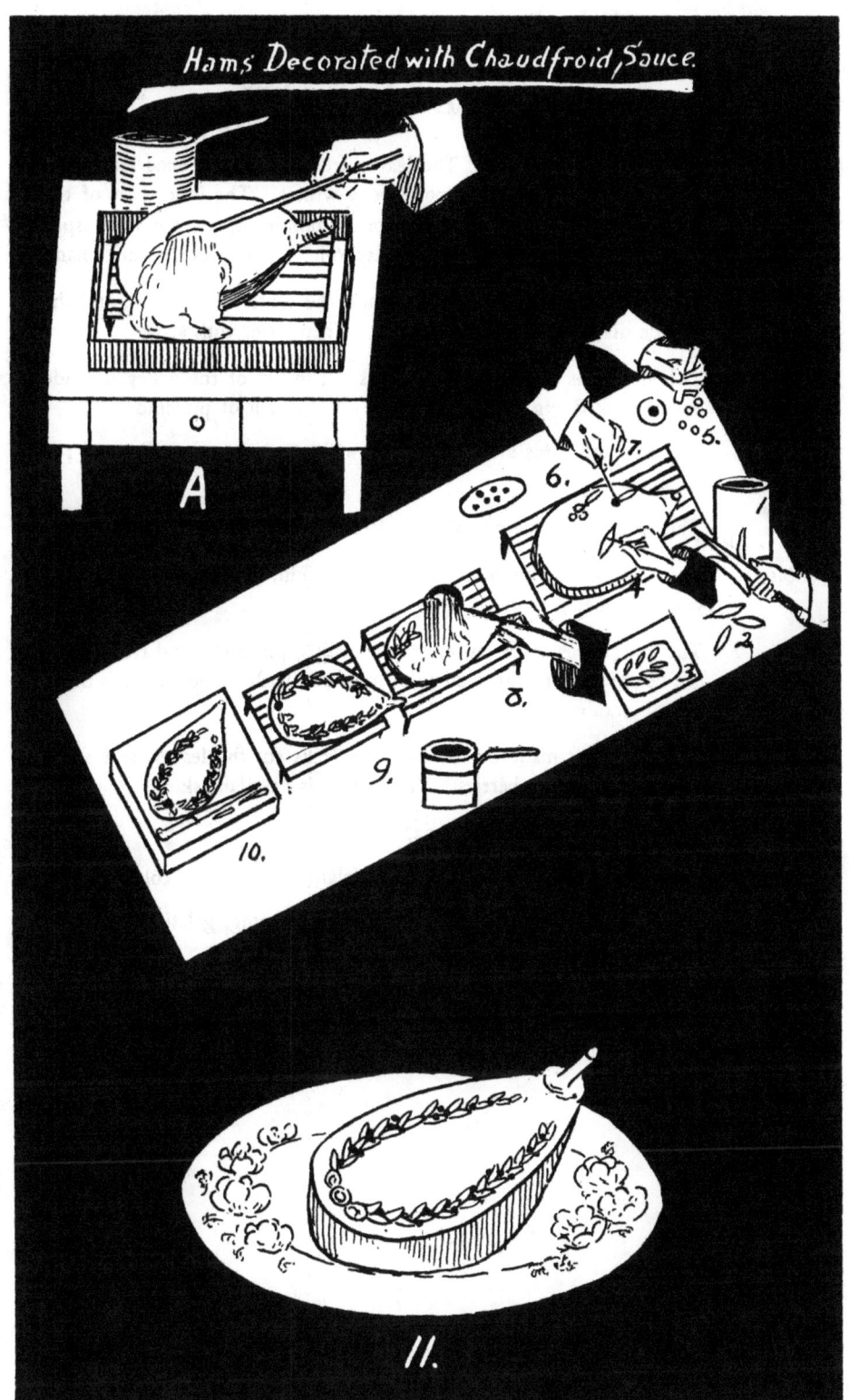

Chaudfroid-Decorated Hams

No. 1. A simple flower design. The leaves are made of blanched leeks, and the flower is made of hardboiled egg whites. The inner part of the flower is the yolk. When decoration is completed, cover it with aspic. Put on a little at a time, using a teaspoon. Then cover the entire ham.

No. 2. Make the long petals out of eggplant, the center of pimento, and the outside diamonds of cooked carrots. Then cover with aspic.

No. 3. This design is made of chive leaves. The lily of the valley is made out of cooked egg whites and the big flower out of pimento.

No. 4. The dice and cards are made out of white turnips and truffles and red pimentos.

No. 5. This design is made out of thin strips of eggplant skin.

No. 6. This design can be made of eggplant skin, truffles, or painted on with charcoal gelatin.

No. 7. The butterfly is made out of white turnips, pimentos, and truffles. It can be painted on with fruit coloring if you wish. The border is made out of cranberry halves.

No. 8. This design is made out of blanched leeks for the leaves, and small cranberries for the berries. The ribbon is eggplant skin.

No. 9. This can be painted with cocoa.

No. 10. This can be made out of truffles, eggplant skin, or fruit coloring.

No. 11. This design can be painted on with fruit coloring, gelatin, and cocoa painting used together.

No. 12. Black thread is used for this design. It can be used only on an artificial ham for display purposes.

Decorating Ham with Gelatin

This method is less known to most cooks. It is interesting to do and beautiful to see if you have a knowledge of painting. The gelatin powder is dissolved in hot water and mixed with charcoal powder obtainable in any drug store. Mix well and apply with a brush, using cocoa painting rules. You can get any gelatin color desired. It is used for show pieces only.

Decorating Ham with Black Thread

This method also is used for decoration purposes only. Hams can be simulated out of rice, corn meal mush, or any substitute suitable for table or window decorations only. This is another little known method but attractive in final results. Have a picture of the design you are going to make. Cut black thread to desired length, and, with a needle, put thread in liquid aspic and place on ham. Later, use a teaspoon to add more aspic.

Transfer Pictures on Ham

An easy way to dress up a ham is to use the transfer pictures you used as a kid. Take a transfer paper and place it on a dry ham, already covered with Chaudfroid sauce as shown in No. 1. When in the proper position, rub a sponge over it, being careful not to move the paper. Take one side and pull it off to see your design. This is usable for artificial hams for window decorations or food shows. If used for real food, remove before slicing ham as it is not edible. There are hundreds of selections, of course, and can still be found in dime stores.

How to Decorate Cold Chicken

Before decorating or glazing, a chicken must be free from any fat or overcooked meat. It must be dry and thoroughly cold. The Chaudfroid sauce should be nearly cold, and not too thick, but like a medium cream sauce. The glazing must be done quickly and immediately placed in the ice box. If you have a walk-in ice box, you can do the glazing there. However, even if you are not fast, you can do a fine job. Do not have the glazing too thick, as it will form lumps on the chicken. Always keep everything clean.

No. 1. The cold chicken is placed on a wire rack. Place a tray underneath to catch all overflow sauce. Glaze chicken with nearly cold Chaudfroid sauce, starting with the head and pouring towards the back. Pour swiftly and cover all. Put into the ice box and let cool for 15 minutes, repeating the glazing as often as needed. Be sure chicken is entirely covered. Three glazings should be sufficient. Then give entire chicken a coat of aspic and place in ice box again.

No. 2. The vegetables used for garnish are leeks, carrots, and black olives. On a board, cut blanched leeks two to three inches long. Place into soft aspic. Cut carrots into triangular shapes and place in aspic. Cut olives with round cutter and place with others.

No. 3. With needle and pincers, carefully take the garnish from the aspic. Place three leek leaves in front of the chicken breast. Make the border using carrots, then olives, then carrots, etc., until completed. Place in ice box again and let cool.

No. 4. Now remove from the ice box and continue decorating the legs. Place in ice box once more. While waiting, prepare aspic so it is cold, almost jelled.

No. 5. Glaze the entire chicken with aspic, applying it very carefully. Place in ice box again. Repeat operation until fully covered.

No. 6. You can place the chicken on a rice sockel. (Sockels are explained in their own section.)

No. 7. Or, use a cornmeal sockel on a large platter with various cooked vegetables all around. You can use asparagus tips, artichoke bottoms filled with fresh peas, cauliflower, water cress, and carrots cut in round balls. Shown here are two potato baskets with carved vegetable rose. Place chicken on sockel with aspic, triangular limes, and paper frills on each leg bone.

No. 8. Slice decorated chicken with the aid of a large carving fork inserted

into the lower carcass. Slice breast as shown. You may remove garnish before slicing. Legs are carved by holding the bone with one hand on the frill or with the fork inserted into the leg. Then slice from the top down. When serving, always try to give a little white meat together with a bit of dark meat and some vegetables.

No. 9. Dinner set for six, with glazed cold chicken as center dish. Use candle holders which you can make out of wax, and decorate with wild wax flowers.

No. 10. The cold chicken after being glazed with Chaudfroid sauce is decorated with small cooked or canned mushrooms. The side leaves are made of blanched leeks or eggplant skin. The border around the leg is of black olive halves. Place in ice box, and when cold, glaze with aspic.

No. 11. The daisies are made of hardboiled eggs. Outer leaves are of egg whites, the inner center of the yolk, or of boiled carrots. The dots are pimento, and the half-moons are green pepper or cucumber skin. The half-moons along the legs are made out of green olives.

No. 12. Place fresh red or black cherries on top. The stems are made from eggplant skin, leaves from blanched leeks, and the border from truffles, or carrots, or pimentos. Or, use black olives in place of truffles.

No. 13. Thinly sliced seedless oranges are placed on top of the chicken, starting at back and coming to the front. Side decoration is made out of blanched leeks or chives.

No. 14. After chicken is well glazed, additional chicken is sliced from another. Make the slices uniform and place on the chicken breast from back to front. Alternate overlapping slices from left to right. Alongside the slices, make a border with capers or small radish slices. The rest can be decorated with black olives, pimentos. Cut pimento strips, for example, and place over legs. This form of decoration, of course, requires two chickens.

No. 15. The coconut palm is made out of cooked green asparagus. The top leaves are leeks or eggplant skin, and the coconuts of truffles or fresh asparagus heads. The mountains are made out of thin pieces of eggplant skins, and the grass of chives or leeks.

No. 16. This cold roast chicken is not glazed with any sauce, but is decorated with various fruits. A fresh cluster of grapes may be placed on top of the chicken, and leaves made of eggplant skin or leeks. Legs are decorated with black cherries, and the front of the breast with a wreath of egg white pieces. This must be heavily glazed with aspic when completed.

No. 17. This roast chicken has orange slices and fresh strawberries on the top, strawberry halves on the sides.

No. 18. Shows a roast chicken decorated with date halves placed in the middle. There is a peach half on the sides with a semi-circle of red cherries as a border.

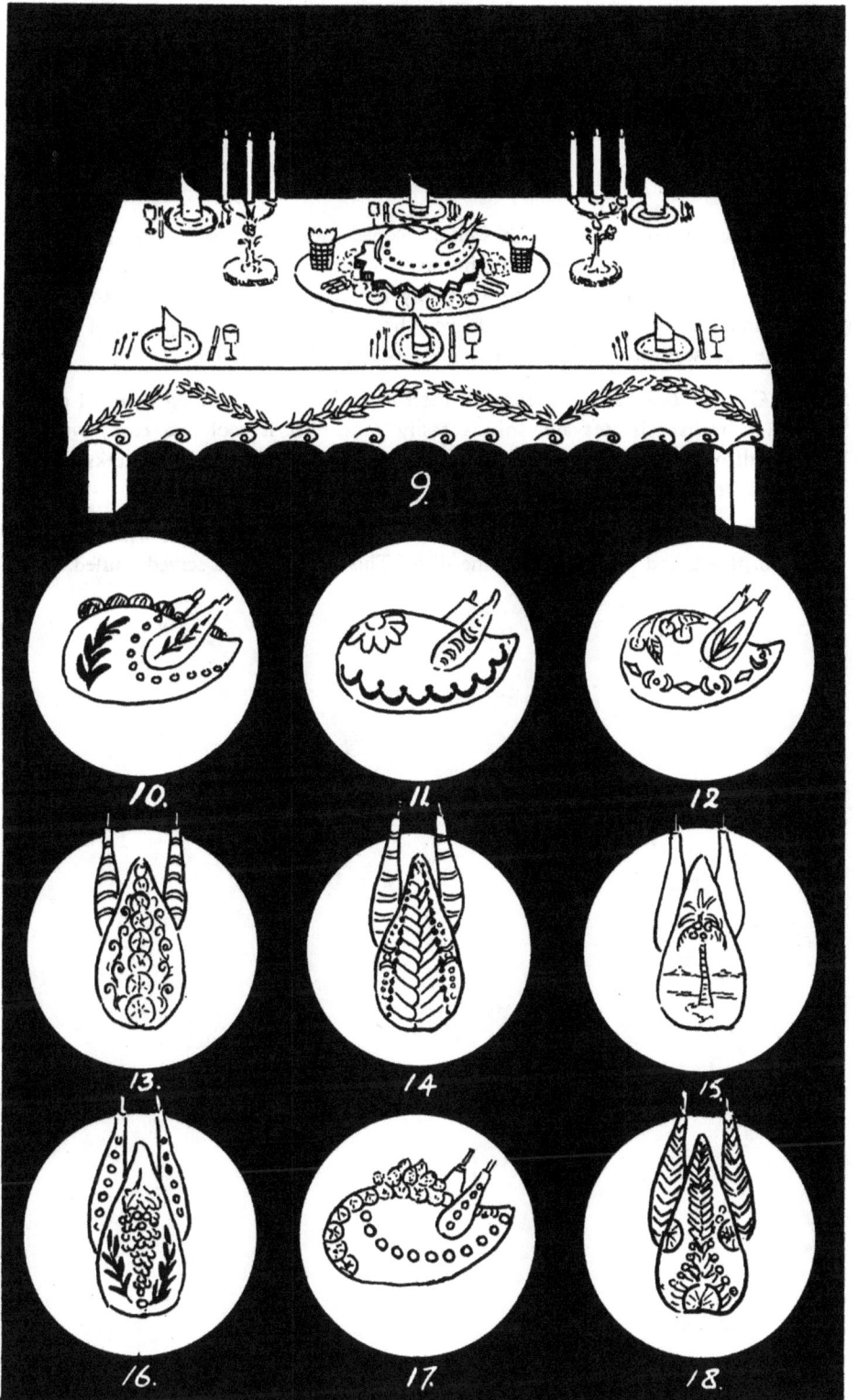

Decorated Breasts of Chicken

(Jeannette)

Cook a young chicken with well-developed breast until it is three-fourths done. Let it cool in broth. Cut the breast into three slices lengthwise. Place chicken slices on a wire netting or pastry rack. Cut an equal slice of cooked Virginia ham and place under a chicken slice. Cut a corresponding slice of imported goose liver (foie gras) and place on top of the chicken.

Give the goose liver the form of the former breast, by molding it round on top. The liver is soft and this is easily done. Let it cool and cover with Chaudfroid sauce. Decorate with fresh blanched tarragon leaves, leeks, or chives, truffles, and stuffed olives. Glaze well with chicken aspic.

When cold, place on a rice sockel with some lemon shells filled with lemon jello, sliced, and placed around the dish. This dish must be served chilled.

Decorated Chicken, Parisian Style

Two chickens are required to make Parisian style. Boil a young hen until it is done. Let it cool in the broth. When cool take off the entire breast. The two legs and front carcass and two wings remain. Clean the inside of carcass and fill with gooseliver and form to its original size. Place in ice box and when cold cover with Chaudfroid sauce. Take the second chicken which is raw and put through a fine sieve. Season with salt and pepper, little cream, two egg whites with little Madeira Wine. Mix this well. Dice cooked smoked beef tongue into small dices, also the half cooked breast of the other chicken with some truffles. Add this to the raw meat. Place in ice box one hour. Now take a sauce pan about three inches in height and twelve inches in diameter. Butter well the bottom. Have a pot of hot water with four teaspoons in it. Hold one teaspoon in left hand and one in right hand. With your right hand scoop one teaspoon three-fourths full of raw meat. With the left hand scoop it out of your right hand and place into sauce pan. Place next to one another. This will form your meat in Olive shape. Continue this until all the meat is used up or the pan is full. At this time add white wine to cover it. Then cover with strong chicken broth. This is the broth from the other chicken. Now cover with a cover and put on stove and let it simmer five minutes. Remove from stove without lifting cover. Let cool overnight. These odd shaped breasts are called *Quenelles*. The object is to make them equal in size and somewhat pointed as the picture shows. The next day place the Quenelles on a wire netting and cover again with Chaudfroid sauce. Decorate with small designs and then glaze with aspic. Place in ice box for one hour. Now place your first chicken on a clean platter and on the front of the chicken place each breast of chicken. Build from the bottom upward. Add a little chopped aspic to hold together. When this is finished decorate the rest of chicken and cover with aspic. This is not easy to make and requires experience.

How to Prepare Fish

No. 1. Large fish usually are used for buffet decoration. Fins are cut off, and the fish is well cleaned and washed.

No. 2. It is an art to cook a large fish so that it will not split open. Extreme care must be taken. The stomach and mouth are sewed up. The gill also is fastened. If the stomach appears sunken, fill it with sliced onions and bread to be removed when fish is served.

No. 3. The fish is then wrapped in a towel or napkin, but not too tightly as the fish will expand during cooking.

No. 4. Tie fish with string as shown, closing the ends, and, once again, being careful not to tie too tightly.

No. 5. Place fish in cooking utensil large enough so that fish is not bent. Fill with cold water to two or three inches over fish and add sufficient salt. To one gallon of water, add one glass of vinegar, a few whole peppers, a small bunch of fresh parsley, four stalks of celery, one or two peeled onions, one peeled carrot, one lemon, three bay leaves, and six cloves. Add all this to the water and let it come to a slow boil. When it boils, set it on the side off the stove so it will simmer for 20 minutes. Cover fish, set it aside, and let it cool overnight in the fish water. Next day, remove fish from napkin, place on a fish platter, and keep cool in the ice box. Glaze the fish in the same way as chicken, or ham. Use a fish sauce or Chaudfroid sauce. The rest of the decoration methods are the same. This fish is decorated right on the skin as shown here, and, after being decorated, they are glazed with aspic only.

No. 6. After being cooled, the fish is decorated with cranberries or red pimento for flowers, blanched leeks for leaves, and eggplant skins for stems. When finished, place fish in ice box and glaze two or three times with aspic. Use a large fish platter with plenty of room at each end.

No. 7. Make daisies of hard-boiled egg whites, centers of egg yolks, leaves of blanched leeks, and stems of eggplant skins. The border is made of pimento.

No. 8. This is a diamond design, cut with a cutter. Alternate truffles and egg whites, and make a border of sliced radishes.

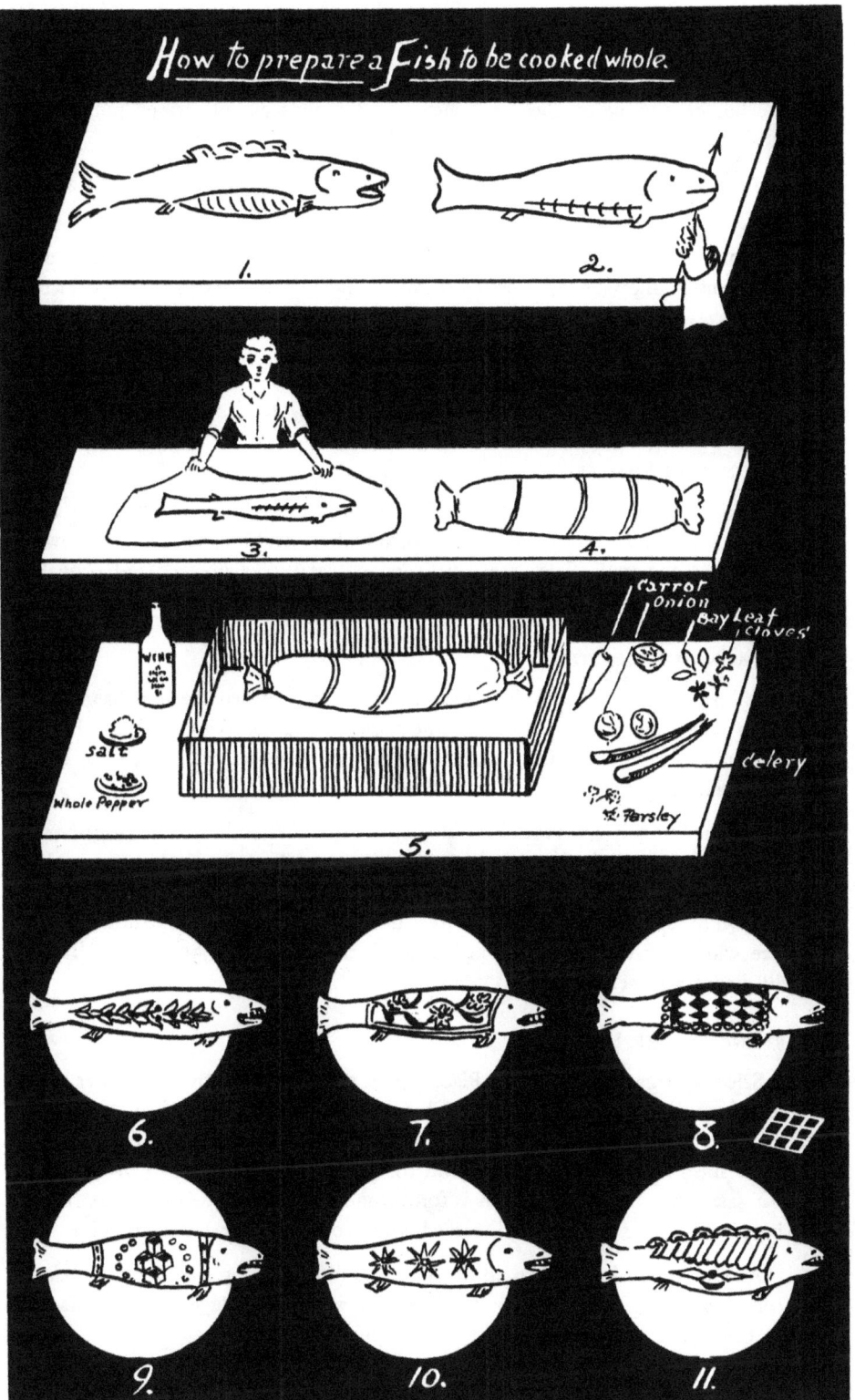

No. 9. This design is made of egg whites, truffles, and cooked carrots. The border is made of sliced radishes, and the ends out of striped pimentos with capers.

No. 10. Flowers are made of egg whites with egg yolk centers. The side flowers are made out of carrots with black olives as centers.

No. 11. This fish is decorated with cooked marinated mushrooms on top. Sides contain slices of cut smoked salmon. Borders are butter cream. Two large leaves are made out of blanched leeks with black olives or truffles.

Decorated Lobster

Cooking the Lobster

Select large and perfect lobsters. Live lobsters are cooked in salt water or fish stock for from fifteen to twenty-five minutes, according to size. Remove from water and cool. They are usually cooked a day in advance and cooled overnight.

Preparing the Lobster

With scissors, cut along shell underneath the tail. When the skin has been cut on both sides, you can pull out the meat without breaking the top shell. The claws are untouched in this case. Wash out the empty tail. Clean the entire lobster so that it has a uniform color.

Prepare a finely-cut vegetable salad mix, and add aspic. Blend together. Place lobster on its back, and fill with this mix. Place in ice box to cool. Slice lobster meat from the tail in thin slices. Place slices on a wire rack and cover with aspic or Chaudfroid sauce. Decorate the slices with truffles and glaze with aspic three times. The lobster itself should also be glazed. This will give it a shine.

Setting Up the Lobster

Select a large silver platter. Place a rice sockel on it with the lobster on top. Now place on the back of the lobster, the decorated slices of meat, starting at the head and gradually moving back, overlapping the slices. Additional lobster slices may be placed all around the platter. Vegetable salad or lobster meat salad may be served in fancy forms, and shaped and decorated to suit. This picture shows a rice sockel, carved with acorns and oak leaves in color.

Another method of setting up the lobster is to cut the top shell up the back. Remove the meat from the top, and then fill with vegetable or lobster salad, and place your lobster slices on top of your salad.

How to Use Leftover Lobster Shells

One can make some very artistic designs from lobster shells, including baskets, vases, figures such as cooks, musicians, Indians and many others.

Set shells together with quick-drying plaster of Paris. Or, you can use wax for this purpose. Shown here is a whole lobster with parts numbered. There are ten parts which should be carefully laid out on the table just as you see them here. No. 1's are the long feelers, No. 8 is a shell which is found underneath shell No. 5. To make the figure of an Indian, make some plaster of Paris and fill shell No. 2 with it. Insert shell No. 8 in front to make the shirt. Clip off section of front claws No. 3, and set together with No. 6. These two parts make the arms. For the head, use the front claw, Nos. 9 and 10, intact. The headdress is made of the entire tail, No. 7. The legs are made of No. 3. The shoes are made of one part of the pincer, No. 9. All these pieces are filled with plaster, wire is put through the plaster, and the pieces are set together.

Set the entire man into a plaster base. Let it stand upright overnight, and, the next day, clean shells and paint it. You can dress the figure in a variety of uniforms. A simple butterfly can be made of Nos. 7, 9, and 1.

How to use Left-over Lobster Shells.

How to Serve Pheasant

If you wish to serve pheasant artistically, it requires some preparation. Once pheasant was used only during the hunting season, but today they are raised on farms and can be served the year around without being expensive. When the pheasant is killed, you should be careful not to damage the plumage. This can be used very effectively.

No. 1. The bird is killed and kept in an undamaged condition. Remove both wings close to the body. Do not let any blood get on the feathers. Remove the tail close to the body. It must be cut off—not pulled off. Remove front half of feathers to give you No. 2.

No. 2. Shows wings, tail, and pheasant breast with the neck and head in one piece. No. 1. shows with an arrow where to cut off the wings. It also shows with an arrow where to cut the tail on top and bottom. Indicated by an arrow on top neck is the point where you should start to pull loose the skin with all the feathers on. Peel it carefully until you get to the lower neck which you cut. Keep peeling the skin until you arrive between the feet at the point shown by the second arrow. This will give you the head with the neck and the breast plumage from the back down to the belly between the feet, all in one piece. The two wings with the bones in them, and the tail with all its long feathers, are each in one piece. This is No. 2.

No. 3. Brush the wing feathers with a brush, so they will fall into place. Insert wire into the marrow of the wingbone and push it up to the first long feather as indicated by the dotted lines. Let the wires be exposed about three inches and then clip off.

No. 4. Insert the wire through the mouth, following the windpipe. Make a knot in the wire so it will not pull through. The knot must be in the mouth which is closed. If mouth does not remain closed, tie with string.

No. 5. The tail is made the same way. A smaller wire can be used. Push wire up the tail feather as indicated.

No. 6. This shows a bread sockel, well-fried, and placed on a platter. Three inches are kept for a border. Tail feathers are stuck into the bread sockel in the center of one end.

No. 7. The wings are stuck into the bread on each side about mid-way in the sockel.

No. 8. The neck is inserted in front in the middle of the sockel, with the bread well-covered by the breast feathers so the bread cannot be seen. The neck and the wings can be put in accordingly as the wire can be bent.

No. 9. The actual cooked pheasant is now placed on the platter between the wings, neck, and tail in such a way that it will not come into contact with these. This is easy since your platter with the pheasant on it also has a border.

No. 10. When served, the cooked pheasant is not visible. The guests are surprised to find the cooked pheasant on the platter. This can be done with any other bird, if the plumage is in good condition. When serving the pheasant remove both wings and carve it in front of the guests or bring it back into the kitchen after the platter has been shown to all the guests.

How to Make Rice Socles

The purpose of a rice sockel is to allow you to serve your food in a more attractive manner. They are used a great deal on buffet tables.

The rice used in a sockel should be the best obtainable. Wash it in cold water six or seven times until the water is clear. Let the water drip off the rice. Fill a large container with water, more water than rice, and let it come to a boil. Add the rice and let it cook for five or six minutes. Stir only two or three times. This is called blanching the rice. Pour rice in a sieve, and let the hot water drip off.

Line a casserole with a wet towel, and sprinkle rice evenly all around this towel. Sprinkle over the rice, ¾ oz. alum powder per pound of rice. Also, add ¾ oz. salt per pound of rice, and one pound of melted mutton kidney fat per pound of rice. This fat must be white. Mix this with the rice, close the towel, and place in a tightly-covered casserole. Put this in a double boiler and steam in the oven for two hours at 300 degrees.

Clean your meat grinder and rub it with lemon. Grind the rice through the finest blade. Work rice with spatula until fine, then add to your mold. Pack well so no air holes will appear, and fill to the top. Place in a cooler overnight. When needed, use a little hot running water and the rice will fall out of the mold easily. Check to see if there are any defects. The sockel is now ready to put on the platter. You can do a bit of carving if you wish. You can use fruit coloring also, if you desire to have it in color. Plain hand carved is usually the finest.

It is important that the mutton fat be pure white. This can be obtained the following way. Break up the mutton fat, which must come only from the kidney, into small pieces. Remove all blood stains and skins. Place in a crock and fill with cold water to stand overnight. The next day, pour the water off and render fat slowly, which will take about thirty minutes. When fat is clear, strain through a towel and let it cool. You will now have clear white fat for your rice.

The top figures show the different molds which can be used for sockels. The form must be clean and oiled. When rice or cornmeal is used, you must pack it well in the mold so that there will not be any air pockets. To remove sockel, place the mold in hot water for a few minutes and put it upside down. The sockel will come out very easily.

No. 1. This design is plain and two inches high. The corners on top and bottom are sharp.

No. 2. Cut out olives or truffles with round cutter. Use same cutter to cut holes in the sockel. Place olives or truffles in the holes. Other vegetables can be used, such as carrots, orange peel, radish skins, or green pepper. Black on white, however, always looks well.

No. 3. The leaf design is made from leeks, well-blanched, and cut in uniform size. The pieces are pasted on with a liquid rice mix. Measure heights and space leaves equally, so the design will be exact.

No. 4. The double-band design can be made out of leeks or, if red is desired, of pimento. Black can be made of artificial truffles. The height should be three inches.

No. 5. The flower design is made from leeks. You can use pimento for the flower with yellow lemon rind in the center. Use chives or leeks for stems

No. 6. Mark the center and place leaves exactly on the line. They can be black, red, or green, or black and white, red and white, or whatever you prefer.

No. 7. This should be three inches in height. Make two narrow bands of artificial truffles, leeks, eggplant skin, or carrots. Small roses placed in the center are carved out of carrots.

No. 8. This mosaic design consists of seven dice. Cut out egg white for the top square, one eggplant skin on the right, one of carrot on the lower left. This makes a single die. Build them together to get the complete design. To make a good job, a cutter is necessary. The other part of the design is made of leeks or carrots.

No. 9. The same as No. 8 but arranged around the sockel.

No. 10. Cut leeks, carrots, and eggplant skins in $\frac{1}{4}$ inch strips and as long as your sockel is high. Space these strips evenly around the sockel.

No. 11. Same as No. 2, but a double row.

No. 12. Leaves are made of leeks, cut the length of the sockel. The bottom can be made of black olives or red pimentos. This looks good on a white sockel.

No. 13. Make a middle line and mark spaces one or two inches apart. Place a round olive top in the dot, and cut leaves in half-moon shape from eggplant. Yellow dots with green leaves also will make a good combination.

No. 14. This must be spaced exactly. The borderline can be made of leeks and the inner design of cooked carrots, cut in Julienne.

No. 15. This can be made of blanched chives or leeks with a small round ball of pimento, at each end.

No. 16. This design is good in black, green, or eggplant brown, must be exact.

No. 17. Same as No. 16. Also can be made of artificial truffles, must be exact.

No. 18. Use half slices of eggs for this design, or, you can use white turnips and cooked carrots.

No. 19. You can use almost any vegetable to make this triangular design.

No. 20. Measure the distances. First, place a long leaf made of leek, green pepper, or eggplant. Then place two leaves next to the long one. A half-moon can be made of truffles or carrots or pimentos. The dot is green or black olive.

No. 21. You can use many colors in this design. You can make the rose of beet, cut the bottom flat, and paste it on. The leaves can be made out of leeks.

No. 22. This design has a vine made in brown out of eggplant cut thinly enough to bend. The leaves are made of leeks. A small cutter can be used to cut red berries out of pimento. Red currents also can be used.

No. 23. This grapevine design is very attractive. It is made especially effective by using rice of the same mixture as that of the sockel, for it is then all white. Take the rice mixture when hot and put through a fine sieve. Stir until smooth. Put in a pastry bag and put the vine, leaves, and roses right on the sockel. The mixture should not be too hard or too soft. If you want it in color, you can use fruit coloring. Brush on with a soft brush. You also can make leaves of leeks or green peppers, the vine of eggplant, and the grapes of white turnips. The grapes are cut out with a small Parisian or potato-ball cutter, and can be touched up with blue color.

No. 24. This ribbon can be made of green, brown, red, black, or yellow. Use pimento, leeks, eggplant, or truffles.

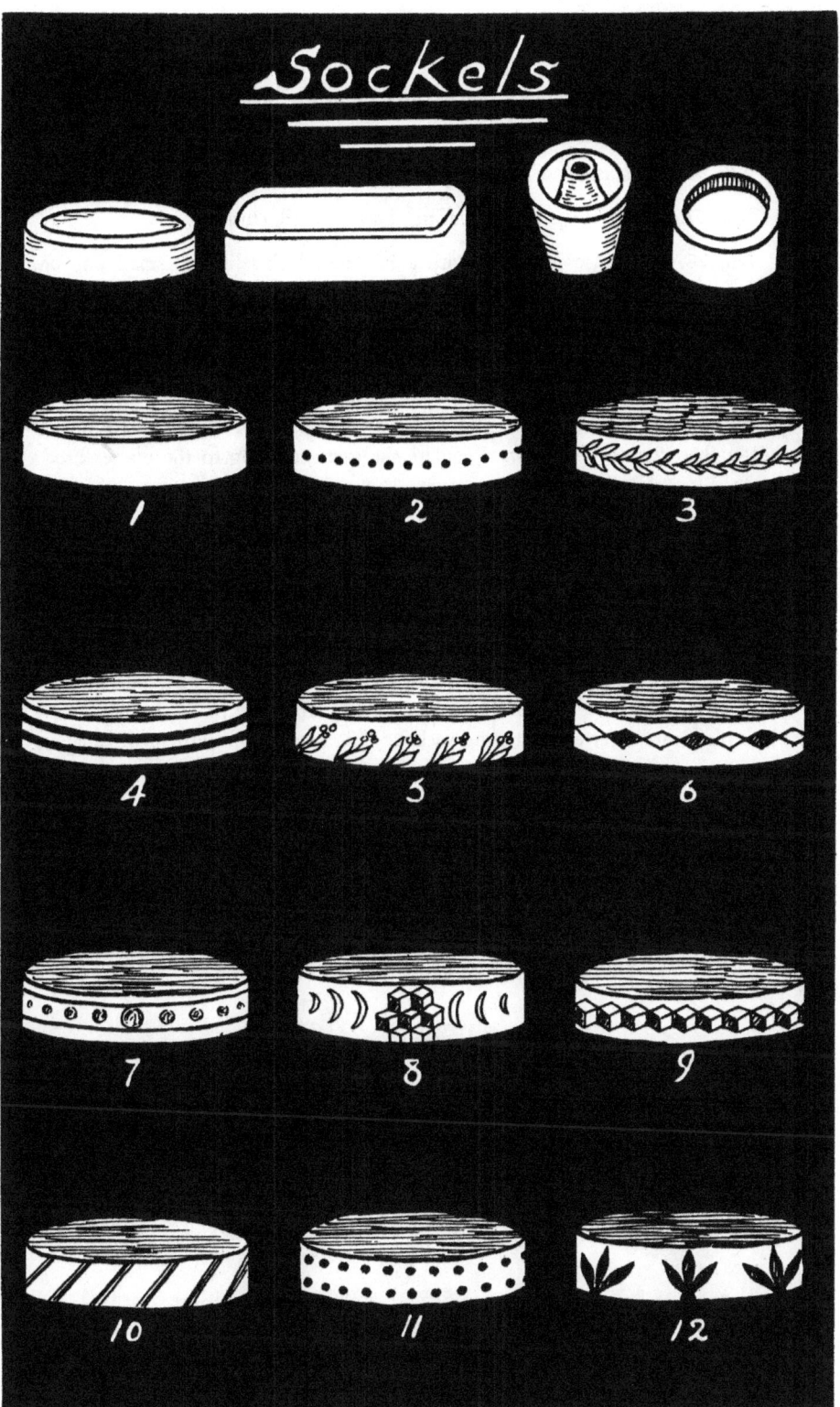

No. 25. This triangular design can be made of carrots and artificial truffles, or pimento, or eggplant.

No. 26. This is hand carved with simple wedges.

No. 27. This also is carved, using a half-round chisel.

No. 28. This also is carved with a half-round chisel. The small one on top is carved with a small paring knife. The lower one is three inches high. The top one is two and one half inches high. The top one should be three inches shorter in length and narrower in width than the bottom sockel. The platter should be the same in length as the upper sockel.

No. 29. This is a triple sockel, hand carved. Each level is two inches shorter than the one below it. Regulate the size according to the platter used.

No. 30. This is a sockel with five terraces. Space the sockels as mentioned above. It is hand carved. You can make the lines at first with a pencil. A small chisel will do a perfect job with the aid of a ruler. The round design is cut out with a cutter and filled with carrot. The small dot can be of black olives inserted the same way. The bottom sockel can be four inches in height; the next one, one and one half inches high, the third sockel can be three inches high; the fourth sockel two inches high, and the fifth sockel, one and one half inches high. They are all, of course, each shorter than the previous one. Small black olives are inserted in the top sockel. This is filled up with small canapes, fish, or eggs of all kinds. It also can be used for small hors d'oeuvres.

Sockels

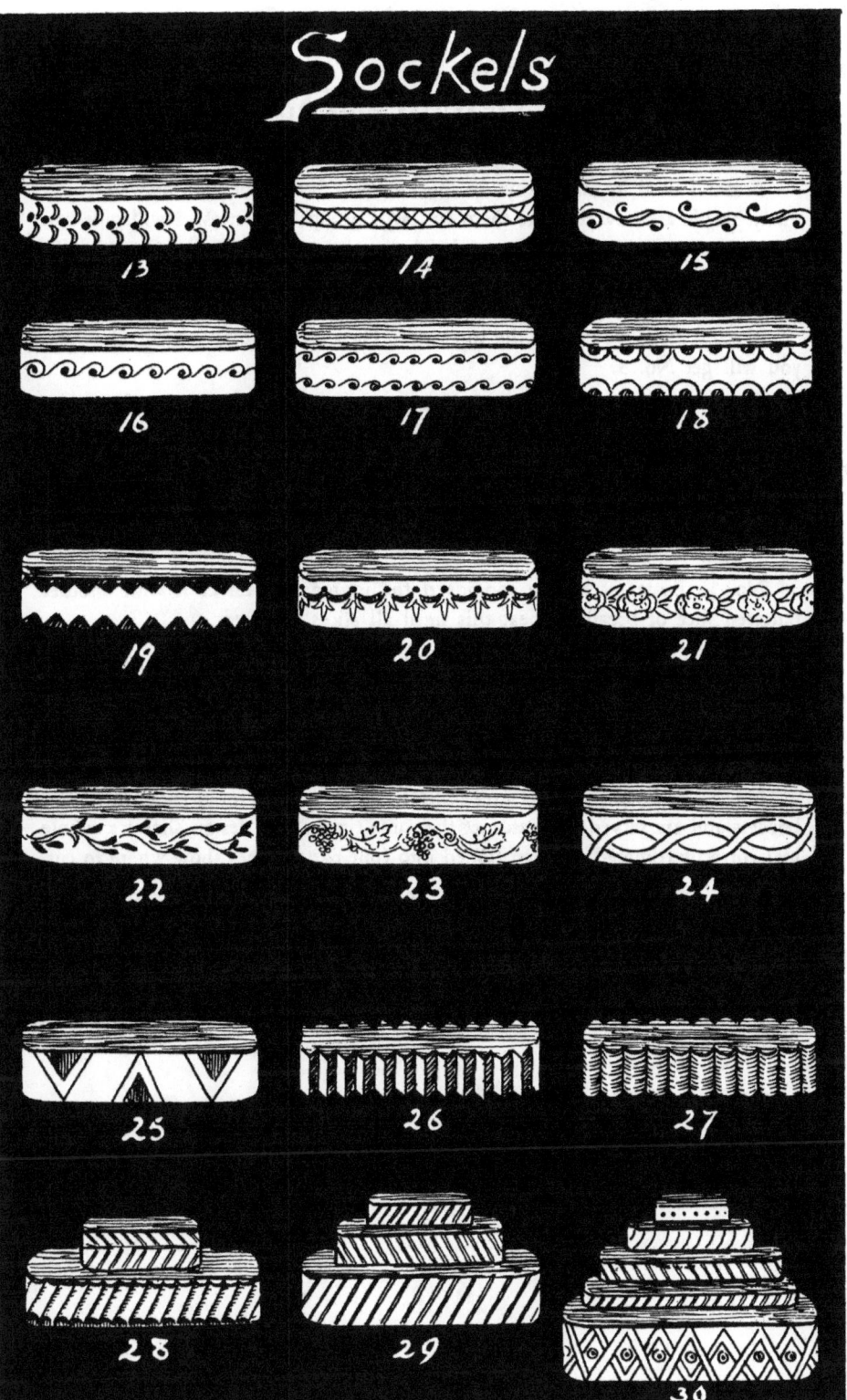

Bread Designs and Socles

Bread is used in many ways in the kitchen. Sandwiches are one way, and many people ask how to make them for large groups or parties. I will give you some ideas on making different sandwiches.

No. 1. The dotted line shows what must be cut off, cutting lengthwise.

No. 2. First, we cut off the top rind. Then cut the other three sides, and you will get No. 3.

No. 3. This shows the bread trimmed and squared. Cut straight down for large individual sandwiches. Butter and add contents, and then trim and cut in half.

No. 4. Trim bread properly and cut thin slices lengthwise. Place on top of each other as in No. 5.

No. 5. Butter each slice and insert the ingredient. Cover it with another buttered slice of bread. Repeat this until all slices are used.

No. 6. Shows the finished sandwich, and how various sizes can be cut. The straight dotted line shows a full-sized sandwich. The dotted line at an angle shows half-size triangular-shape sandwiches. To make finger sandwiches, cut one and one-half inches wide.

No. 7. Croutons or fried bread slices are often used for decorating platter borders and are served and eaten at the same time. This design shows a whole loaf correctly trimmed and partitioned into four parts. Lines show where to cut.

No. 8. This design is one-fourth of No. 7. This is cut in half again.

No. 9. This design is cut through twice, making the crouton smaller.

No. 10. This design shows how to cut triangular croutons. They are $\frac{1}{4}$ inch thick.

No. 11. This design shows how to cut half-moon croutons with a short round cutter. These are deep-fried.

No. 12. This shows plain round slices.

No. 13. To make a crouton more effective, you can cut them in triangular form and stamp a round hole in the center. These are fried in deep fat.

No. 14. This sockel design is used a lot. Cut one full loaf of bread. Trim as in No. 3 and cut in half from upper left corner to lower right corner. This results in two halves as shown. It is used mostly for cold meats, or lobsters.

No. 15. This is a pyramid sockel. It is used for a centerpiece. It also can be fried in deep fat.

No. 16. This design is made from No. 3, cut with deep grooves. This should be the same length as your platter, so measure the bread accordingly.

No. 17. This shows how the round croutons should be pasted on a platter after they have been fried, with little water and flour paste.

No. 18. This design is double. It is made the same way as the others.

No. 19. This shows how to fry croutons in deep fat. Fill a pot half full of fat, and heat to 300 degrees. Place bread in basket and cook until a light brown. Large long sockels will be cooked first on one side and then the other.

No. 20. This shows how to carve wedges in the bread.

No. 21. In this, only the sides are carved.

No. 22. This shows how the sockel must fit the platter. A border of two inches is free. Food is placed on top of the sockel and on the border of the platter. Meat and fish, or other seafood, can be served on top with vegetables around the sockel. Both ends have a carved flower imbedded in parsley or water cress.

Nos. 23, 24, 25. These designs show how to use the croutons on a platter. Creamed spinach is served with the croutons browned in butter. These designs also are used for meats, such as roast tenderloin, chops, fillets, steaks, tongues, or cold meats, hot fish, with or without sauces, and seafood of any kind. This will give your platter a modern look.

Nos. 26, 27, 28, 29, 30. This shows sockels cut in different shapes and combined. You can make them larger according to your need. These are used for hot or cold foods, decorated lobsters, fish, finger sandwiches, decorated meats, hams, tongues, gelatins, chops or roasts of all descriptions, salads, or fresh fruits. In No. 30, silver spears are used.

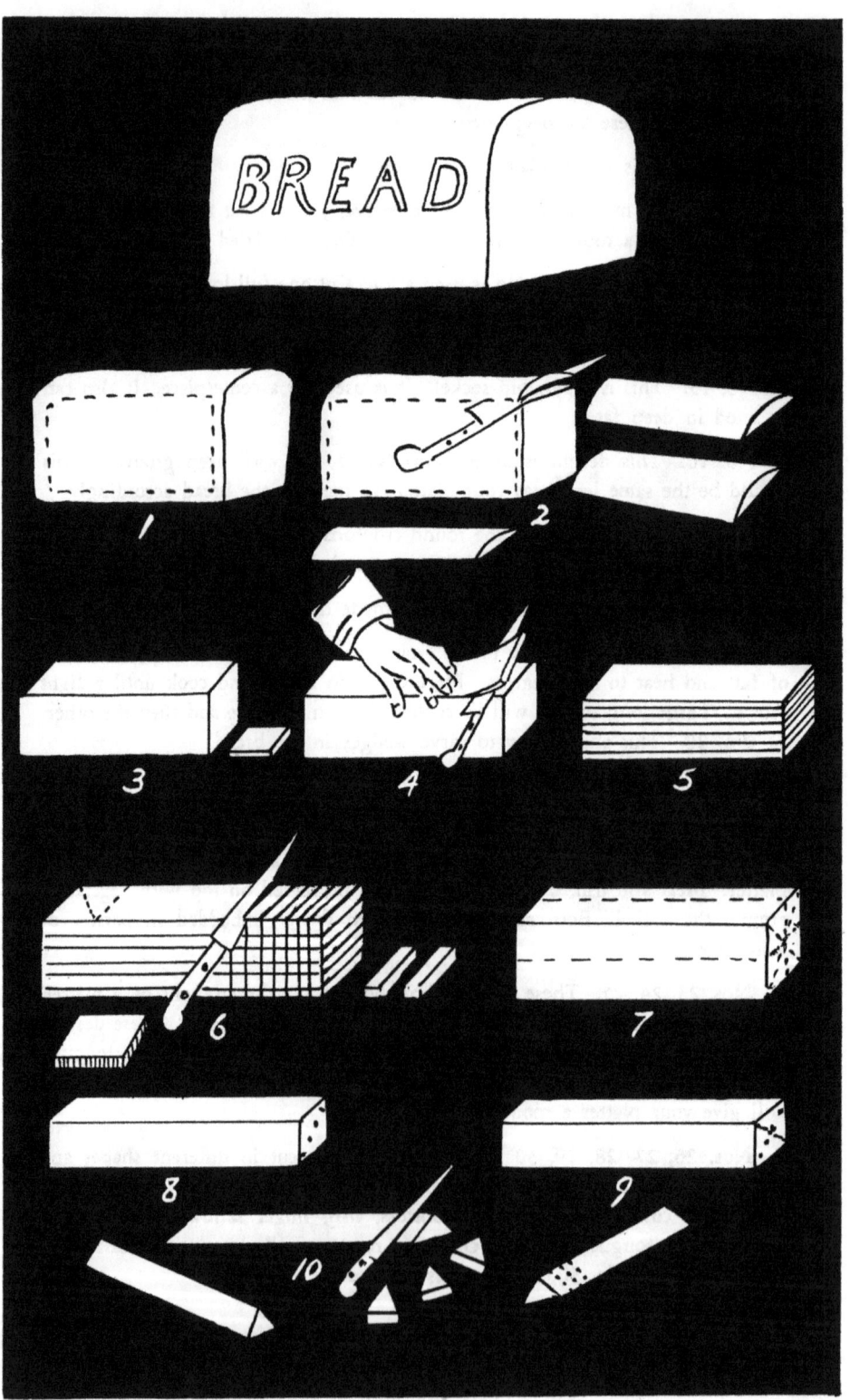

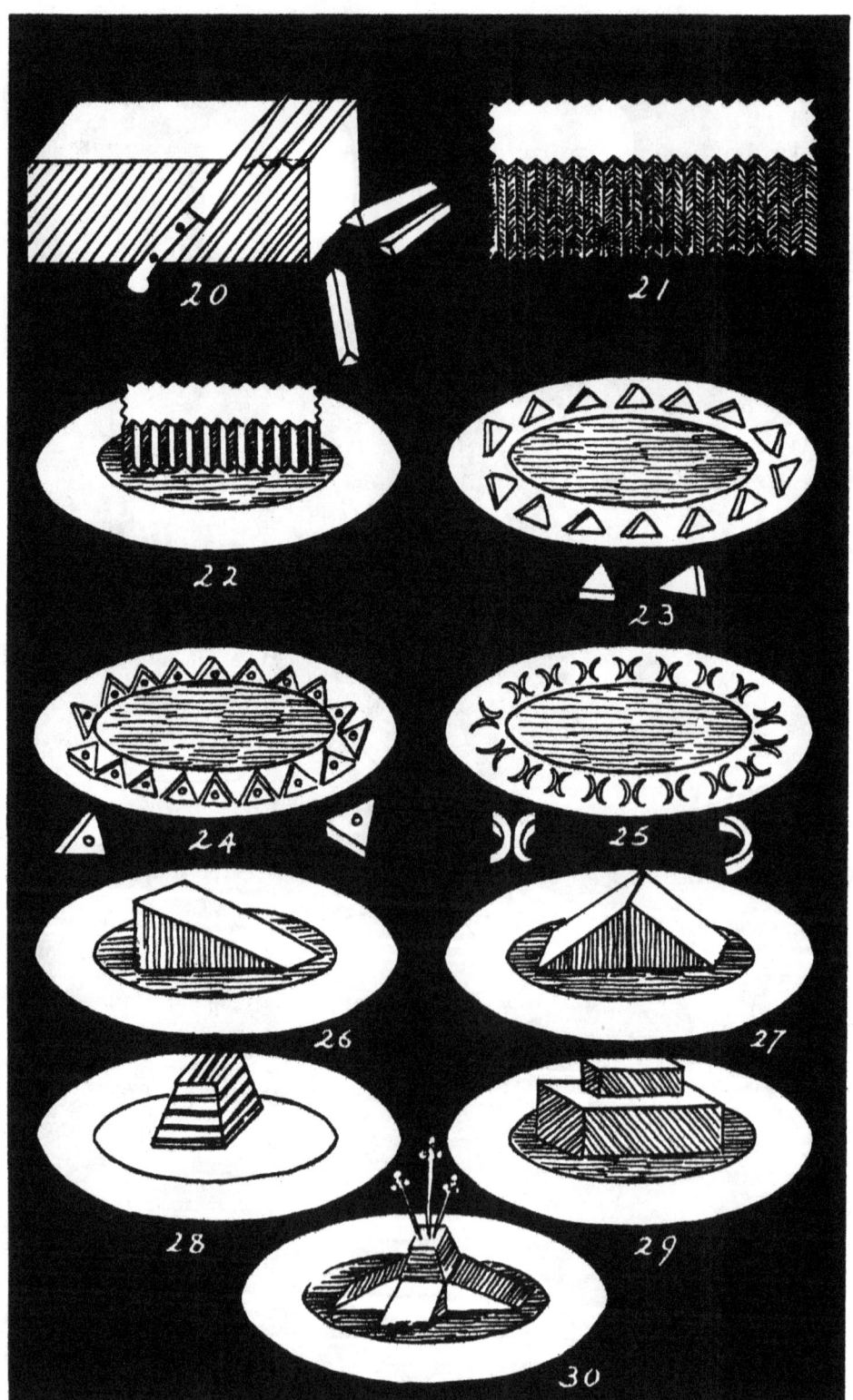

Butter Service

The serving of butter in an attractive manner is a problem to most housewives. Many cooks have not taken the time to study different ways of serving butter, so I have undertaken to give you a few ideas.

No. 1. This is the old method of just slicing any thickness desired.

No. 2. One pound of butter can be cut with a machine in any size you wish. Place butter in machine, and pull one wire down and the other across. This gives you butter tablets.

No. 3. Butter curls are used a great deal in Europe. They require a special curled and peaked butter knife. This is shown in the right hand here. Also have a pitcher of hot water into which the knife can be put. Pull the knife over the butter, holding the left hand below knife so that the butter will drop into the hand. Place in a bowl with ice so that curls will remain hard. This can be served on butter plates or any way you wish, three curls per person.

No. 4. Butter balls are made with a large Parisian cutter. Cut balls even-sized and place between two wooden boards which are grooved. Roll from side to side until you have a round ball with a pointed design. Place in ice box.

No. 5. Julienne of butter is made with a grate. It is well to immerse the grate in hot water and then grate the butter over it. Place butter in a dish in the ice box. You can arrange the strips on a plate like a bird's nest. Put little butter balls colored various colors—blue, green, or red—into the nest. You can use vegetable coloring for this purpose. This is very effective.

Nos. 6, 7. These show how to cut butter with various cutters.

No. 8. Shows how to use cutters. Immerse cutters in hot water so butter will fall from them.

No. 9. Cutting half-moon.

No. 10. This shows wooden molds. The one is round and has a plunger with a leaf on it. Fill the round form about ½ inch, then push the butter out and you have the leaf form. The lower one is a larger design also carved in wood. Put in cold water and the butter comes out as a leaf. Use one leaf to a person.

No. 11. Shows various cutters you can obtain in your neighborhood.

No. 12. After you have made your fancy designs, fill a bowl with crushed ice and put them on top to keep until ready to serve.

No. 13. Butter is put into a kettle and creamed with a wooden spoon. Stir until it becomes fluffy.

No. 14. After you have creamed your butter, place in a pastry bag. Put in a rose-leaf tube and pipe out roses and leaves on wax paper. When paper is full, place in ice box. To make them is quite an art.

No. 15. Have a dish of boiling water on hand with several extra spoons in it so that you will always have hot spoons with which to work.

No. 16. Scoop out of creamed butter, hollow egg-shaped butter rolls. Place them on a plate in ice box to harden.

No. 17. You can arrange the egg-shaped butter rolls this way to serve to your guests.

No. 18. Shows various wooden molds which can be obtained from various hardware stores. There are many different patterns.

Radishes

Radishes are obtainable the year around. They are known to everyone and are indispensable in the kitchen. They can be used fresh as they are, for relishes, in slices for salads, and for garnishing. Select medium-sized ones for full flavor, and these also are best for color. Radishes also are carved and can be used for platter decoration. I will show you different ways to carve them.

No. 1. The radish rose is made by cutting five leaves on the outside of the radish. Leave the inside for the guest to eat. This simple cutting does not need any elaboration. Cut off the top and bottom and lay in cold water. The petals will soon open.

No. 2. If you want the inner part to stand out more, follow the dotted line and remove this meat.

No. 3. Remove the shaded portion here. While not necessary for design, it makes the radish easier to eat.

No. 4. The correct radish as it should look when finished.

No. 5. This is a six-petal radish with the bottom cut off. These are served mixed with olives and celery.

No. 6. Radishes with the top trimmed like this do not keep well, and should not be used too often.

No. 7. This is a white radish. Select a large one and mark as this picture shows. This will form a dice.

No. 8. This shows perfect dice. The holes are made and replaced with black olive pieces. These can be served effectively at card parties.

No. 9. A large radish with good color, thinly sliced for platter decoration.

No. 10. Use cutters of various designs and cut out flowers. These also can be used for platter decoration.

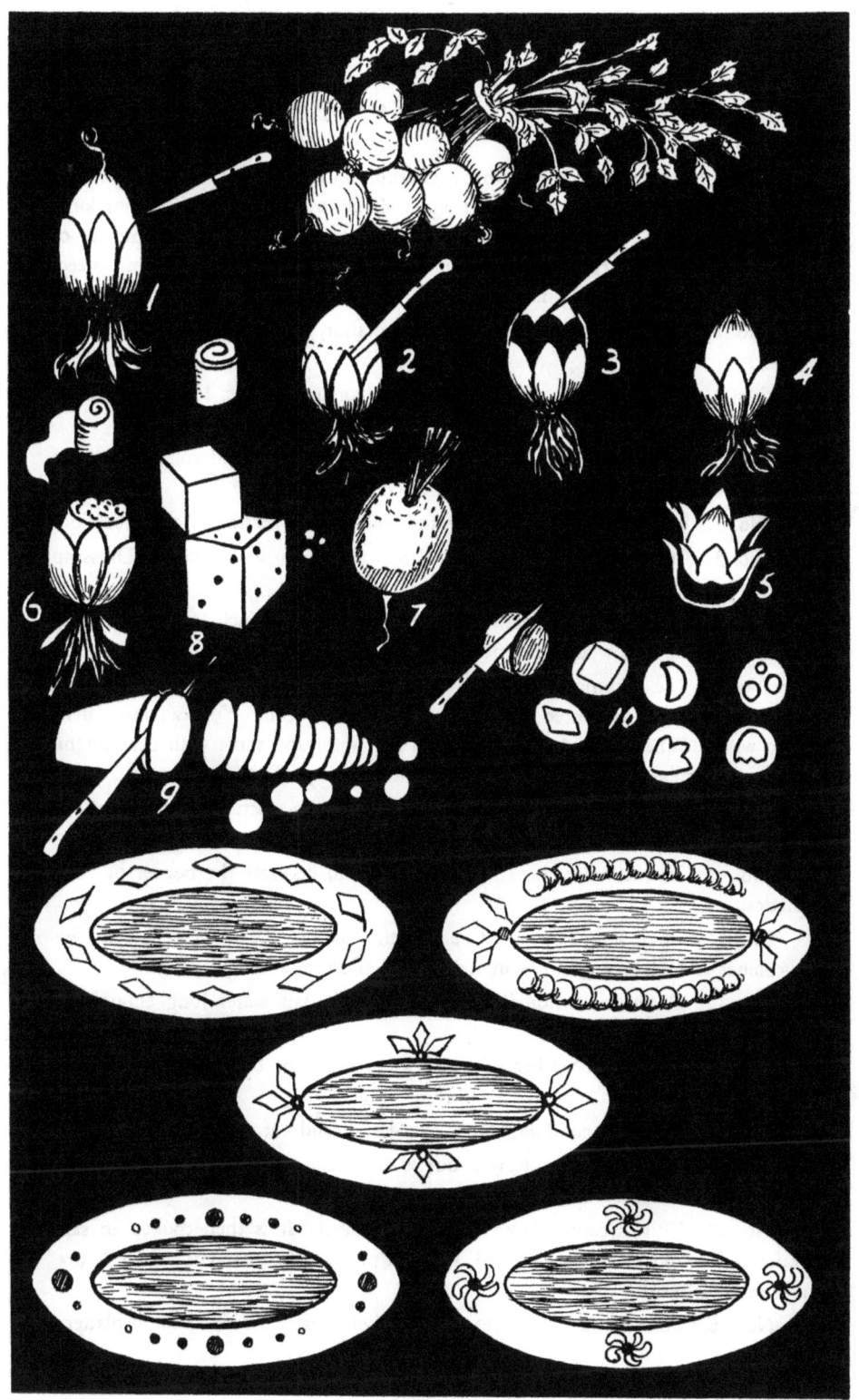

Cucumbers, Pickles, and Gherkins

Many people do not know what a gherkin is. It is a small undeveloped but genuine cucumber. They are picked when about two and one half inches long, and placed in a barrel and covered with salt or sweet brine. The pickle, of course, is the larger, fully-grown cucumber. The best cucumber is medium-sized. They are used for salads and decoration.

No. 1. Slice gherkins and lay them in rotation on a platter or on the food itself.

No. 2. Half gherkins cut lengthways and again in slices, leaving about $\frac{1}{4}$ inch uncut.

No. 3. Press down with a knife on the slices in No. 2 and you will get the fan-shaped gherkin often served in the kitchen.

No. 4. Remove skin of cucumber and cut in slices for salads or decoration.

No. 5. Cucumbers sliced and placed in rotation for a fine salad. Dressing can be poured on later.

No. 6. Peel a medium-sized cucumber and cut a two-inch length for vegetable and then hollow out the meat.

No. 7. The cucumber of No. 6 hollowed out. Do not make it too thin. Cook in salt water for three minutes and immediately cool. You can leave it in cold water. When ready to use, reheat in hot water and serve with peas in the hollow cucumber. Garnish the platter. This is very effective.

No. 8. Cucumbers washed but with skin left on. Scrape with a fork to make grooves and later slice. This is a good method for salads.

No. 9. Cut cucumber slices in half and use to decorate the border of your platter.

No. 10. Take a medium-sized cucumber. Cut out the inner center of the cucumber and serve vegetables in it. This is effective at a fine party.

No. 11. After the inside is removed, cook in salt water long enough to soften.

No. 12. Fill the cucumber with slices of carrots or beets. It gives a nice contrast.

No. 13. This is a gondola. Mark the design and cut out.

No. 14. The gondola hollowed out so that food can be served in it or so it can be used to serve cold sauces.

No. 15. This is carved from a small cucumber. It is then cooked in salt water and placed in vinegar and oil, salt and pepper. Let stand for three hours and serve as relish.

No. 16. This shows half slices of cucumbers neatly arranged on a platter.

Potatoes

It is my intention to give here the names of the various types of potatoes served in the larger hotels and restaurants. This will show you how to prepare them at home or at any place of business.

No. 1. Boiled potatoes can be peeled and cooked whole if they are of medium size. Or, cut in half.

No. 2. Shows how to cut them in quarters.

No. 3. Shows the *wrong* way to hold knife.

No. 4. Shows the *right* way to hold knife.

No. 5. Trim potatoes to a uniform appearance. Cut three edges off. This may take some practice.

No. 6. These are called half-moon potatoes. They can be made in various sizes, and they are usually fried in butter on a slow fire.

No. 7. Natural potatoes usually are boiled. This shows just how much should be cut off the potatoes to get the shape of Natural potatoes.

No. 8. Chateau potatoes are cut the same way as the Natural, only larger. These are usually put in a roast pan in the oven.

No. 9. Rissole potatoes are cut as are the Chateau, except, the point of the potato is left on. These are usually roasted in the oven.

No. 10. Olive potatoes are self-explanatory. They are the size of an olive and are fried in butter.

No. 11. Fondantes potatoes are large Chateau potatoes cut in half and roasted to a light brown in the oven.

No. 12. Large Chateau, made as above.

No. 13. Large Rissole, made as above.

Numbers

The carving of numbers is essential in vegetable carving. There are birthdays and anniversaries at which carved numbers are especially appropriate. To get the best results, follow directions carefully and do clean-cut work.

No. 1. Cut on all four sides.

No. 2. Trim so you can cut the thickness desired for the number. Cut lengthways with knife.

No. 3. Cut carefully to give it the right shape.

No. 4. Cut and trim to get final figure as shown in No. 5.

All numbers are made in the same basic way. Some have curves and others are straight. So, if you know how to make one, you can make the others.

Letters

Letters are carved in the same way as numbers, but are harder to make. They must be uniform in size. This is gained as the start, when you trim or square the vegetable. Rutabagas often are used in place of potatoes because they are larger.

You can spell out names, "Happy Birthday," or other greetings for the occasion.

It is effective to carve your letters and arrange them close to each other, fastened by toothpicks, on a bread sockel 12" to 15" in length, 4" to 5" high, and 3" wide. Place on a platter with a napkin to make an appropriate centerpiece. The guest usually is surprised to see his name appear in this manner.

A little green parsley or water cress placed near the carving is always effective.

The carvings also make effective window decorations.

Beets cannot be used for letters as they lose their color. However, vegetable coloring can be used to color the letters.

When not in use, place the carvings in cold water and keep well covered. When placed in the ice box and with water changed twice a week, the carvings will keep to be used over and over.

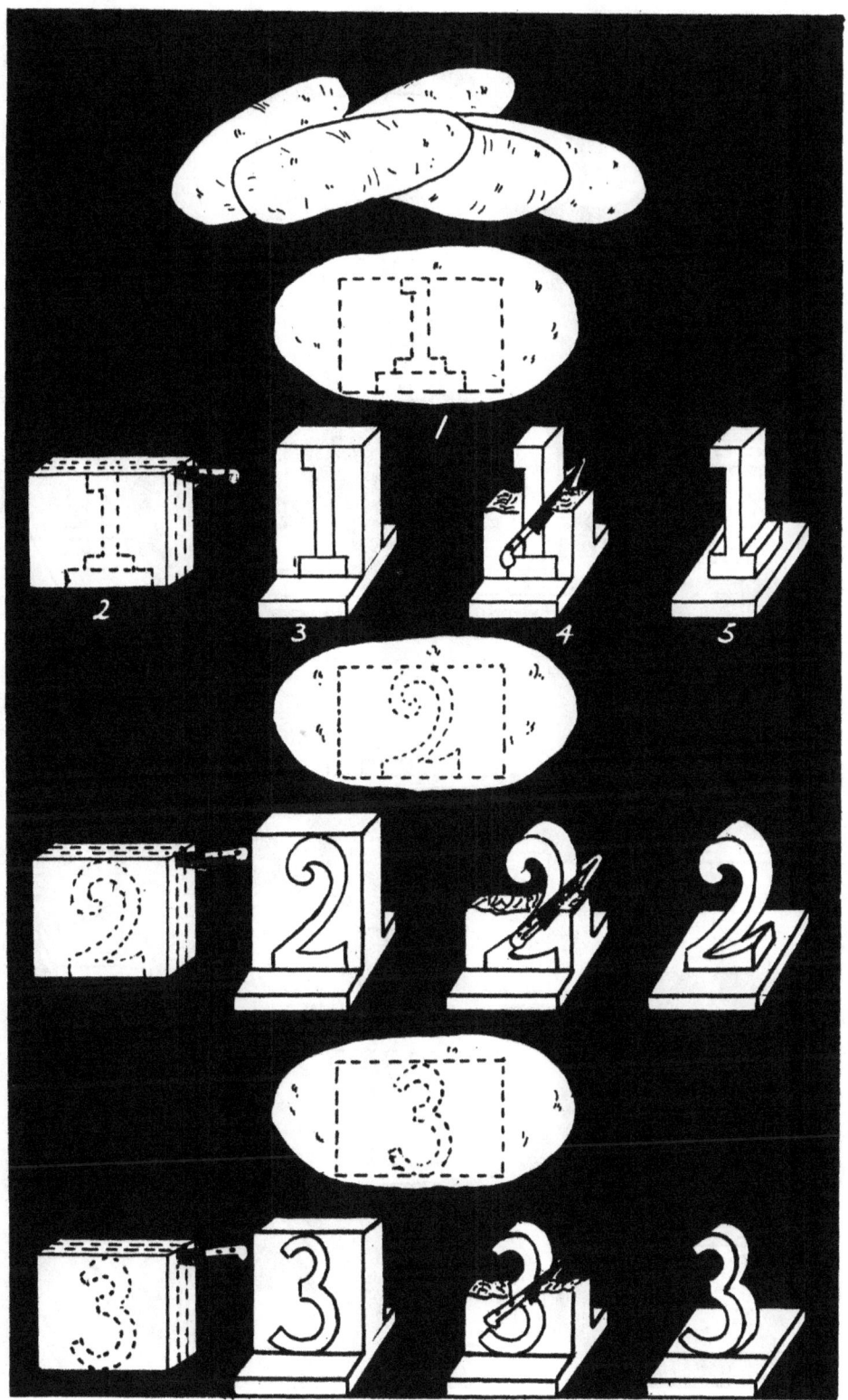

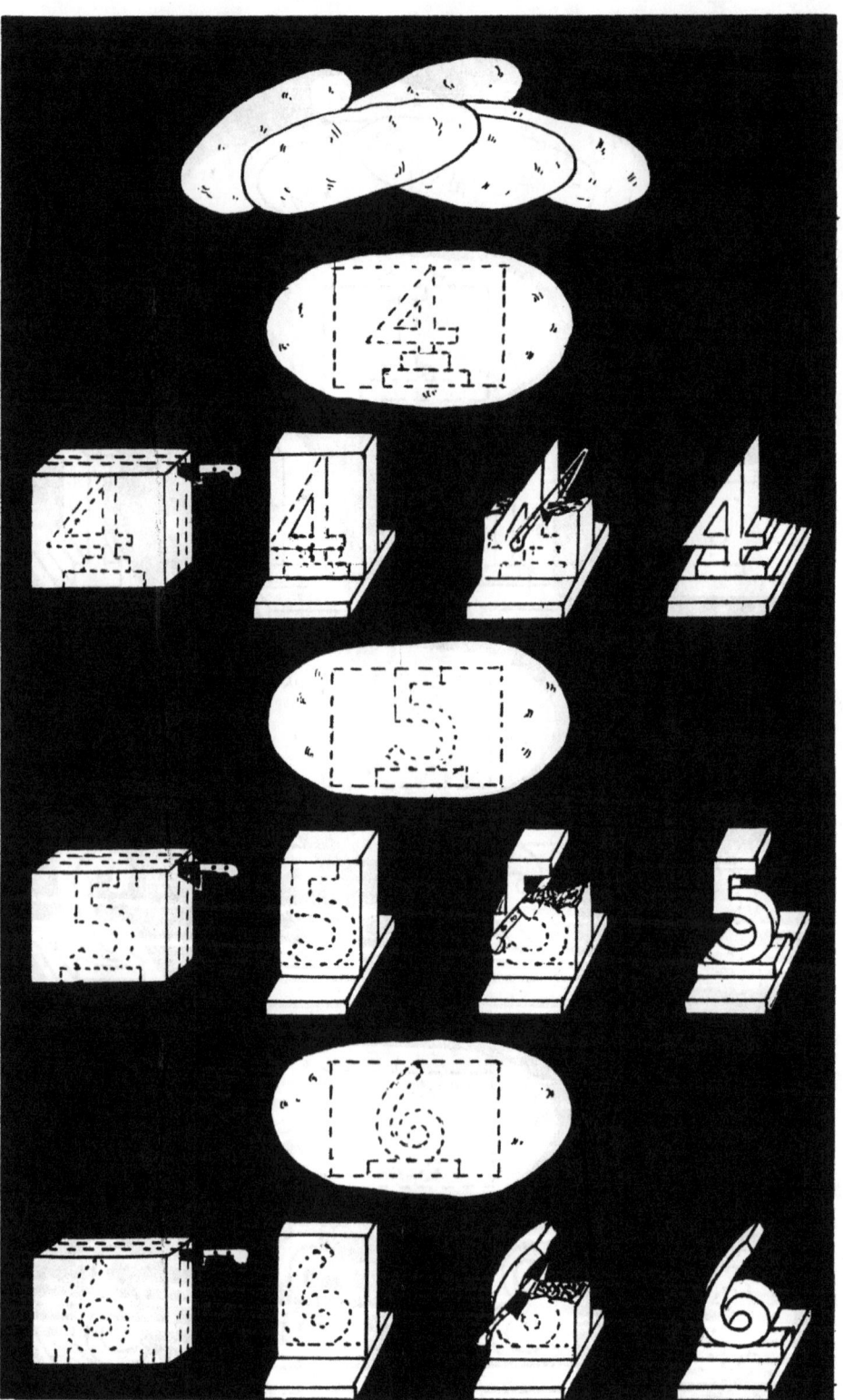

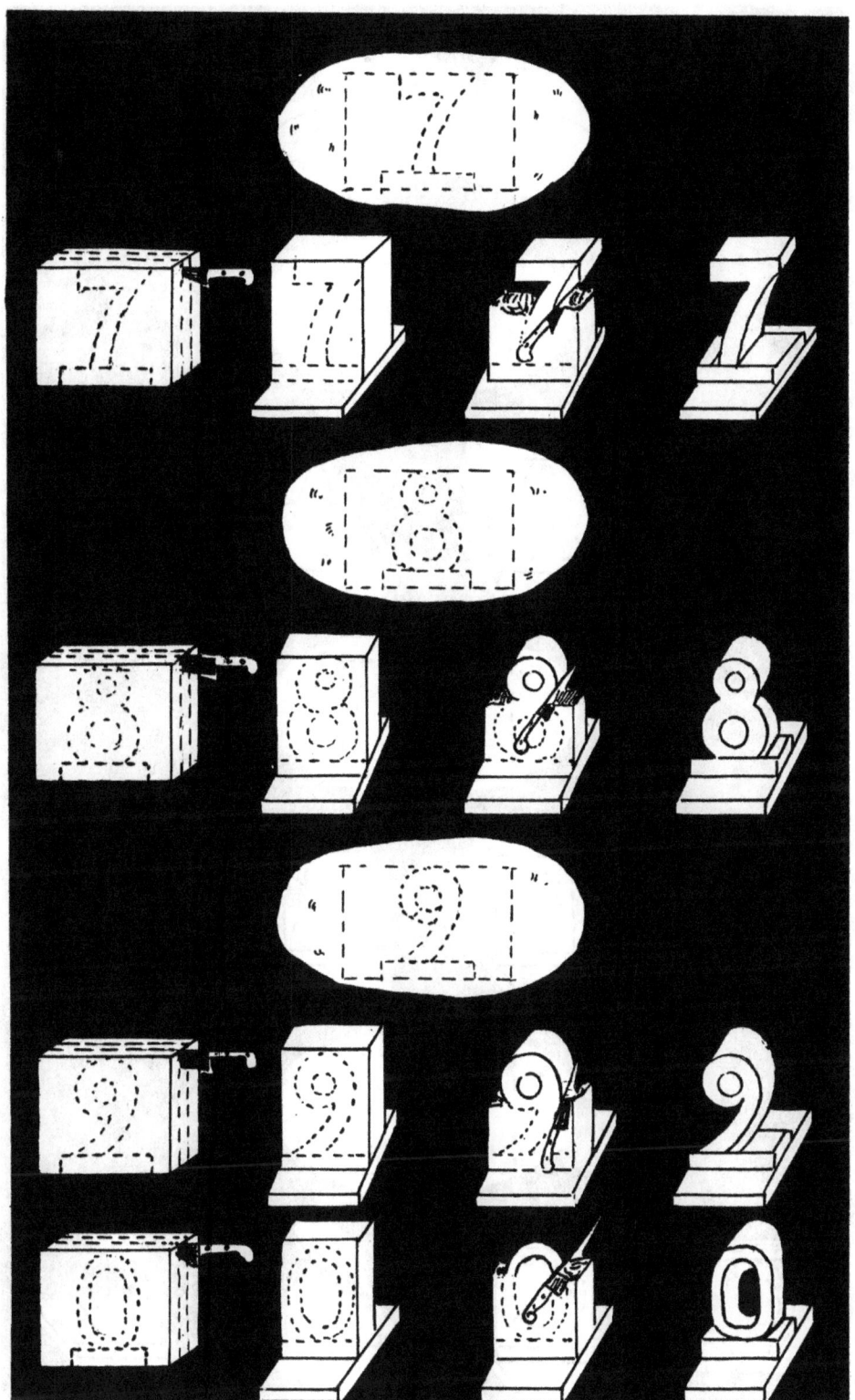

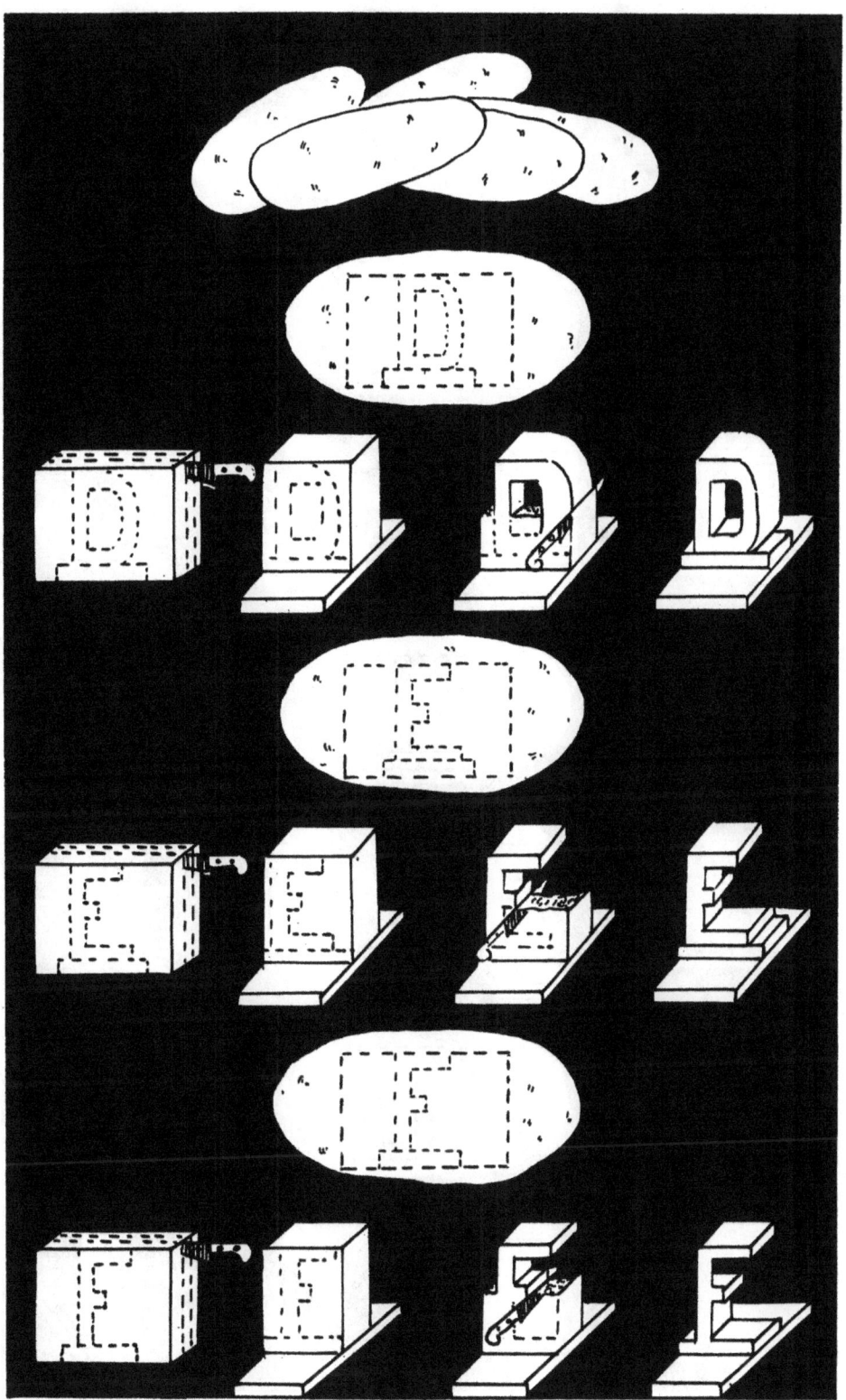

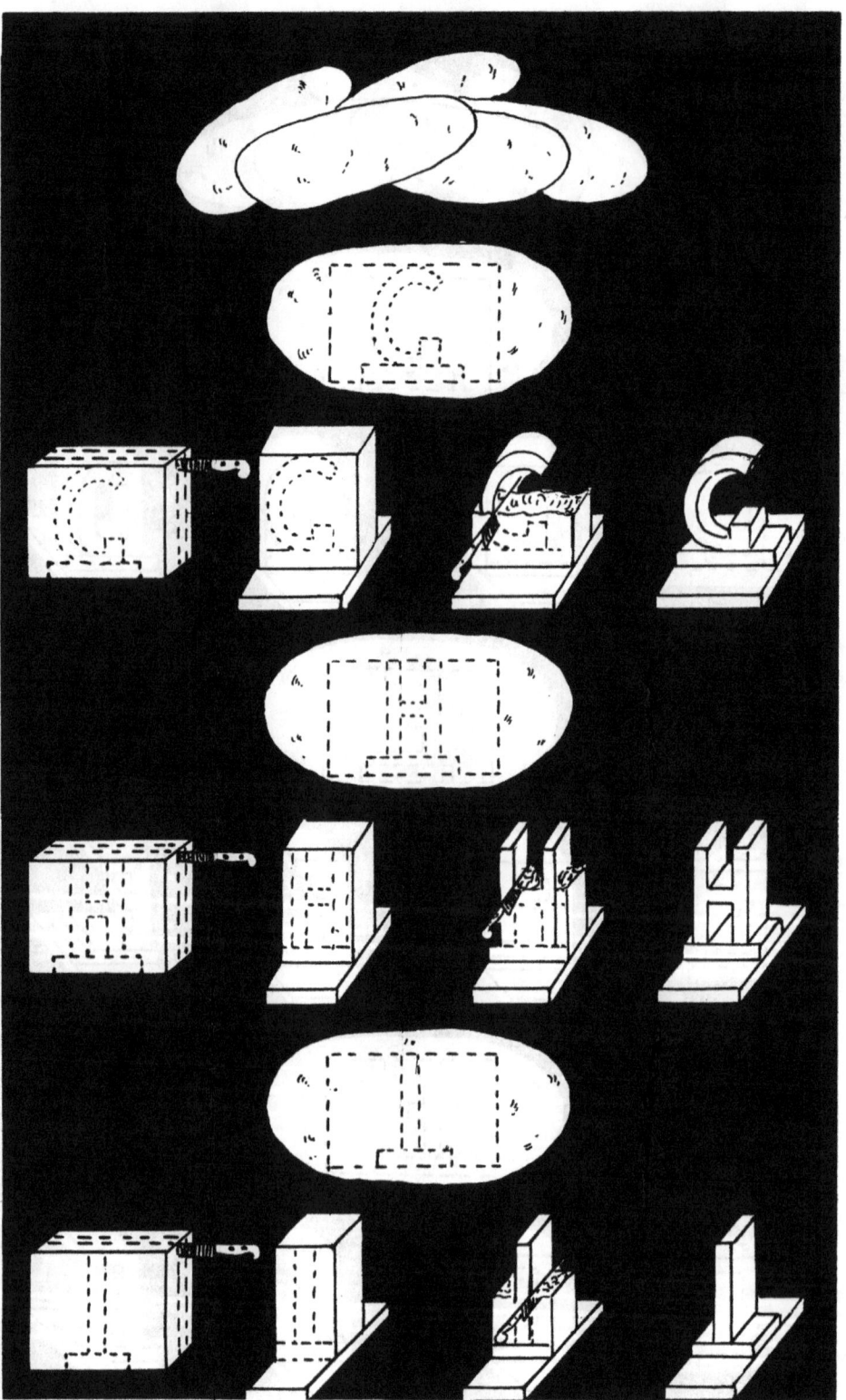

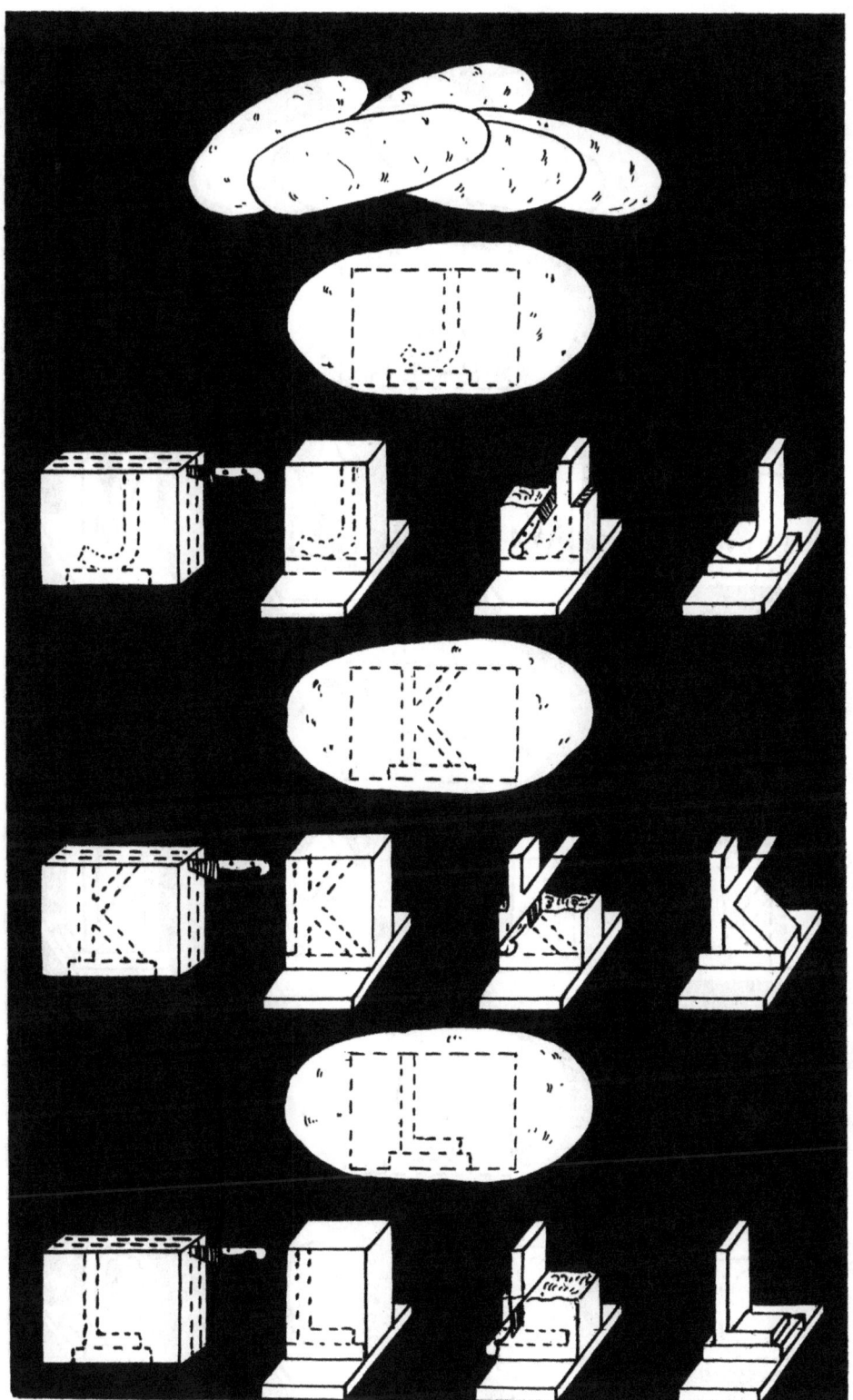

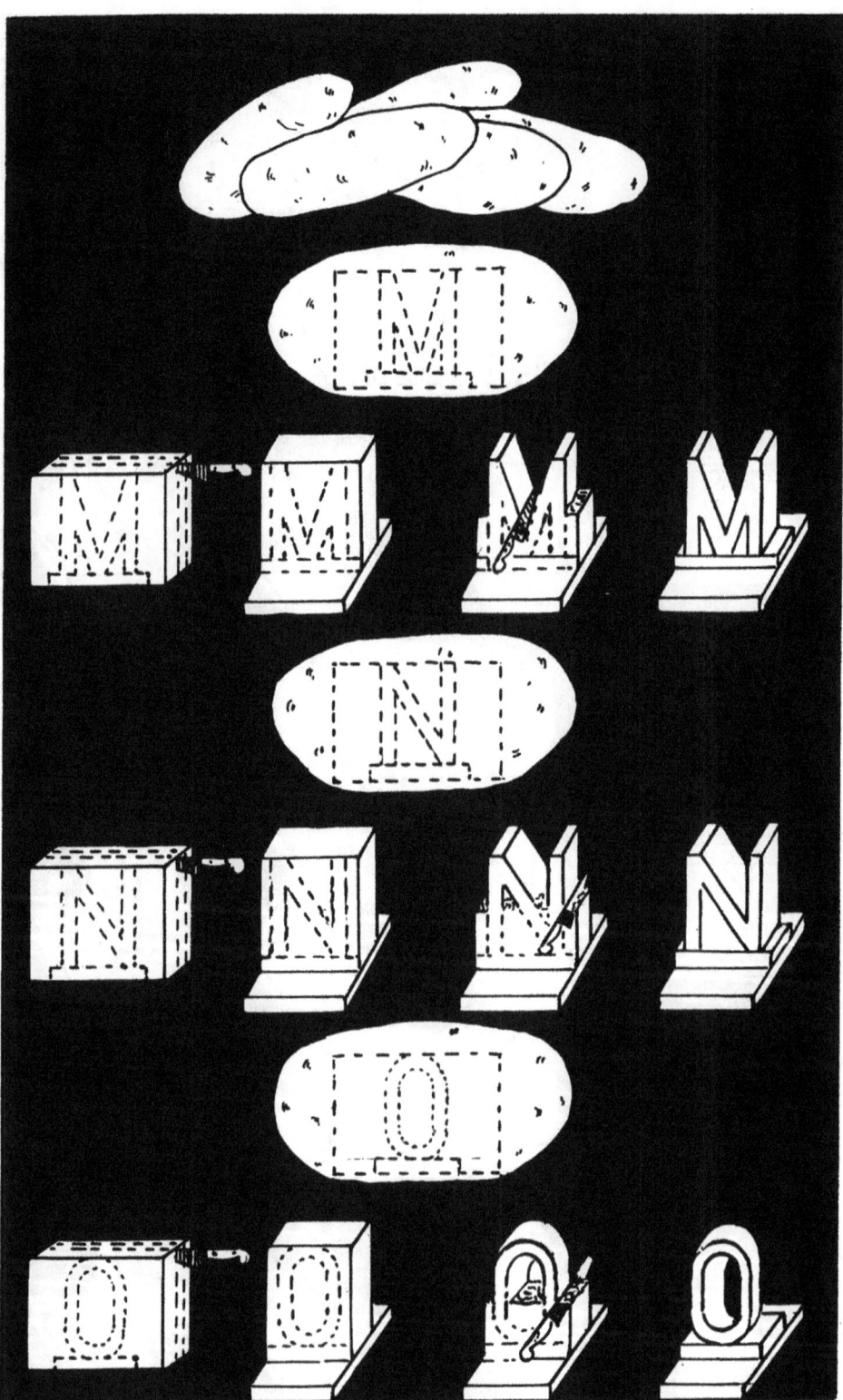

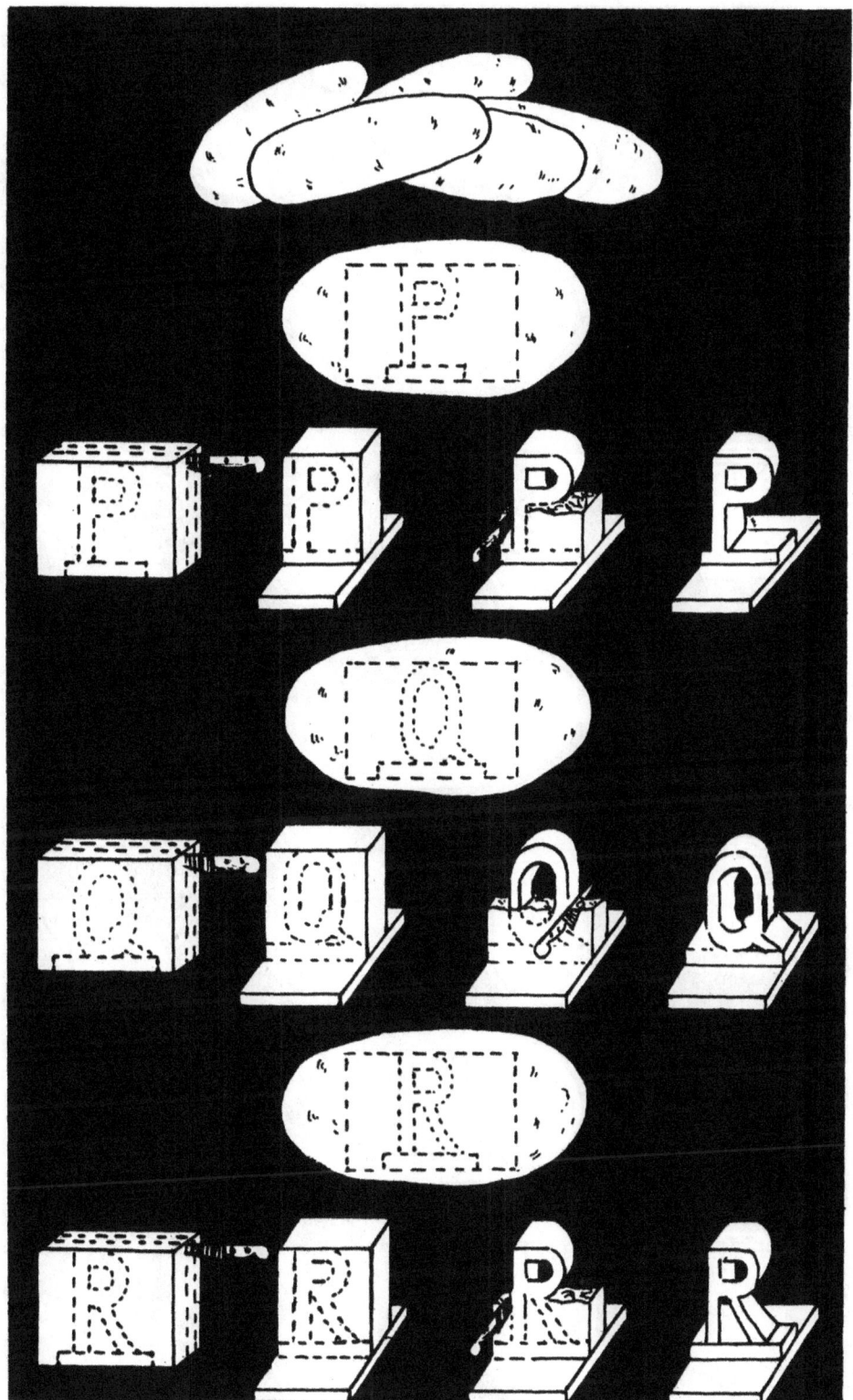

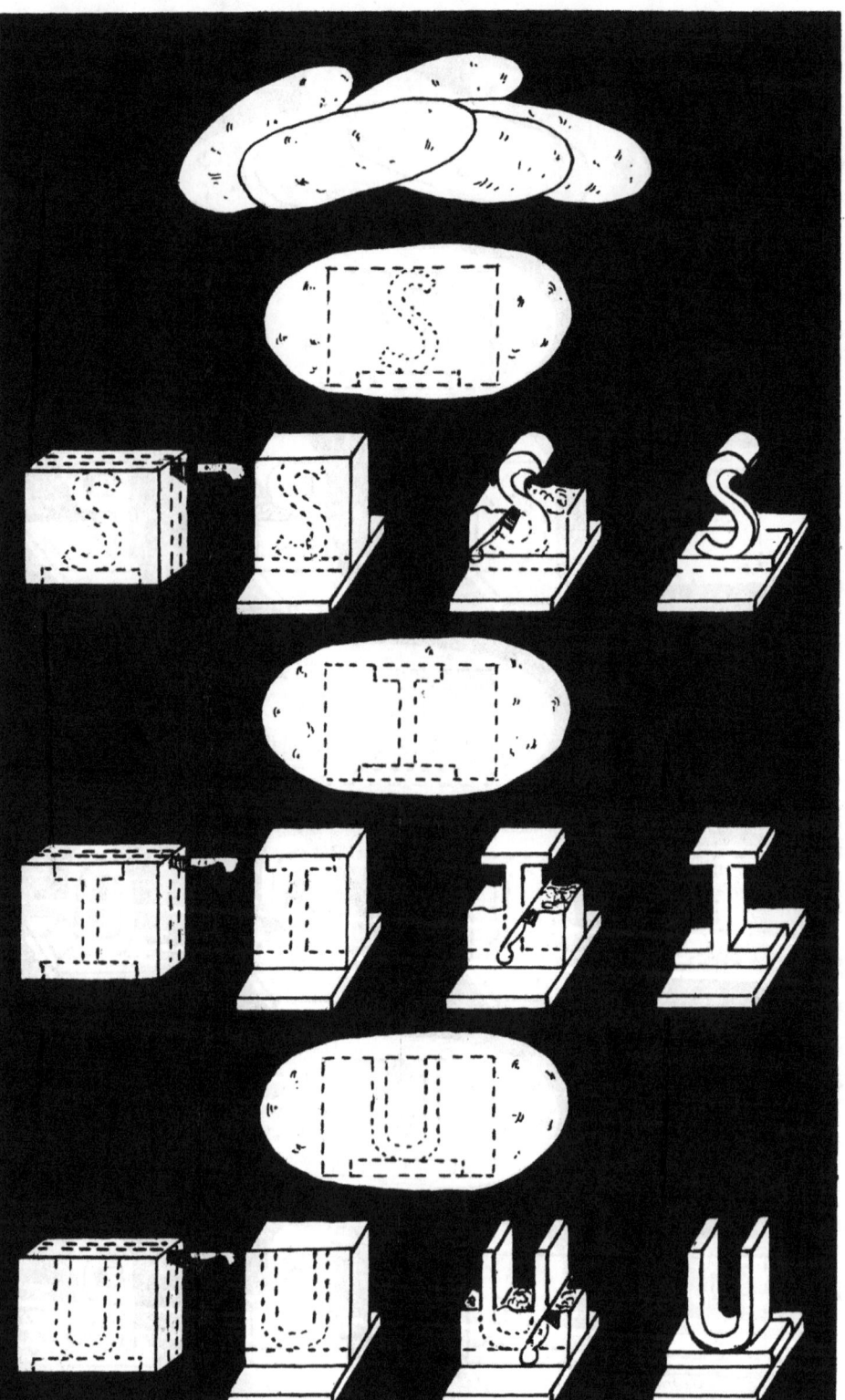

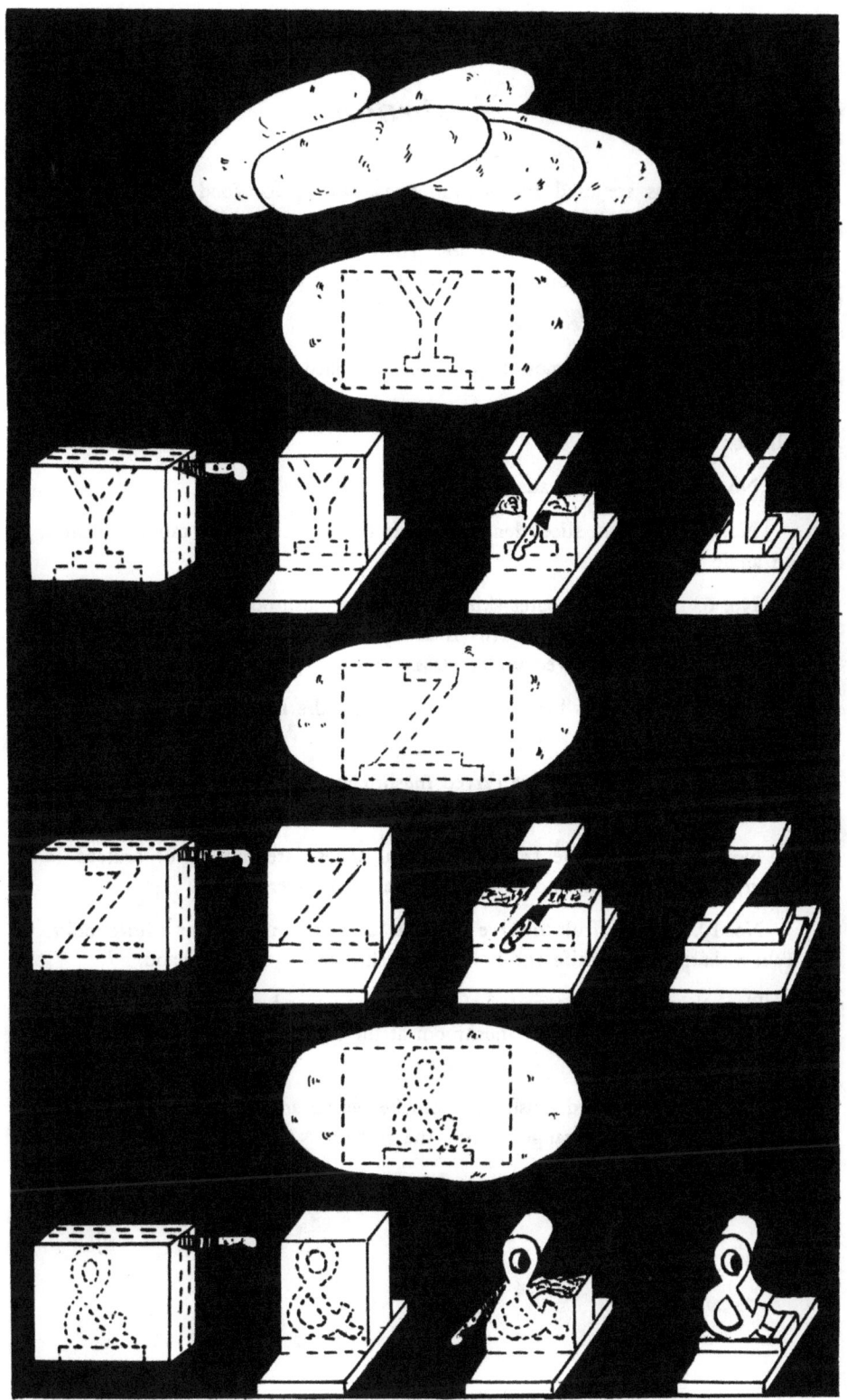

Mushrooms

Mushrooms are used for decoration as well as for food. All mushroom decorations are edible. They should be fresh—not over two days old. Rub them with lemon juice to keep them white. There are various ways to prepare mushrooms. They can be broiled, sauteed in butter, or baked in cream.

No. 1. Fresh perfect white mushrooms.

No. 2. The stem removed; ready to be washed.

No. 3. The stem can be used for many purposes. For example, you can slice or dice them.

No. 4. Mushroom heads sliced.

No. 5. The stem sliced lengthwise. If they are long, you can cut them at an angle.

No. 6. Remove the outer skin and rub the mushroom with lemon to prevent it from turning black. This is always done for creamed mushrooms or when they are to be served under glass.

No. 7. This shows how to press a star into the mushrooms with point of knife.

No. 8. Shows three large carved mushrooms on a piece of toast. This is how they look when broiled or creamed.

No. 9. Rosette made from mushroom. These are broiled or sauteed in butter, placed on toast, and covered with a glass cover.

No. 10. It is difficult to carve a rosette. Have the mushrooms a little moist. Take a sharp paring knife and hold the mushroom in your left hand.

Place the knife in the center of the mushroom and cut from the center to the edge, slightly turning the mushroom at the same time. This gives you the round curve.

No. 11. The cooked mushrooms can be placed around the border as well as it serves for food arranged inside the platter.

Carrots

This design is used in carving an alligator from a carrot. The carrot should be large and somewhat crooked at the end so as to make the tail appear as natural as possible.

No. 1. This shows how to cut the carrot smooth and mark your alligator design. Cut away the part on the side which is not needed and begin to carve on top.

No. 2. Give the alligator a rough outline as shown here and carefully carve the details.

No. 3. After the alligator is made, it can be colored with vegetable coloring: ground—light green; the alligator—dark grayish-green; the mouth—red; the teeth—white, and the eyes, white and black.

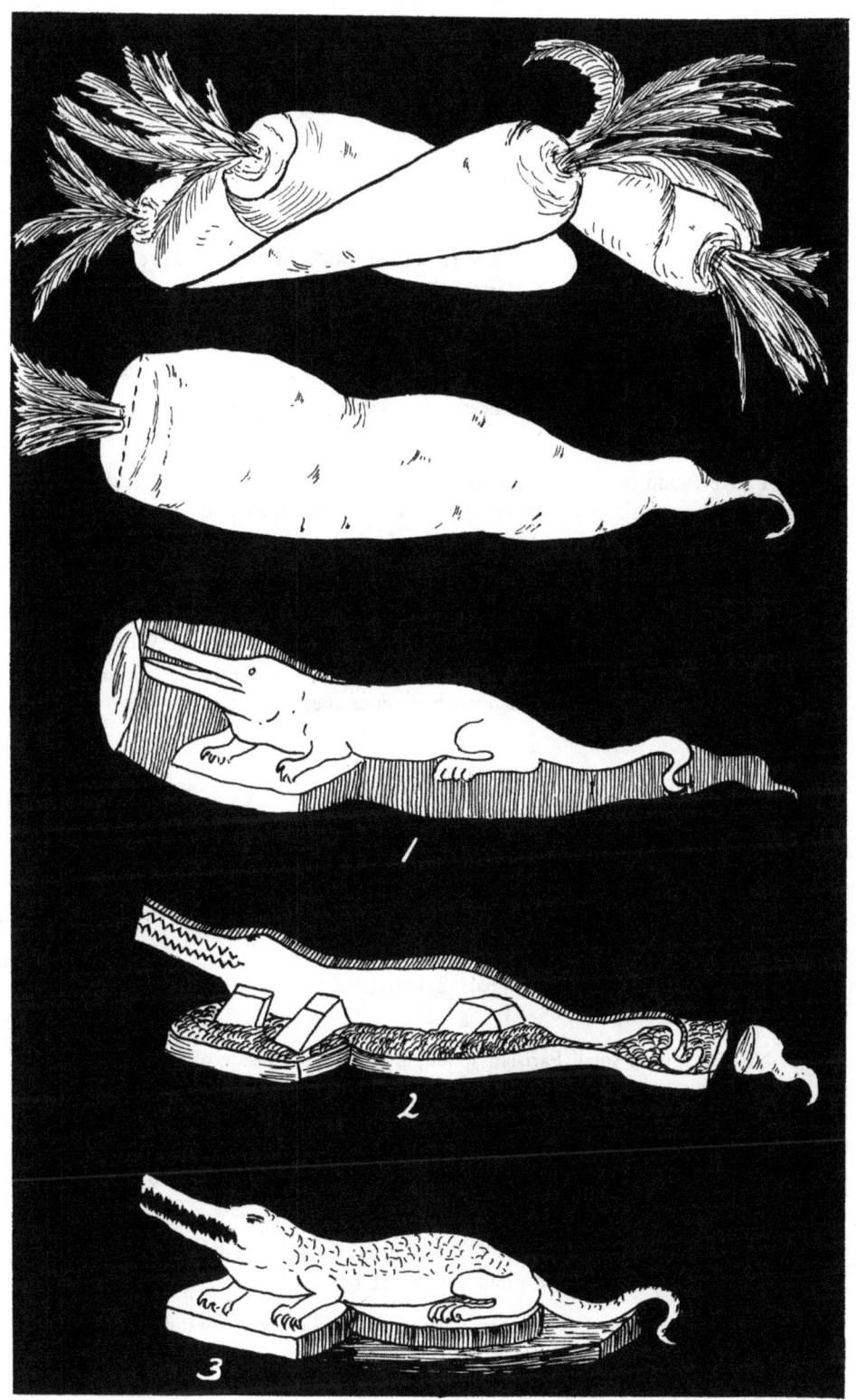

Flower Carving

Flower carving is one of the most popular of all carvings. It has many uses. There are no rules for making flowers. The rose is made more than any other flower because it is easier to make, perhaps. The water lily, lily of the valley, narcissus, and iris are very seldom made. I would advise that you try the simplest flower as a starter. Practice to become perfect. When you have reached perfection with one design, try more difficult ones. Do not become discouraged, because practice makes perfect. It is good to make your flowers in season and adaptable to the occasion. They are carved out of white turnips, potatoes, rutabagas, red beets, and carrots, and add much to your platter decoration.

I have found that children love to do vegetable carving. I have had some from fourteen to sixteen years of age who have developed into artists. If they like it, they will, of course, be more successful.

It is well to use vegetable coloring to color the flowers. It can be put on with a fine brush. Do not over-color, or use loud colors. Never place flowers in water after you have colored them as the color will dissolve. When your party is over you can then place them in water and put into the ice box to use over again. You must then retouch them as they will have lost their color.

Wild Roses

No. 1. The roses are carved out of white turnips or potatoes. Peel the potato and then cut in half. Space or mark your design in the middle.

No. 2. Trim the potato on all sides until you reach the outside leaves, about one inch thick.

No. 3. With the aid of a paring knife, follow the rose leaves until all excess potato is removed.

No. 4. With a small Parisian spoon, scoop out the inside of each rose leaf as in No. 5.

No. 5. The striped lines on the leaves indicate turned-up edges.

No. 6. When rose is fully cut and completed, cut it off the potato and paste on the platter.

No. 7. This shows how the finished rose is placed on the border of the platter. They can be colored pink, yellow, or red.

No. 8. This is a cutter design often used for border decoration.

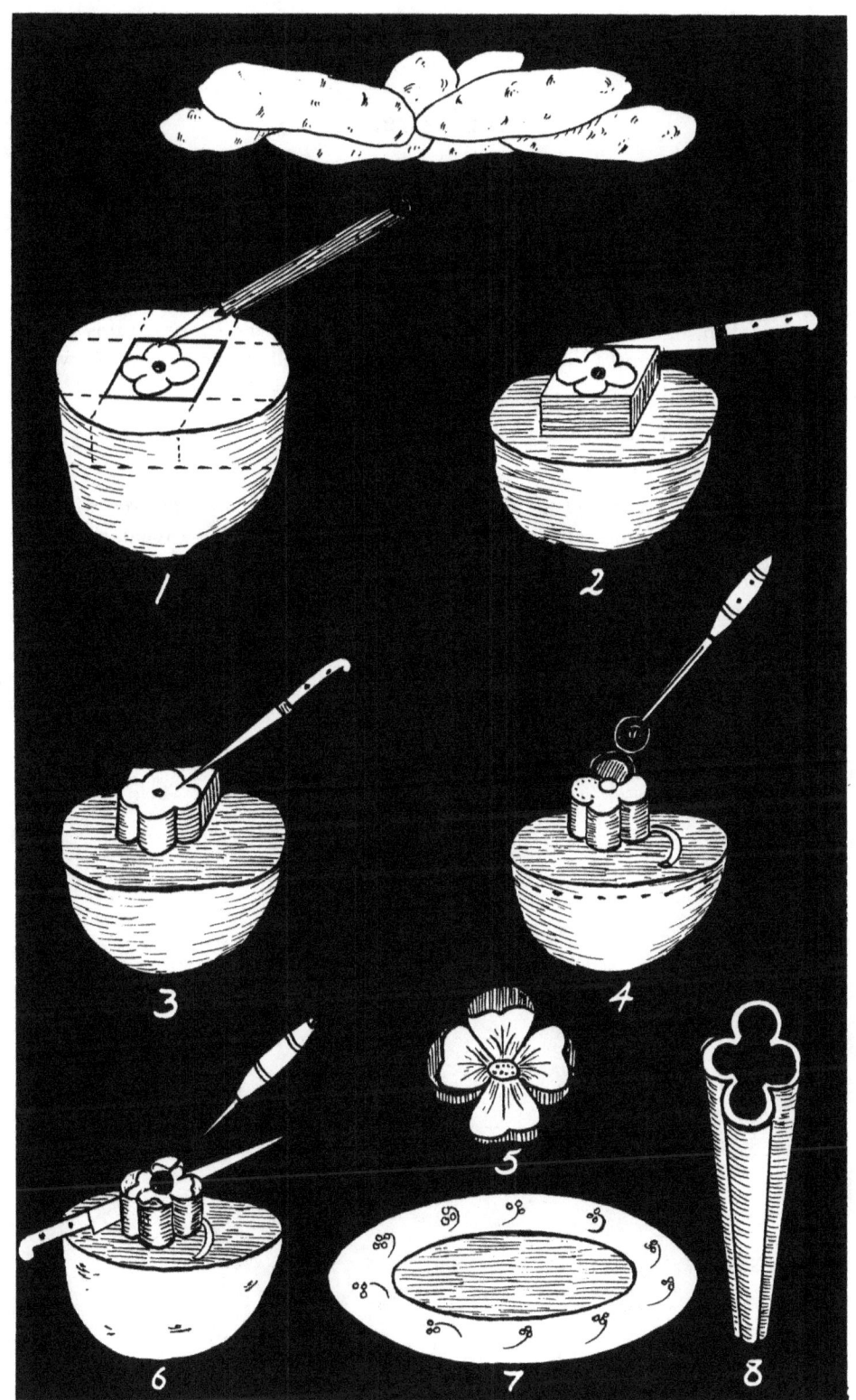

Daisies

No. 1. Peel the white turnip and cut it in half. The design is marked in the middle.

No. 2. When you have marked your design, cut with the tip of your paring knife 1/4 inch deep following the line of your leaf. Cut all the way so it stands out as shown. Cut again from the inner ring all along the leaves towards the outside until a small piece falls out as shown. This will form your leaf. Carve the stem later.

No. 3. This shows the design after it is all cut out. You can omit the stem if you wish.

No. 4. The leaves of the marguerite now can be made any shape you wish. You can make them oval as shown in No. 2. This is done with a round chisel, or you can reverse the chisel and make the leaf partly sunken or hollow.

No. 5. The marguerites can be attached to a fine wire with a few leaves also cut from the same turnip and placed in a vase cut from a large turnip. The vase is carved with scenery by a method explained in the section, "How to Make Vases."

No. 6. Shows how attractive a platter will look with marguerites placed around the border.

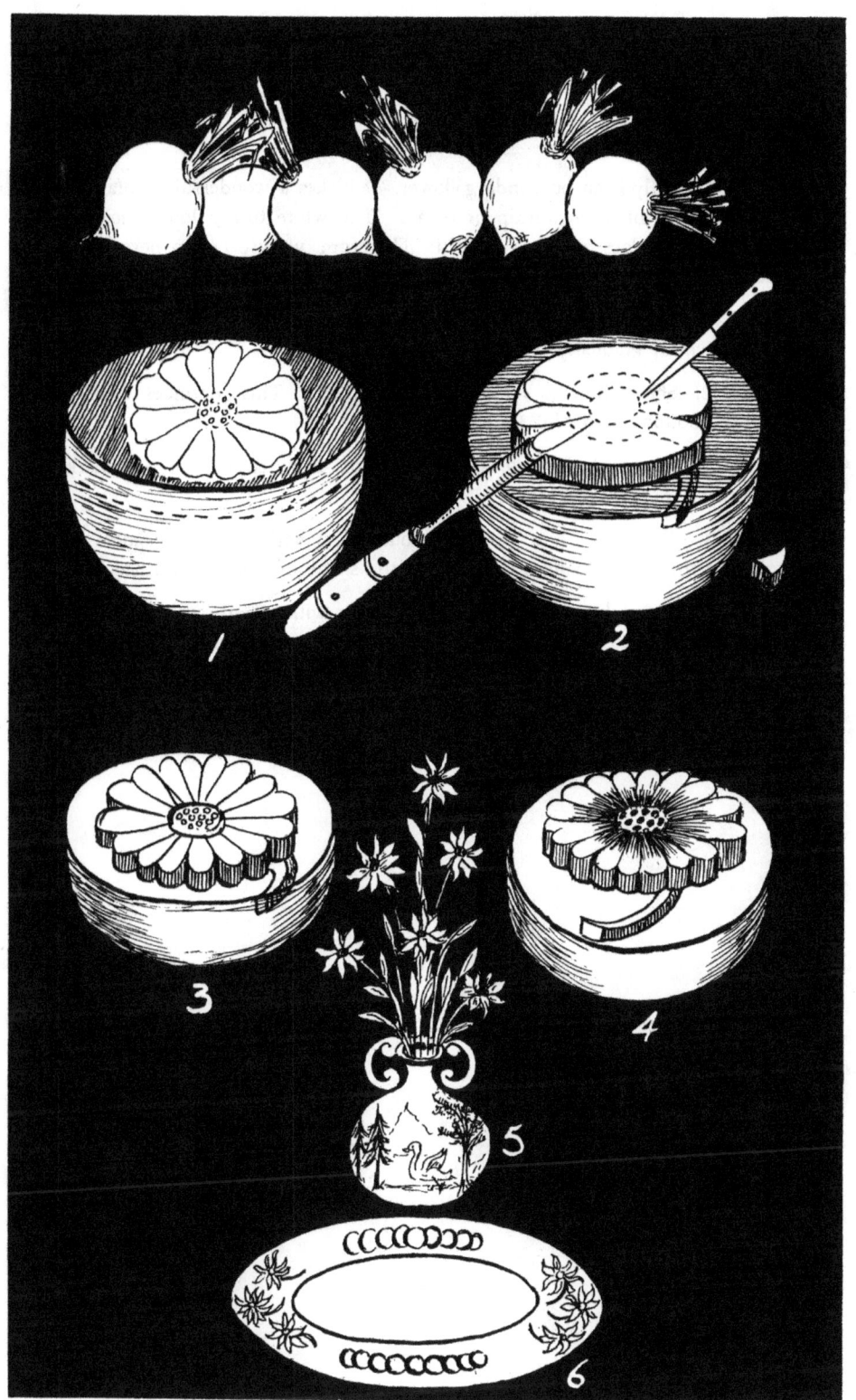

Calla Lilies

The calla lily is an outstanding flower. It makes a wonderful decoration. It is made out of white turnip or potato. The white turnip looks nicer than the potato, but does not keep as well. Therefore, we use potato here instead. They keep a long time in cold water in the ice box if the water is changed daily.

No. 1. The potato is peeled, and the dotted line shows how to begin. Remove the meat gradually until you obtain No. 2.

No. 2. Shows how to remove meat gradually. This continues until you reach the bottom as in No. 3.

No. 3. This shows lily exposed and cut out. Now cut out the part marked here with a dotted line.

No. 4. This shows how we hollow out No. 3 with a Parisian spoon. We scoop out the meat leaving a thin leaf in the shape of a nearly finished lily.

No. 5. Shows how we insert a green wire with a little stem cut out of potato also attached, to finish the lily. The center stem is colored yellow.

No. 6. This shows how a bouquet of lilies can be placed on a platter. This is especially appropriate at Easter time. You also can carve two nice roses to place in green parsley, as shown in the picture.

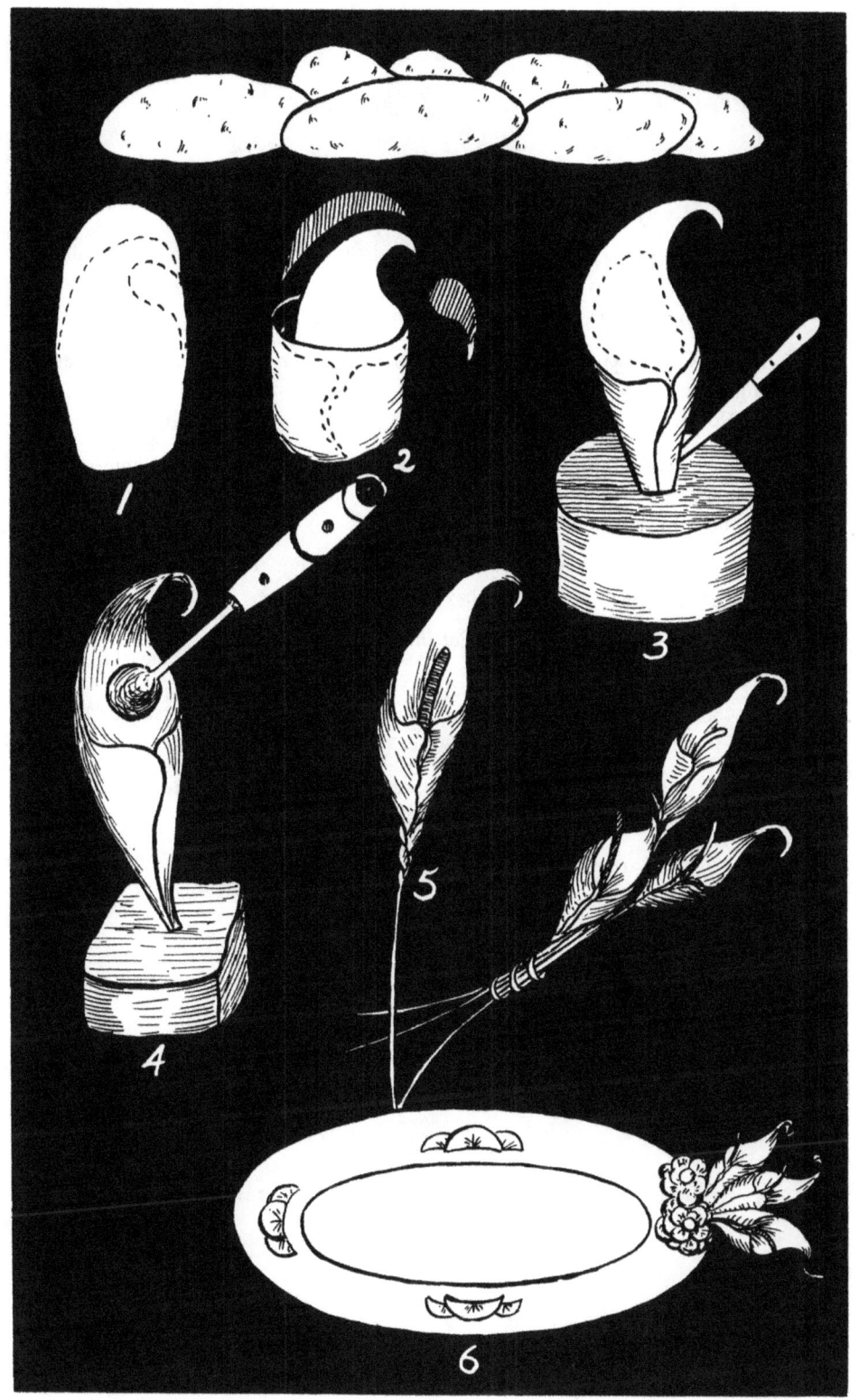

Morning Glories

Morning glory is made out of potato or white turnip. This flower is easy to make and very attractive.

No. 1. Mark the design into the potato with a blue or red pencil as shown here. Make it about 4" in length at the beginning, and when finished it will be about 3" in length. Always cut off from the bottom.

No. 2 Cut the potato off in an oval shape as shown here. Remove the meat, leaving a top of one inch in thickness, and constantly work down until you get figure No. 3.

No. 3. Shows a heavy top. The shaded portion below shows a reinforcement of the potato. The inside is removed with a scoop. You can use a half-round chisel to get a really deep effect.

No. 4. Trim the flower in perfect size. Carve out the petals. Mark them in with pencil at first, and always have an uneven number.

No. 5. This shows the detail. Put in centers which you can buy in a flower shop. Put heavy wire into the stem.

No. 6. This is wire which is used for artificial flowers. You can purchase these in small bundles in any flower store.

No. 7. Wind two or three flowers together and bend in any direction. Lay flat or put into a vase. When coloring, choose soft colors.

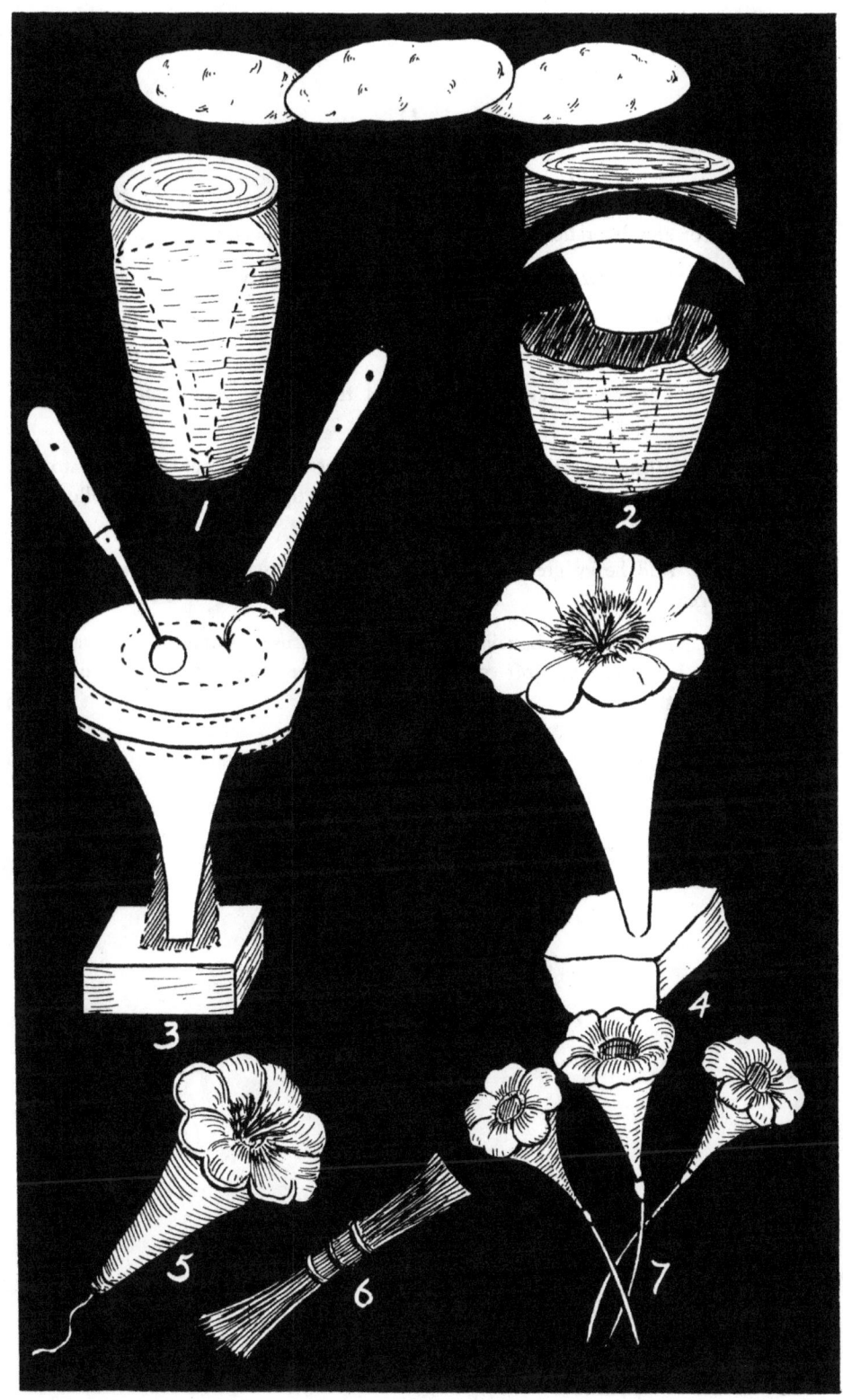

Tulips

The tulip has grace and distinction. Though not easy to make, they are colorful for any decoration. They can be made out of potato or white turnips.

No. 1. Mark your design and count your leaves. They should have five.

No. 2. Remove some of the top and give it proper form all around. Mark distinctly so you can follow.

No. 3. Cut the top and slightly round the bottom. Be careful not to break it.

No. 4. When the tulip has its right shape, cut the inside out with a potato scoop. Be careful not to slip with the knife. Cut the petals thin and hollow out completely to within one inch of the stem.

No. 5. Add heavy green wire to the tulip and insert a yellow center of artificial centers.

No. 6. They look the best in a bunch. You can use a single color or various colors, but always use soft colors. A vase can be made out of turnip or a melon basket.

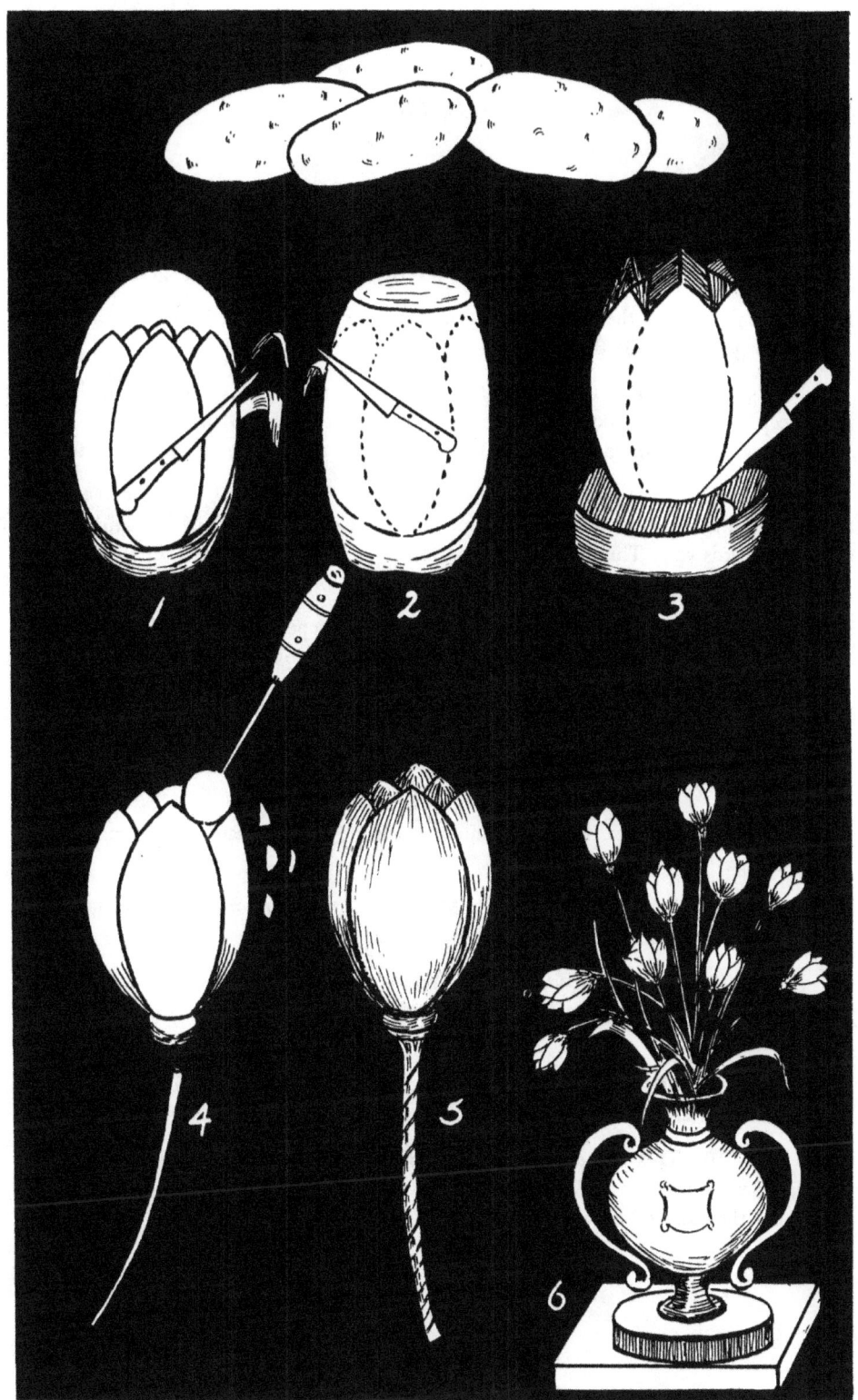

Roses

The rose is used more than any other flower, because it is easier to make. It is found on every platter where vegetable carving is used. They are made from potatoes, turnips, beets, and carrots, and colored various shades. The round leaf is most popular, as the pointed leaf needs more experience in carving.

No. 1. Peel the potato and mark leaves with red pencil in such a way as to get five petals the same size.

No. 2. After you have marked the leaves, insert your pointed knife and keep cutting all around from the top of the dotted line to the bottom of the leaf where the dotted line ends. This is about ¼ inch above the potato bottom.

No. 3. Shows how to take the inside out. Start about ⅛ inch above the dotted line. Cut all around with your knife. Hold the point of the knife out or towards you. This will enable you to cut out the portion between the leaves where they come together.

No. 4. After removing all meat as in No. 3, repeat the operation over and over until you reach the center. Mark with pencil to be accurate. If the uncarved potato is pointed too much, cut off some of the top to make it level. See that the leaves on the outside are even.

No. 5. When the rose is finished, check it and take out all meat from the corners. You can color the rose any color you wish.

No. 6. This rose is more pointed and has 15 to 17 leaves. It is made of rutabaga.

No. 7. Shows a flat rose with 37 leaves. It is done with the usual procedure, but the leaves are cut short by half the length.

No. 8. This is difficult to make. You need a large potato or turnip. Mark the leaves and carve them deep at the base. The end of each leaf is pointed and bent outward.

No. 9. Shows how leaves are carved out of a slice of potato or turnip. Mark them and make them uniform in size.

No. 10. This design shows more thickness. You can cut it with a knife and use a chisel to make the leaves waved as in nature. You can put these under the roses or on a platter.

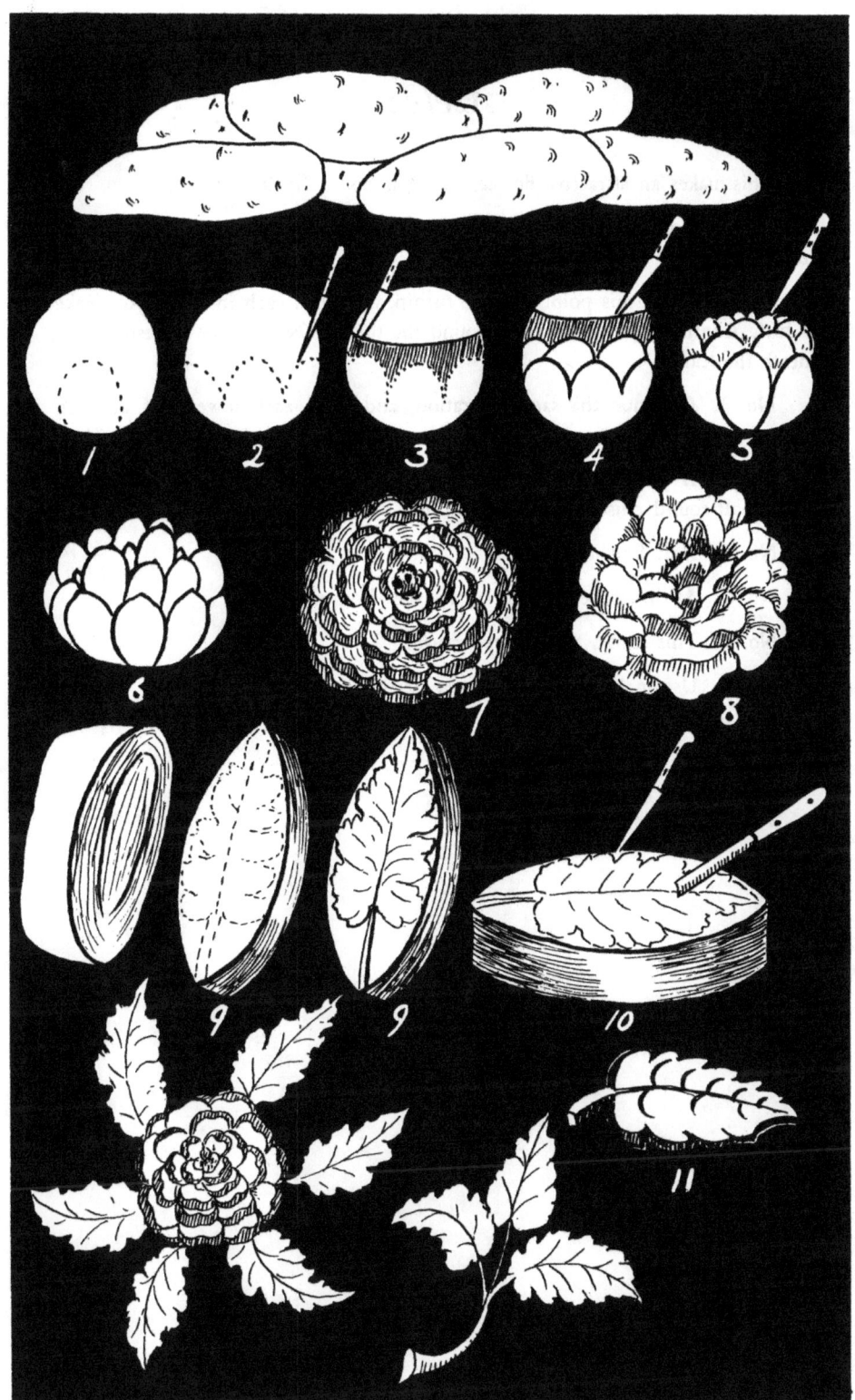

Azeleas

This makes an attractive flower, and it is not difficult to make.

No. 1. Bend the top of a tin can as in No. 1, forming somewhat of a round point.

No. 2. Insert this point into the turnip, and with each insertion you make a leaf. Continue this process all around the turnip. Now, remove flesh underneath the leaf.

No. 3. Continue the same operation, and place each lower leaf between two upper leaves.

No. 4. If you do not use the tin piece to mark your leaf, you can use a small half-round chisel from your carving set.

No. 5. Half finished.

No. 6. At this stage you can cut it away from the base.

No. 7. This shows the finished flower.

No. 8. Use in this way for platter decoration.

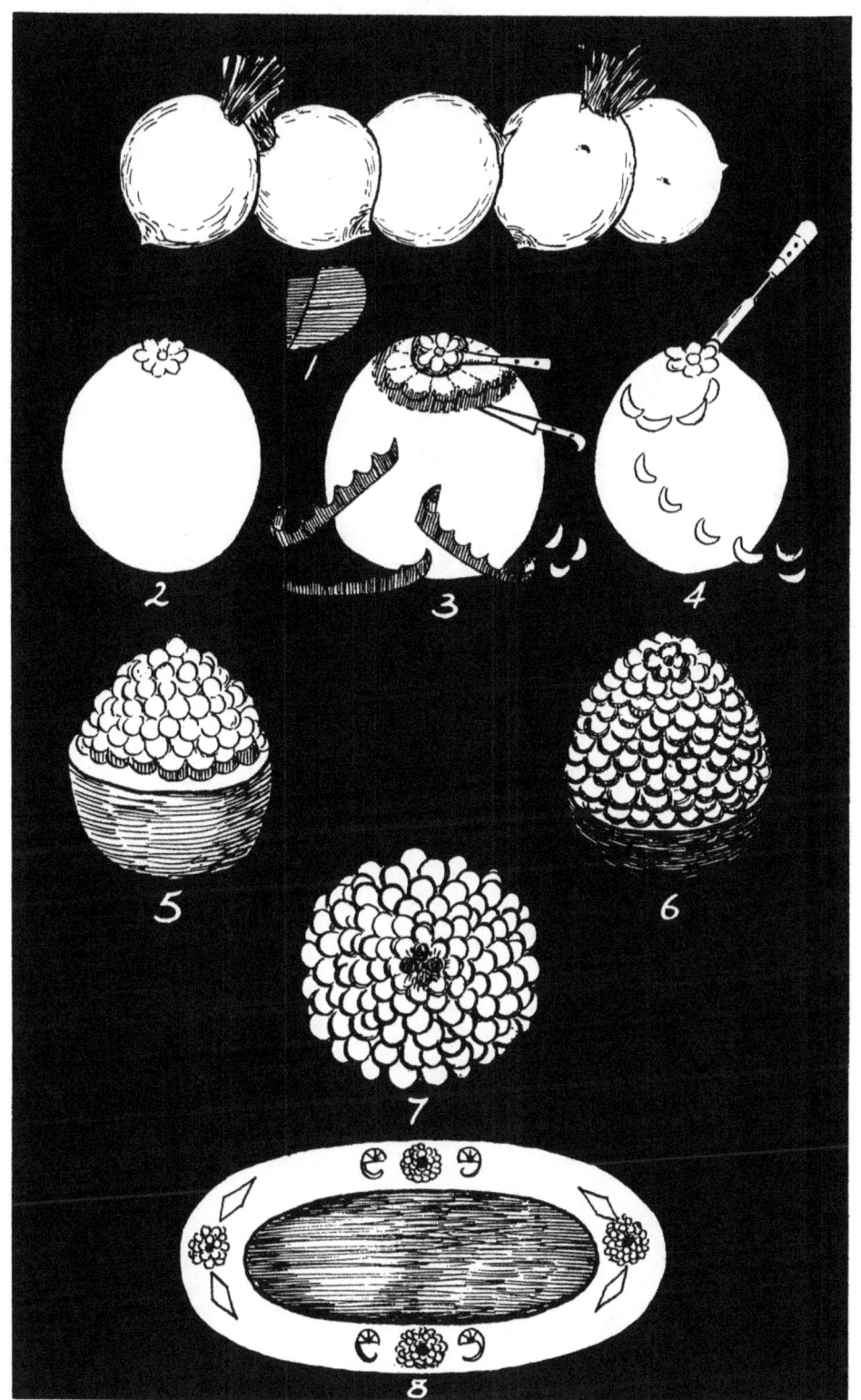

Figure Carving

It is well when carving people or figures to start with something easy. For this reason, I have chosen a snowman.

No. 1. Select a large Idaho potato. Trim it on one side and mark the design.

No. 2. Start to remove some of the meat from the top. Follow the picture.

No. 3. Follow the line as you continue to carve down.

No. 4. Be careful not to carve too much as you can always trim later.

No. 5. Shows how to put in details. Carve a hat, and put it on with a toothpick.

No. 6. Shows the finished product. You can use a paint brush for the broom. The eyes, nose, mouth, and buttons can be made of black olives and inserted in the potato. This will make a nice design for a winter party. You can use it on a platter or any way you wish.

Shoes or Slippers

The shoe or slipper is often made and can be filled with small flowers. Made from white turnips or potatoes, they are very attractive.

No. 1. Peel the turnip and mark the design.

No. 2. Cut along the dotted line until you get No. 2. Carve out the meat until you get No. 3.

No. 3. Cut the shoe to the right shape and get the correct size.

No. 4. Cut out the inside of the shoe and put in details.

No. 5. Other details added. Cut out an additional stand to bring the shoe up higher.

No. 6. Put in details and cut corners.

No. 7. This shows the various ways they appear on sockels or platters.

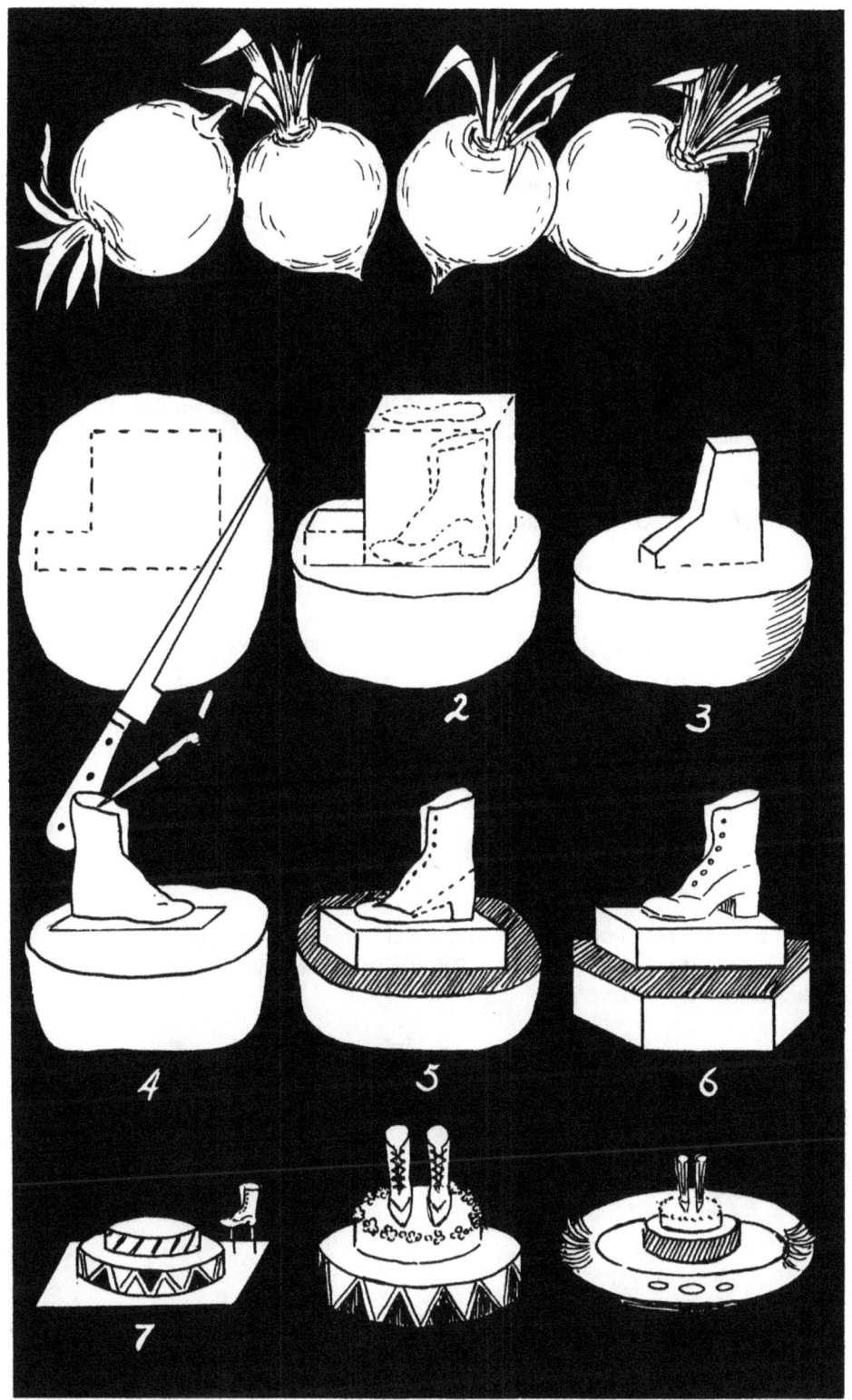

Swans

Swans often are made and are very attractive. They are not hard to make. They are made of long potatoes, white turnips, or yellow turnips, and can be placed on a sockel.

No. 1. Peel potato and trim by cutting off sides.

No. 2. Cut off two slices about ¼ inch thick and mark wings on them, one left and one right. Follow dotted line and cut as in No. 4.

No. 3. This slice is about 1¼ inch thick. Mark the swan on this slice and carve out on dotted line.

No. 4. The wing.

No. 5. Shows how to slice wings.

No. 6. Shows how to press knife towards the wing so the feathers fall in rotation and stay that way.

No. 7. After the body of the swan is made, attach wings to each side.

No. 8. This will be clumsy at first. You must trim and cut in the right proportion. When bird is slender and graceful, carve the tail. Slice again and press with knife so the slices will lie down.

No. 9. Cut head in proportion and put in details, such as bill, eyes, and neck.

No. 10. Add the wings with toothpicks. You can use two toothpicks in each wing to make them firm.

No. 11. The swan complete with sockel. This can be placed in the middle of platter. It will look best white. Put in water, cover with wet towel, and put in ice box to preserve it.

American Eagle

The eagle is historic and picturesque. It can be carved out of a rutabaga. It is very attractive, and you can color the beak yellow, the head and the tip of the feathers white, the legs and feet yellow, the claws black, and the rest of the body oak brown. The log should be light brown or green. It also can be placed on a sockel.

No. 1. Square the rutabaga on all four sides. Mark the bird design, and begin to carve down. Keep the wings about ½ inch thick.

No. 2. Carve down and remove meat slowly. Keep in mind the shape of the body of this bird.

No. 3. Shows the eagle carved in the rough. From now on, carve the details into the eagle. Carve the wings while the rutabaga is firm. Later carve out the legs and feet. The head is carved out last.

No. 4. The eagle looks better when placed on a higher object, so you can carve a sockel for this. If legs are not strong enough, use a wire between the legs and wings and into the sockel. This will give it the needed reinforcement. Be sure to carve out wing feathers so that it will appear natural.

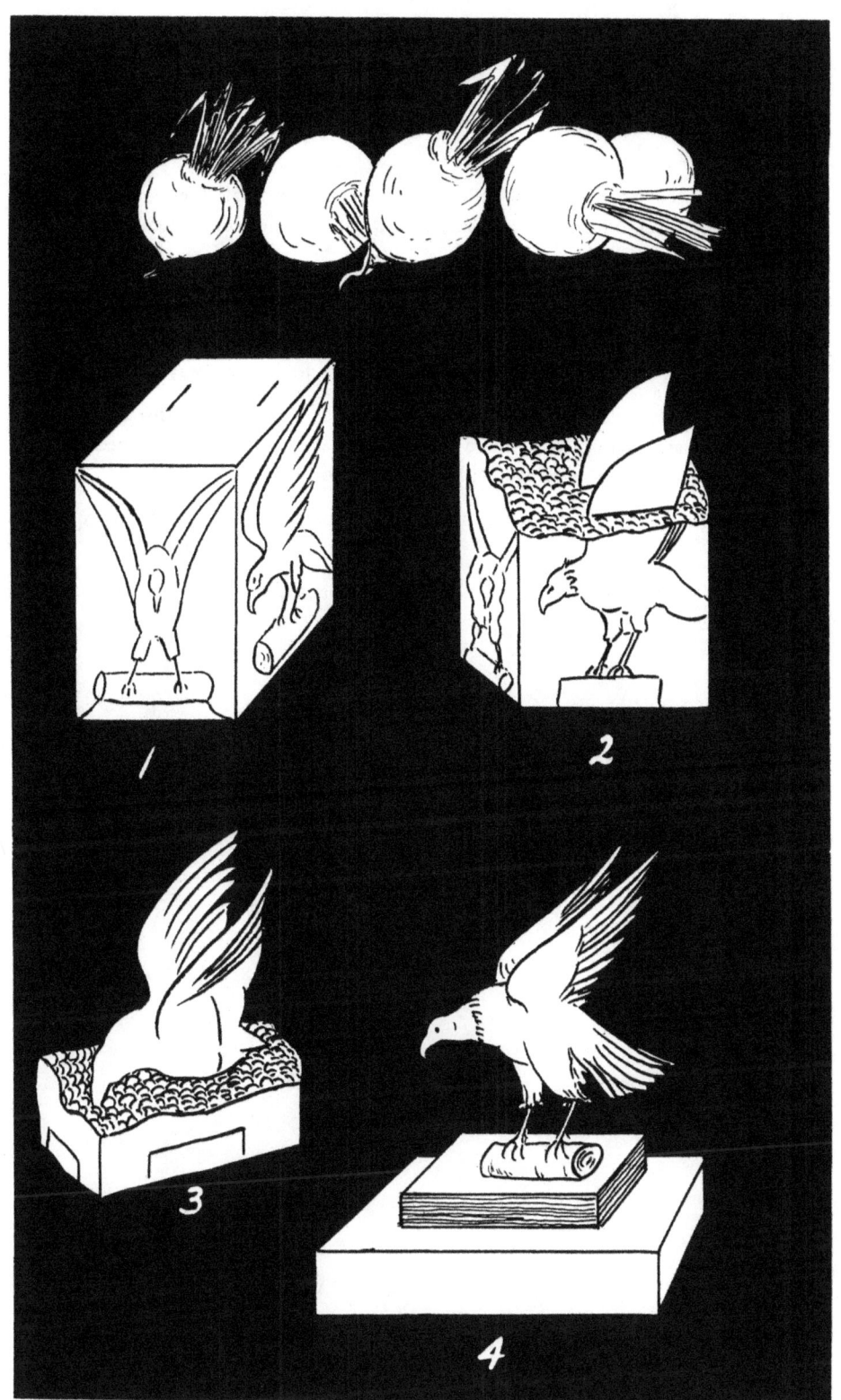

Wheelbarrow

The wheelbarrow is attractive. It can be open with small flowers put in it. You also can serve nuts and cold sauces in it. It is made from a rutabaga.

No. 1. Cut the rutabaga square. Mark the design as shown here. Start to carve away at the wheel and gradually work down as in No. 2.

No. 2. Sufficient meat is left on top of barrow. It is better to make it a bit larger and later remove this excess than to cut too much away.

No. 3. Leave sufficient meat around the legs and the wheel. This will give it strength, and you can work more easily with it. Trim the legs and wheel and remove meat inside the barrow with a potato scoop or knife.

No. 4. Carve out the wheel spokes, the handle, and finish by carving a stand.

No. 5. When it is well made, and in proportion, it will bring you many compliments.

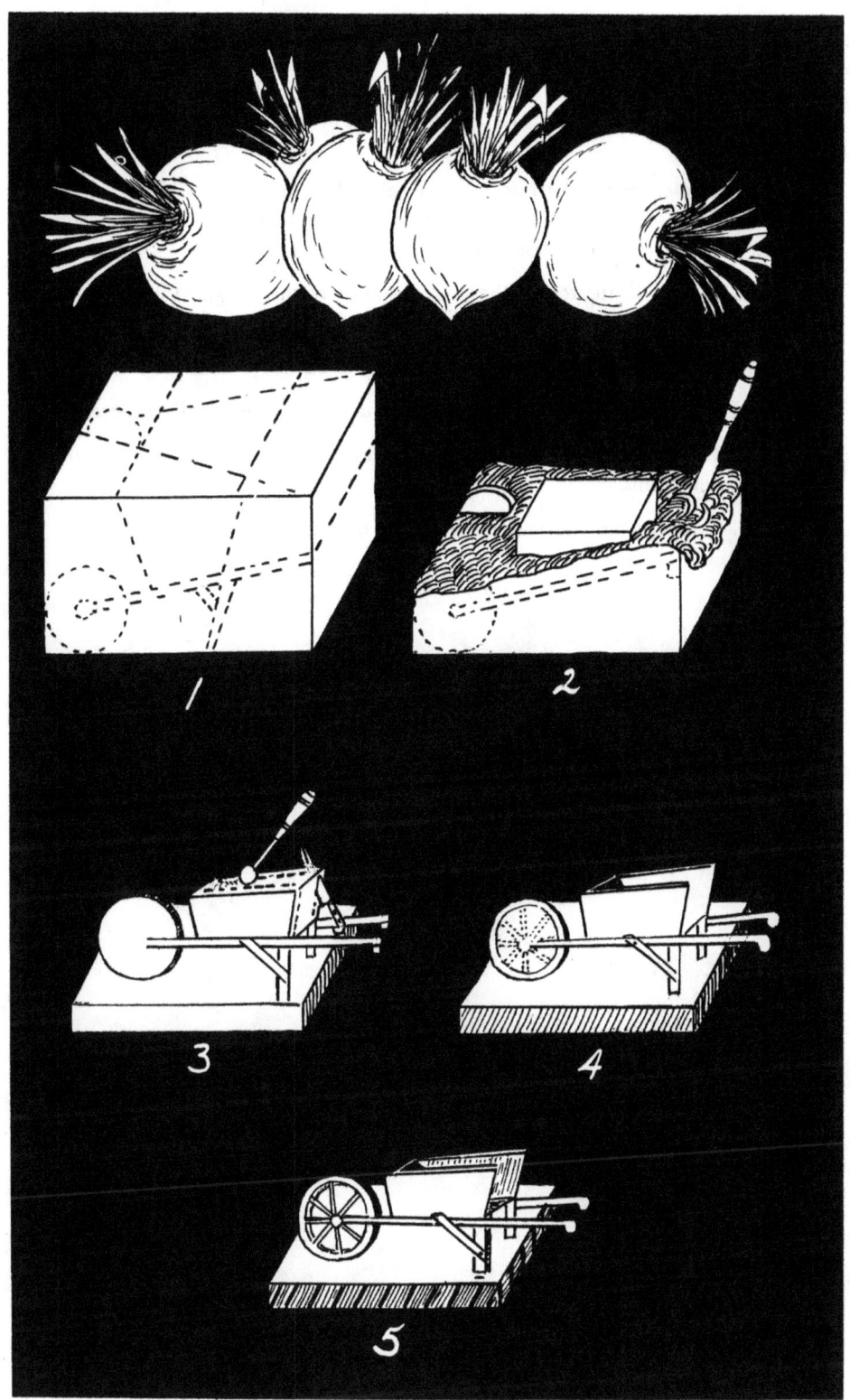

Vases

These vases are very artistic and can be used in many places. They can be made in plain or fancy patterns. If the vase is large enough, you can put flowers in it. You can color the vases with soft colors, also.

No. 1. Cut off the top of the potato, and mark the design. Cut along the lines and get No. 2.

No. 2. If the vase has a handle, it is well to cut the handle first.

No. 3. Remove the meat from all sides until the vase is fully exposed.

No. 4. Cut out the inside of the handle last. If it has a stand, carve it and carve in all details.

No. 5. Shows finished vase. The rest of the vases are made similarly.

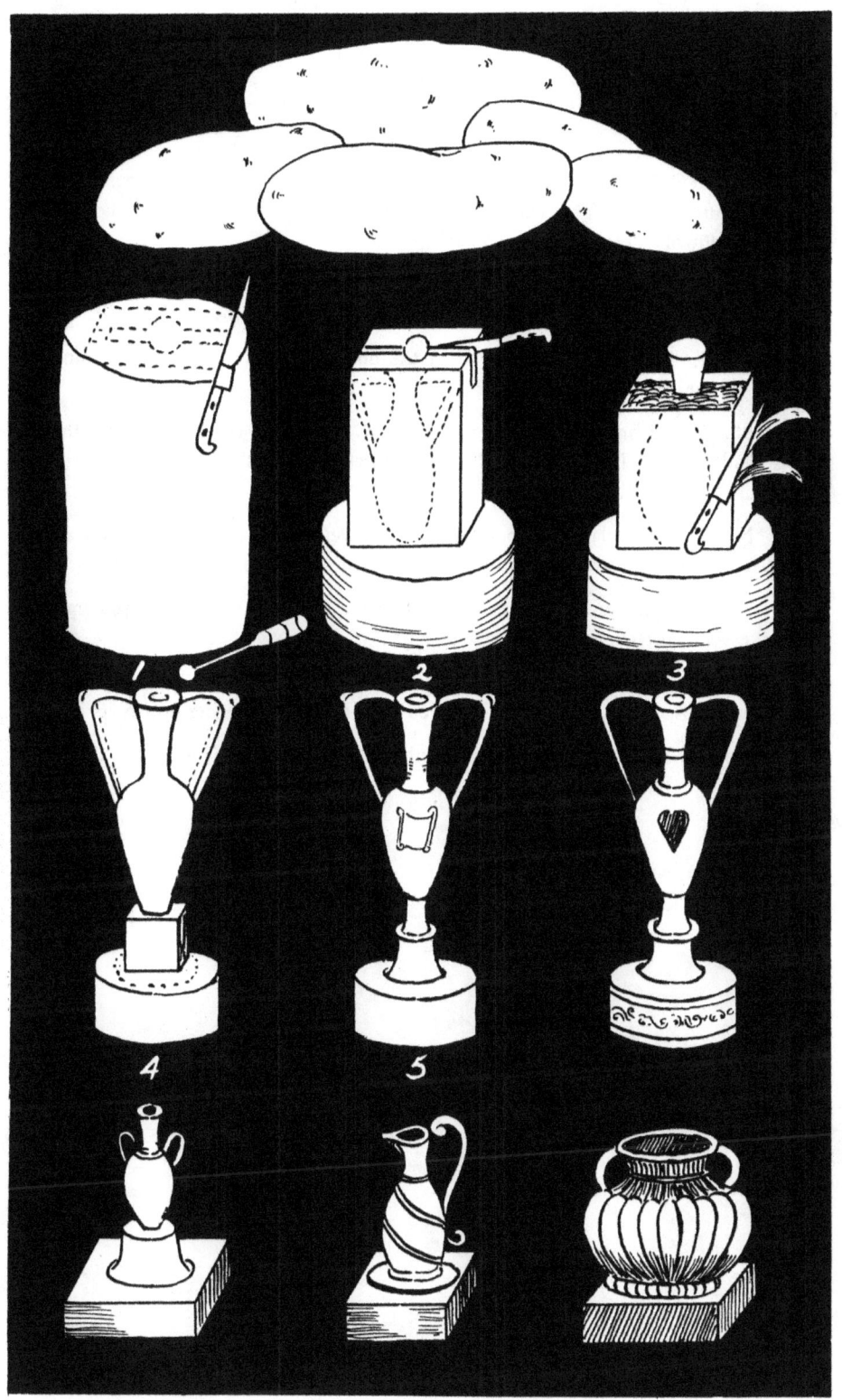

Stand and Sauce Dish

Special dishes are carved to serve cold sauces. These are used mostly for cold buffet tables. They must be well-carved and well-designed. They are carved out of rutabaga.

No. 1. Square the rutabaga and mark the design. Cut along the dotted line, but be sure to allow for handles. This gives you the outline of the dish.

No. 2. Cut out rims as shown in the dotted lines, and cut out the inner part of the handles.

No. 3. To bring out the rim of the dish, you must remove the part that is shaded here. Later remove the inner part of the dish, keeping the walls about 1/2 inch thick.

No. 4. Take a large rutabaga and trim it well. Square it off and mark the design. Cut along straight lines with a long knife, and this will give you No. 5.

No. 5. This stand might be out of balance, but now is the time you must make your corrections.

No. 6. When stand has the right proportion, carve in the grooves. This is done with a small chisel or knife. You must take extreme care not to spoil it.

No. 7. You can fasten dish on stand with toothpicks so it will not fall off.

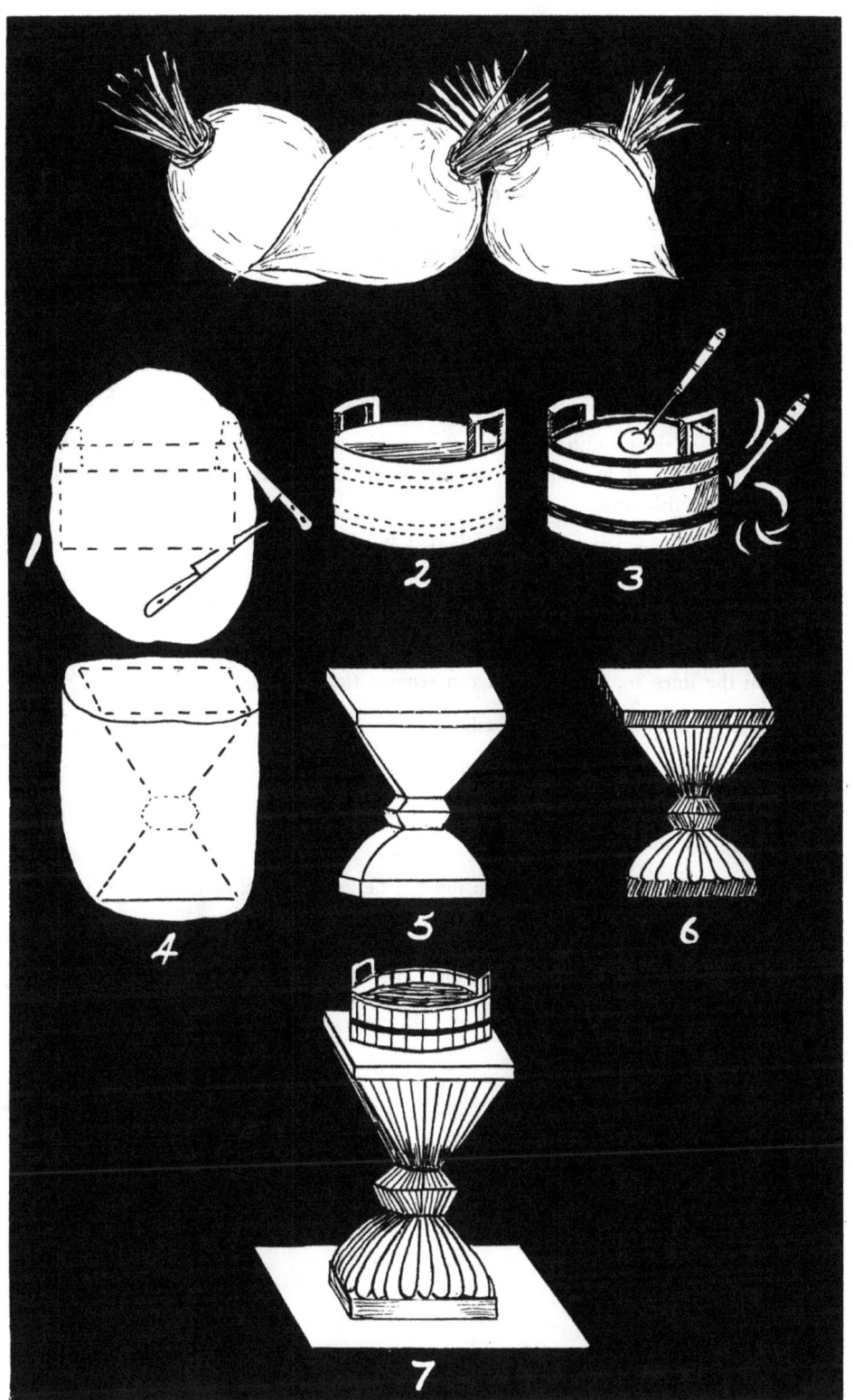

157

Potato Basket, No. 1

Potato baskets are used at parties and on buffet tables in which to serve food. There are various kinds of potato baskets and I have described four popular styles here. You can make them out of potatoes, white turnips, and rutabagas, and as fancy as you wish.

No. 1. Select a large Idaho potato and cut it flat on all sides. Mark a square and trim along the dotted lines.

No. 2. Mark basket design on top as well as on the sides as shown here.

No. 3. Trim on dotted line to give your basket a round shape. It will have a flat top. But, if you intend making raised handles as in No. 4, you must provide for this now.

No. 4. Shows how to cut the top handles.

No. 5. Trim basket to shape and make any corrections needed. Carve lines or grooves spaced horizontally and vertically. If you have no groove or V chisel, you can make the lines with a tin can top bent as shown in No. 9. When the lines are finished, you can remove the insides.

No. 6. Shows the finished basket.

No. 7. A little additional carving makes this pattern.

No. 8. The same procedure with allowance for side handles. Forms No. 10 when completed.

No. 9. Shows how the tin can top can be used instead of a chisel.

No. 10. Finished basket with handles.

No. 11. How to place baskets on a platter with food around them.

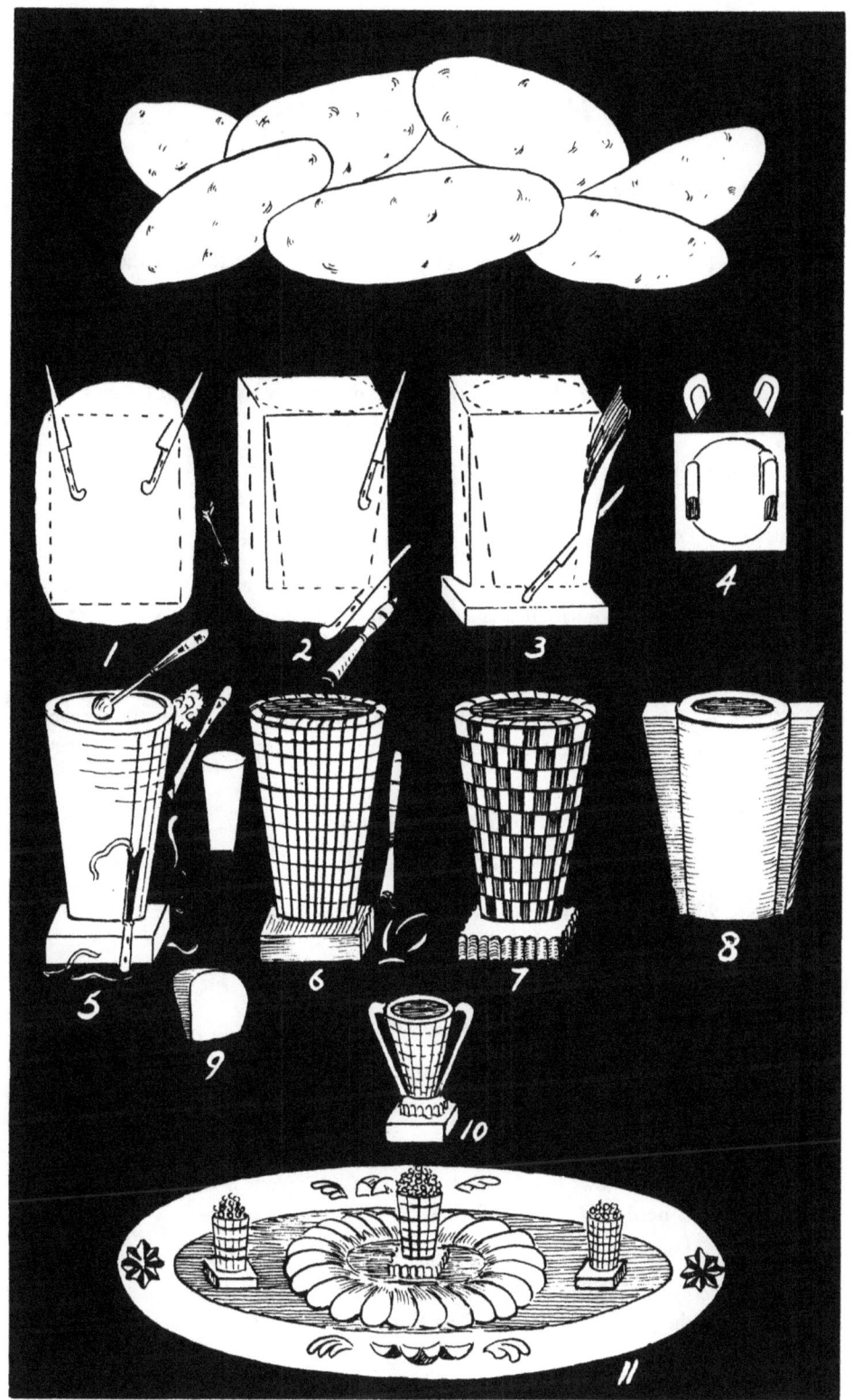

Potato Basket, No. 2

The small braided potato basket is easy to make and can be used to serve peas or any other vegetable. They are very attractive.

No. 1. Select a round potato and peel. Mark the potato with the design of the bottom about 1½ inch high. Cut it through with a knife as shown in No. 1. This will give you the bottom of the basket as shown in No. 5. The remaining portion of the potato is shown in No. 2.

No. 2. Dotted line shows the thickness of the slices which will appear as No. 3 when cut through.

No. 3. This round potato slice is peeled with a peeler as shown in No. 9. Keep peeling until you get a ribbon three to four feet long to use for weaving.

No. 4. No. 4 shows a similar operation but it is wider and used for larger baskets.

No. 5. This 1½-inch slice is used for the bottom of the basket. It has a slight curve, and it can also be made in the shape of a pyramid, narrow at the bottom and wider at the top.

No. 6. Make holes in the bottom. Space properly and make an uneven number. Into the holes, put either spaghetti or macaroni trimmed in even lengths.

No. 7. Shows how macaroni is stuck into the potato.

No. 8. Shows how macaroni is stuck into the potato to get a wider top.

No. 9. Peel the potato slice as shown in No. 3 and No. 4 to get a continuous ribbon about three feet long and without break.

No. 10. Wind the ribbon tightly.

No. 11. Shows the sticks in the basket.

No. 12. Shows how to weave the ribbon around the post. One post inside and the next post outside until you arrive at the top. Use a toothpick to fasten the end.

No. 13. This shows the finished woven basket. Now is the time to make corrections if needed.

No. 14. Put a wire into the finished basket and hold in hot fat, 300 degrees, covering the basket. This will make the basket a light brown. If kept dry and in the ice box, it can be used three or four times.

Potato Basket, No. 3

This basket design is different from the others. It is round, and can be made with or without a handle. Made from a rutabaga, it is very attractive. The handle can be decorated with other vegetable carvings, and the basket can be colored or decorated as you wish.

No. 1. Choose a well-formed rutabaga and peel. Mark outlines and allow 1½ inches for the feet. Do not carve the feet until you are almost finished as this will add strength.

No. 2. Trim the rutabaga, shape properly, and mark in lines all around. This can be done with the half-round chisel as shown in No. 3. Cut off top and carve the lines.

No. 3. Follow lines and carve with a steady hand so as not to carve too deeply. A paring knife also can be used to carve the edges.

No. 4. Carve out the inside with a potato scoop. Keep the walls about ½ inch thick.

No. 5. If you want a handle, insert it now, using a piece of heavy wire. If you have difficulty in making it stay in place, lower it and place it on the bottom of the basket where it will have a firmer hold.

No. 6. Decorate handle with leaves cut from cucumbers or other vegetables. Small roses or a butterfly can be cut from rutabagas.

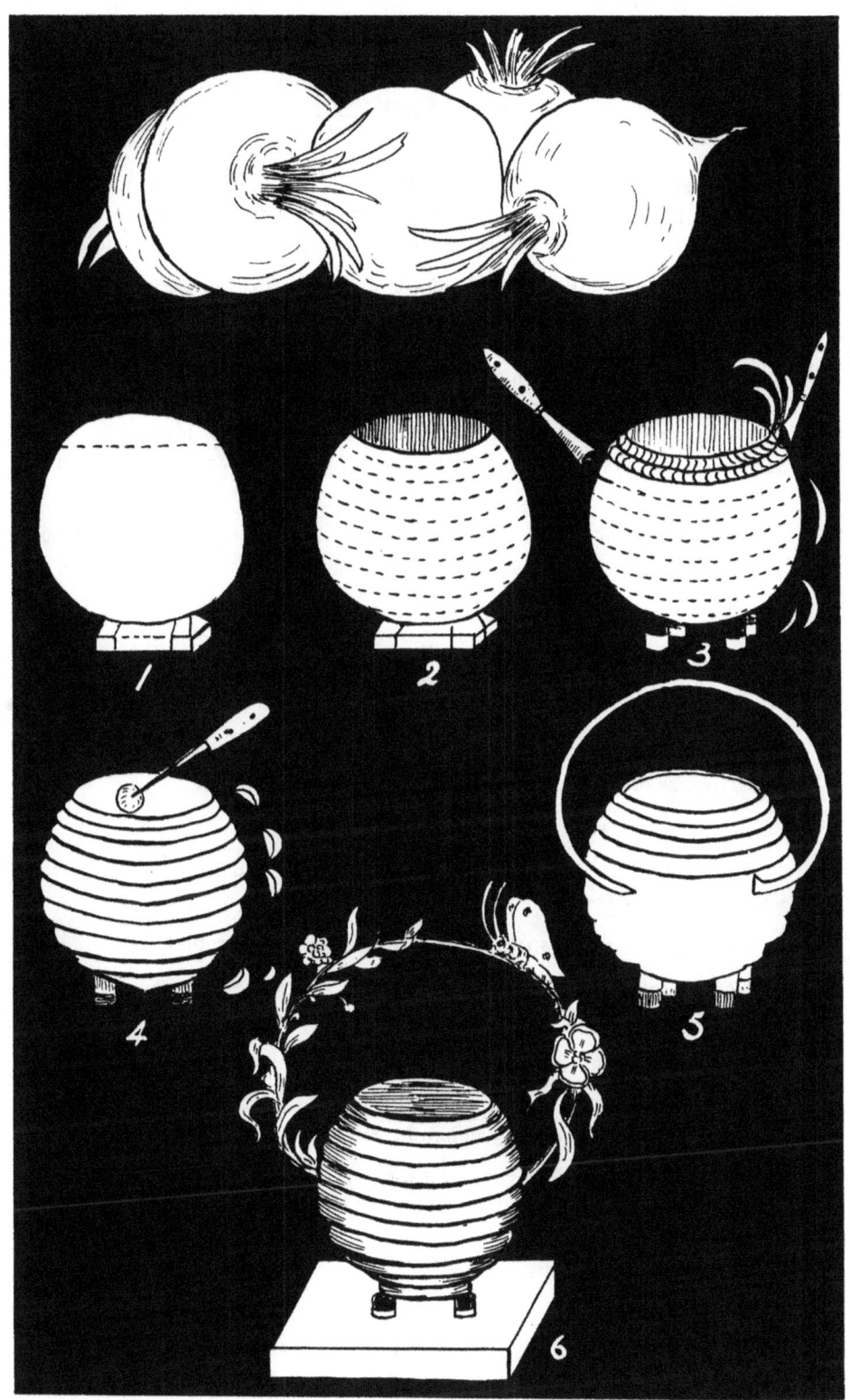

Fruit Carving

Fruit carving is as popular as vegetable carving. The only difference is that the cost is higher. Fruit is seasonable, some having a very short season, and is not always available when needed. Some fruits are very delicate to handle.

However, we in America are fortunate to have fresh fruit the year around. We have many varieties to choose from at all times. Carved fruit is eaten in most cases when carved. When the shell is hollowed out, it is often filled with other fruits. We have oranges, tangerines, grapefruit, melons, bananas and pineapples. These are the ones used for their shells, and baskets, boats, and such things as are made from them. Currants, strawberries, blackberries, red raspberries, cherries, apples, pears, plums, peaches, grapes, and nuts are usually used for filling.

Fruit of any kind makes a good dessert. So, I will try to show you various ways of serving it.

How to Carve Oranges

Oranges are often used to serve fruit or jello. You can make various designs, such as baskets or half-shells, which are very decorative.

No. 1. Select well-rounded orange, and cut off the top.

No. 2. Cut all around the inside of the orange and lift pulp out. The dotted line shows how much to take out.

No. 3. Use a potato scoop if you want to clean it out entirely.

No. 4. This shows how to fill orange with ice cream. Press it down thoroughly. Or you can fill it with other fruits or berries.

No. 5. Decorate the top with whipped cream. Put the top section back on if you wish.

No. 6. Shows how to apply whipped cream.

No. 7. The finished orange topped with four rings of whipped cream. Use the star tube for this purpose. Maraschino cherries cut in strips are used for decoration.

Orange Basket

These are easy to make, no special skill is required, and they can be used on any table.

No. 1. Select an orange with a good color. Mark handle and top of the basket.

No. 2. Cut away the section as shown here to bring out the handle.

No. 3. The handle fully cut out.

No. 4. Remove the inside by cutting along line.

No. 5. After the handle is completed, remove the inside of the half of the orange.

No. 6. The finished basket.

No. 7. An easy way to decorate it.

No. 8. The finished perfect basket.

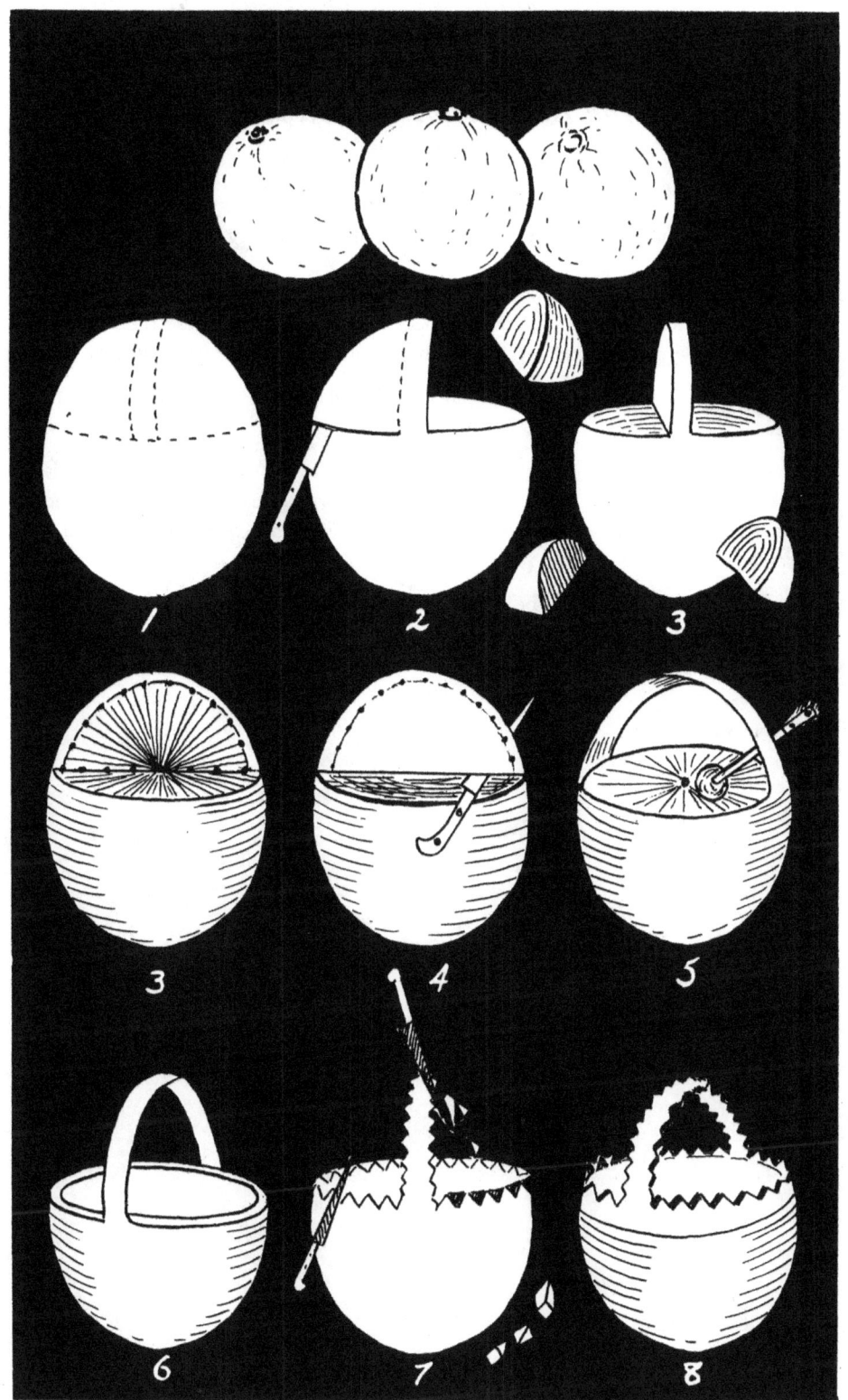

Orange Basket with Double Handle

No. 1. Mark handle as shown here.

No. 2. Cut sections out with a sharp knife, following the dotted line.

No. 3. Shows both handles exposed.

No. 4. Remove inside of orange. Cut along the orange inside the handles. Make a little cut, if necessary, on the bottom to lift the orange meat out.

No. 5. Repeat the same procedure as described with the earlier basket to decorate the edges.

No. 6. With this basket, the single handle is cut in two and the ends rolled inside. The top of the basket can be cut with a half-round chisel. The lines around the basket are grooved with a V chisel and colored to resemble a band.

No. 7. All baskets can be decorated with a silk ribbon and a card with the individual's name on it.

Alaska Orange

This makes an especially nice dessert. The orange is peeled completely and the meat removed. Ice cream is packed in the skin, and it is then put into the ice box. Do not leave in the ice box too long as the orange will blacken.

No. 1. First mark the orange so you will know where leaves are to be carved. They must be perfect in shape so that they will fit when you close them.

No. 2. Cut leaves along the dotted line. Peel off until you reach the bottom.

No. 3. Shows orange with skin completely removed down to the bottom. Remove skin in one section without breaking at bottom.

No. 4. Shows how skin should look when orange is removed.

No. 5. Put ice cream inside leaves so they will close properly.

No. 6. Form the ice cream to shape and carefully close the leaves. Close them one by one and press against the ice cream so that they remain closed.

No. 7. The finished orange, ready to be served. Keep in cooler to serve later, as Oranges Surprise.

Orange Gelatine

The orange gelatine is used for decorating other dishes. Also, it can be used for gelatine salads. It is especially attractive when different colors are used.

No. 1. Select orange of good grade, uniform shape, and bright color.

No. 2. Cut orange in half.

No. 3. The two halves from No. 2.

No. 4. Remove orange meat carefully so that it can be used. Cut sections out with sharp knife.

No. 5. Shows the clean orange half filled with gelatine. Place in ice box, and it is well to let it set overnight.

No. 6. Do not place on top shelf of ice box if left overnight, but put it on a lower shelf.

No. 7. Shows how to cut into slices. Use a large sharp knife for this.

No. 8. The finished orange gelatine in various colors is shown here. A bit of whipped cream adds to the appearance, or it can be used for decoration of other foods. This is appreciated by your guests.

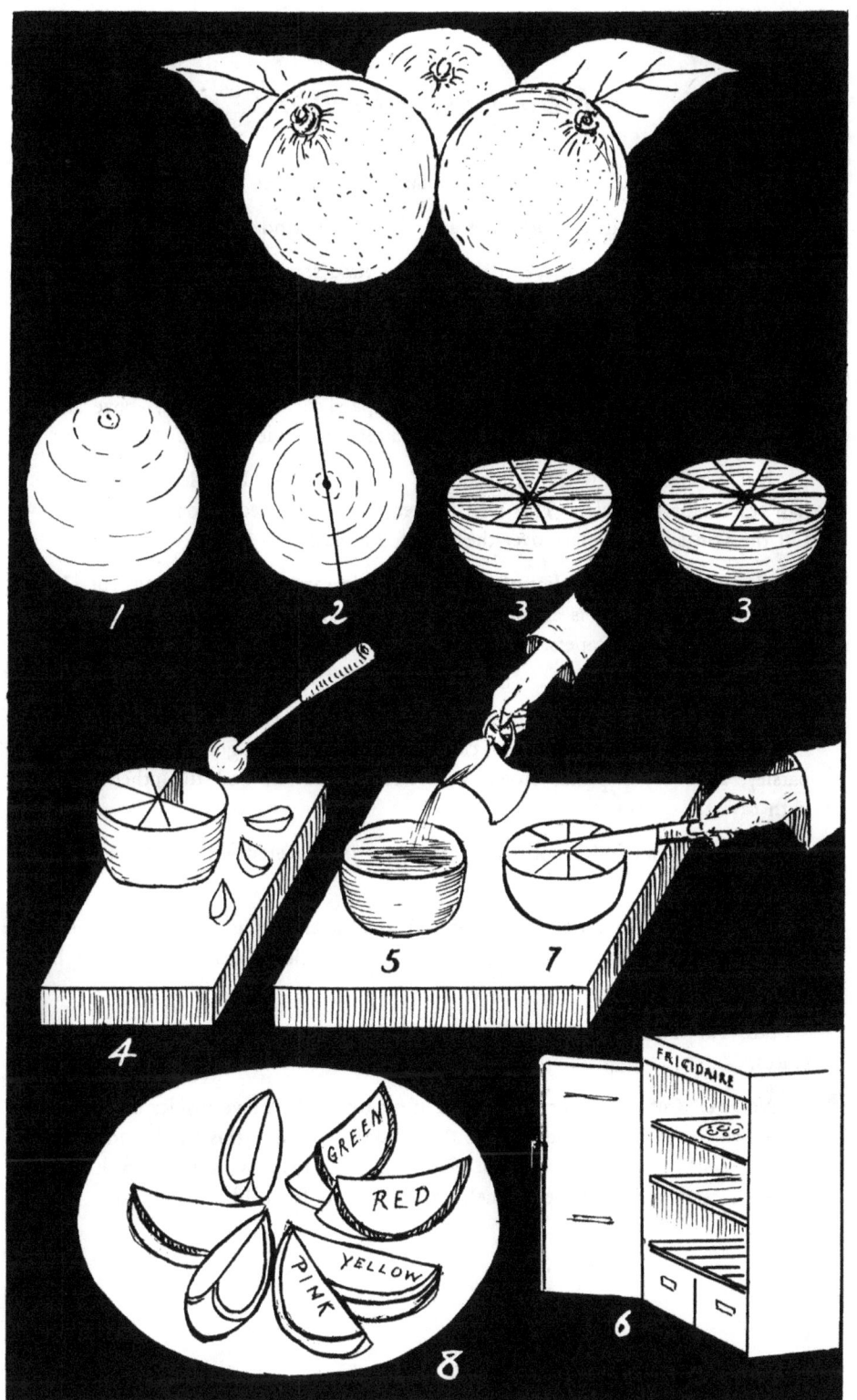

How to Cut Lemons

No. 1. Just plain, sliced lemons, placed on a platter as a border.

No. 2. Whole lemons grooved and sliced with rind on. Place on platter.

No. 3. Lemon sliced, cut in half, with dotted sections representing portion covered with chopped parsley. The center has red Hungarian or Spanish paprika on it.

No. 4. A full slice of lemon with half of meat cut out. Skin is rolled inside. This also can be sprinkled with fine parsley. Both designs, above and below, can be used on food itself, or as platter border decoration.

No. 5. Second row shows lemon cut in six wedges. Each lemon is cut in half, each half cut twice. This type is used for platter decoration or tea glass. Cut the skin side and place over the top of the glass.

No. 6. Shows a full slice of lemon with skin removed and the ends cut. In the center of this slice is an anchovy ring. The anchovy is wound around the finger and filled with capers. This is placed on the food itself, as it can be eaten. This is served with fish.

No. 7. Lemon sliced with skin on. Pieces are cut from the slice as shown here to form a cross. Each section can be a different color: green with chopped parsley, red with paprika, brown with anchovy butter, and the other black with caviar.

No. 8. Shows full lemon slice partitioned and covered with different items as was No. 7.

No. 9. To make a basket, cut out each side of an end and cut out the meat from the handle also. The bottom is trimmed a little so that the basket will stand.

No. 10. This shows the basket when finished. It can be used to serve cold sauces.

No. 11. Cut into a barrel shape. Cut off top and remove insides of lemon. Mark two bands on the side, remove the yellow skin along this band, and place little capers here to represent nails. Fasten the top again with a toothpick and place a carved radish on top of the cover. Use this for cold sauces, also.

No. 12. Shows a pig made out of lemon. Choose a lemon with a hard end. Cut a groove here and color a red mouth. With the aid of a toothpick, prick the skin and place firm capers or whole peppers into the holes to make eyes. For the ear, cut triangular cuts toward the nose, lift up from behind, and press forward until they remain in position. For a tail, cut rind and roll it up. Use toothpicks for the feet. It can serve as a toothpick stand.

No. 13. Lemon is cut in zig-zag half to get this design.

No. 14. This is the progression of No. 13.

No. 15. Cut No. 14 in a thick slice to make this star.

No. 16. Cut lemon in half. Remove meat and fill with lemon or lime jello. After cooling, cut in half, quarters, etc.

No. 17. To make this Eskimo hut, cut off both ends of the lemon to get a large slice from the center. On top, place a half lime with a door cut in it. The border is made by winding fillets of anchovy around your finger to place on the lemon.

No. 18. Cut a thick slice of lemon for the bottom. The second lemon is carved to the border. Remove meat to the border and fill with fish salad, anchovy salad, or use for an appetizer.

No. 19. Take a large lemon and cut as shown here. For a steering wheel, use a toothpick with a slice of carrot. Make the wheels in the same way, and use carrots for lights.

No. 20. The head of the penguin is made of stoneless olives. The eyes are made of hard-boiled egg whites. The center of the eye is a black olive. The bill is made of white turnips. The tail is made of eggplant, and the body is a lemon. The wings can be made of eggplant, or of the lemon itself, colored brown. The buttons are made of black olives. The feet are made of toothpicks and pressed into another lemon slice.

No. 21. The airplane is made of a large, long lemon. The propeller is cut from eggplant. The wings are cut out of the lemon itself. The center is cut out, and the wheel is made out of a carrot. The tail is cut from lemon peel, and the wheels are carrot slices, fastened with toothpicks.

Honeydew Melons

There are many sizes of honeydew melons and they have a long season. Also, they are very attractive and, for these reasons, can be used for many purposes.

No. 1. Mark handle and cut sides as shown.

No. 2. Remove meat inside of handle and in the rest of the melon.

No. 3. Use cutter to cut round holes for handle decoration.

No. 4. A basket with curved handle and curved top gives a different effect.

No. 5. Shows how to make a washtub. Mark design as shown here and cut the top on dotted line. Cut out handles and mark boards all around as shown in No. 6.

No. 6. Use a V chisel to carve board and rims. It can be used for many things.

No. 7. A double-handled basket with fancy decoration.

No. 8. A baby crib, suitable for showers. The wheels are carved of rutabaga and fastened with toothpicks.

No. 9. A large honeydew melon with scenery carved on the outside and one plain handle, usually filled with red or blue berries.

Watermelon

Watermelon is seasonable. There has been little variety in serving it, so I will give you a few new ideas on various attractive ways of serving this fruit. Baskets can be made from it, and it can be carved with attractive designs.

No. 1. Cut watermelon this way with a stand on top. Or, put two stands on the top. You can place other fruit on top with the aid of toothpicks to make wonderful table decorations.

No. 2. Shows how to remove the inside of a half of a watermelon. Carve edge like a picket fence. When hollowed out, it is filled with watermelon and other fruits and used for buffet tables.

No. 3. Shows a basket with carving all around the edges and on the long handle.

No. 4. A basket with split handle at each end makes an attractive piece.

No. 5. A boat-like basket with shields on top edges.

No. 6. Shows three standing baskets without handles, all with carved sides.

No. 7. Shows a basket especially appropriate for a graduation dinner. Make the figure resemble the person for whom the party is held.

No. 8. Do not carve designs too deeply. Color with fruit coloring.

No. 9. A bear scene for a hunting party.

No. 10. Watermelon with a carved cover and with hollowed-out lower half to be filled with other fruit. This is especially attractive.

Pineapple

There are only a few ways to serve pineapple. I will try to show you a few of the most attractive ones here.

No. 1. Cut off top about two inches deep.

No. 2. Cut inside on dotted line and remove the inside. This can be sliced or diced and put back into the pineapple.

No. 3. This cover has two strong toothpicks in front and in back to hold it.

No. 4. Fill with fruit and decorate with whipped cream.

No. 5. Following the dotted line, cut about two inches above the bottom. Leave the top leaves untouched.

No. 6. Fruit can be placed on this attractive stand. Care must be taken in arranging fruit not to overload it. Smaller fruits, such as grapes and berries, should be used near the top.

No. 7. This is a bird house, made as in No. 3. Cut a hole in the side for the nest entrance. A bird can be carved out of a rutabaga. Choose a specific type of bird and color it to make it attractive.

No. 8. This is a Bird house with a raised top.

No. 9. Shows a chariot full of fresh fruit. Hollow out the top and, from another pineapple, make wheels. Use some wood for the handle and legs. Instead of putting the top of the pineapple on the fruit, put it on the front of the chariot if you wish.

Napkin Folding

The art of napkin folding has almost vanished. Reasons for this include the labor involved and the scarcity of linen during the war period. But, the paper napkin will never take the place of a linen napkin in a fine dining room. It was only some years ago that the napkin was changed regularly during the course of the dinner.

It is an advantage to know how to fold a napkin when giving a party. Done artistically, it adds to the table decoration. To explain napkin folding is quite difficult, but this simple method should be satisfactory. It is very important to have the napkin square and well starched.

Simple Napkin Folding

Corner Fold:

No. 1. Using a well starched napkin, fold corner 1 to corner 2.

No. 2. This is most popular in the lunch room or busy dining room.

No. 3. The folded napkin may be placed on the plate or beside it.

Half Fold:

No. 1. This is the straight fold. Fold corner 1 to corner 2.

No. 2. If well starched, the napkin will stand rounded.

No. 3. This also is placed on the plate.

Mother Roll:

No. 1. Years ago we used silver or wooden rings into which the napkin was placed. Fold napkin from left to right to get No. 2.

No. 2. Roll napkin starting from bottom. Often names were engraved on the napkin ring, sometimes very artistically.

No. 3. Place on or at side of plate.

The Ruffled Roll:

No. 1. Spread napkin on table. Keep four dividing lines in mind, as shown here, and halfway roll each of these sections.

No. 2. Roll under the first section until you reach the first dotted line.

No. 3. Continue to roll section on section until you arrive at end. Napkin should be well starched, and press creases with hand to make them stay put.

No. 4. Place on plate.

Simple Napkin Folding

Corner Fold.

Half Fold.

Mother Roll.

The Ruffeld Roll.

Two-Point Fold

The two point fold is easy to make and usually placed on the plate. Make sure the table is attractive by spacing all napkins evenly.

No. 1. Spread napkin on table and, as shown by the dotted line, fold over from corner 1 to 2.

No. 2. Here is a three corner fold.

No. 3. Fold at point shown by dotted line.

No. 4. The completed fold.

No. 5. Locate middle of napkin, shown by dotted line. Fold corner over again.

No. 6. Fold corner 1 to corner 3.

No. 7. Turn napkin to put corner 2 at the bottom.

No. 8. Fold back at dotted lines and press down so it will remain in this shape.

No. 9. Finished two point napkin fold.

No. 10. Place on plate.

Two Point Fold

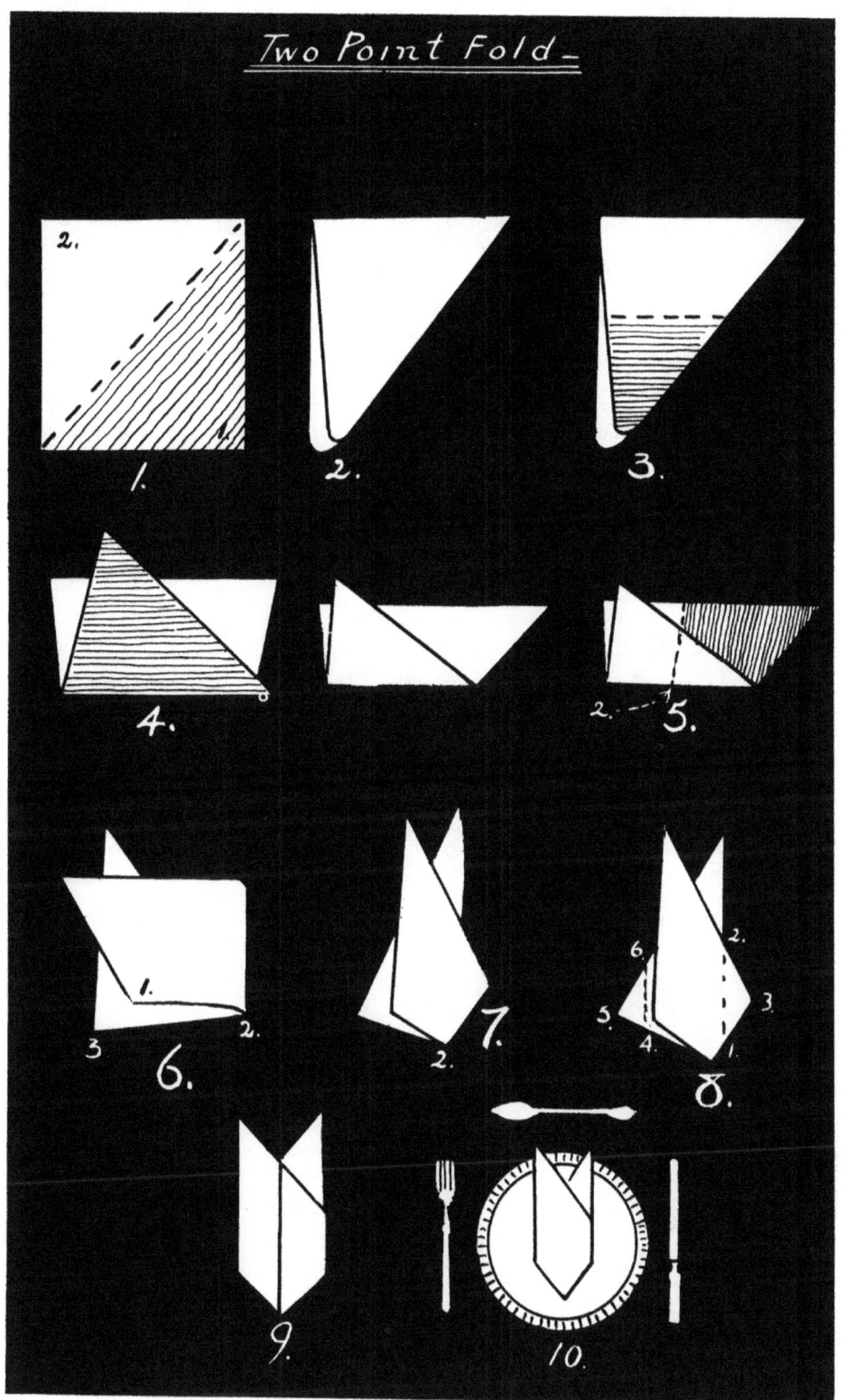

Luncheon Fold

These are used in dining cars, steamship companies, and private parties.

No. 1. Place the open napkin on the table.

No. 2. Fold right corner to meet the left one.

No. 3. Turn napkin so that longer side is near you.

No. 4. Locate the middle of the napkin. Have the open line at your left as shown in No. 5.

No. 5. Find middle of napkin and fold towards left. This will give you No. 6.

No. 6. Fold shaded portion, and insert point into the opening of the napkin and press well.

No. 7. The finished napkin stands upright.

The Lunchen Roll.

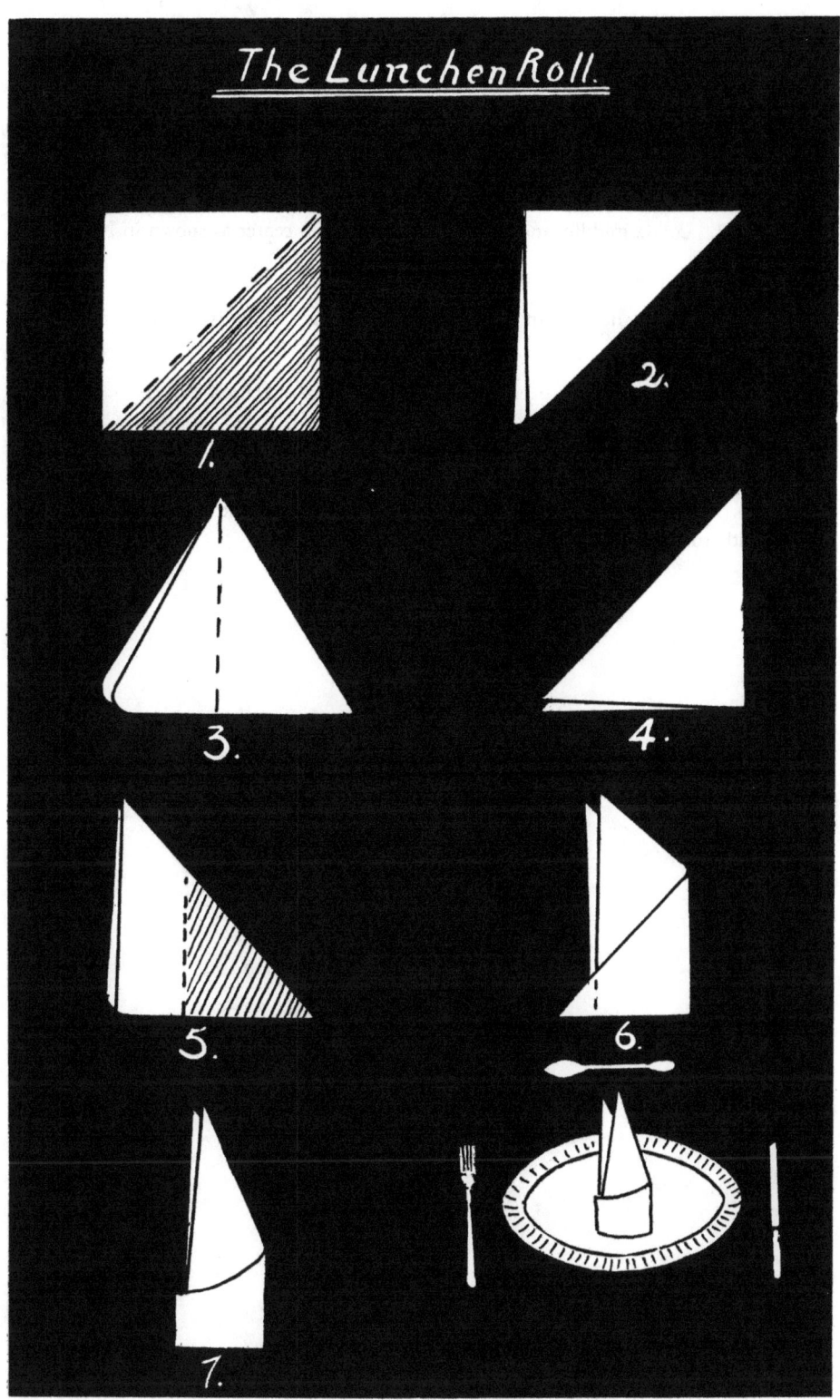

Half Rose and Lily Folds

No. 1. Spread napkin on table.

No. 2. Locate middle, and fold all four corners to center as shown in No. 3.

No. 3. Repeat the same operation.

No. 4. Turn the napkin over, and fold corners towards the center two times on this side.

No. 5. Each side has been through the folding operation twice.

No. 6. Pull out leaves on each corner. Place a tumbler in the center to hold it firm. This is the lily fold.

No. 7. This time, pull the top four leaves up to get the half-rose design. Fill with rolls or fancy potatoes.

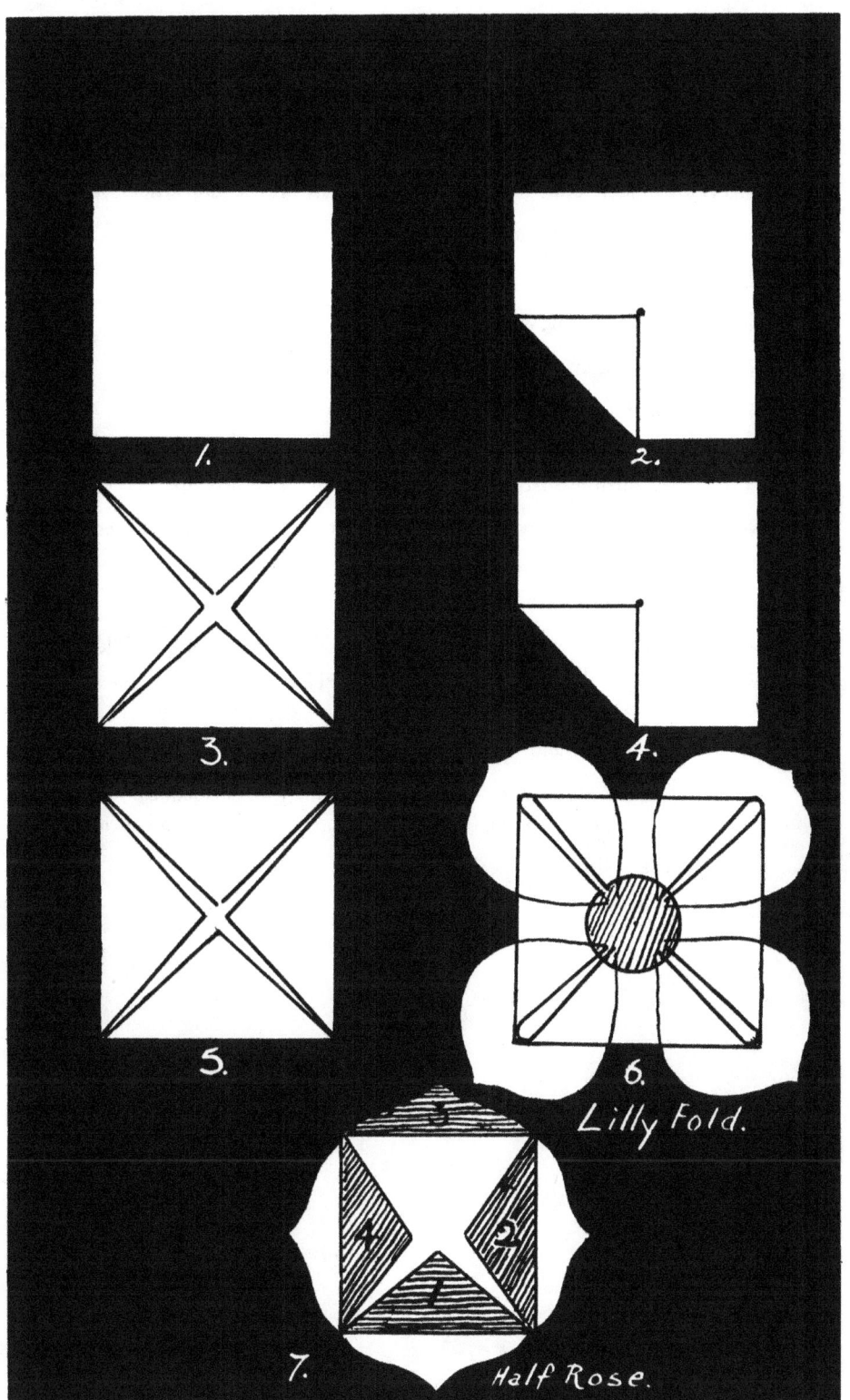

Slipper Fold

This is a banquet fold. It can be put on a plate with a roll inside.

No. 1. Spread out napkin.

No. 2. Fold in thirds.

No. 3. The three folds completed.

No. 4. Mark the middle and fold corner 1 over to line 2.

No. 5. Repeat this same action, bringing down 1 to match 2.

No. 6. This is the front, with both sides of the napkin meeting. No. 6½ shows the back, and the shaded border which is to be turned up.

No. 7. Keep opening towards you. Turn up right border to make even with napkin line marked 0.

No. 8. Turn left border up even with line 0.

No. 9. Hold down point with one finger, and lift up in the middle with another. The sides will open and 1 and 2 will appear. Be careful not to lift it too high.

No. 10. Lift higher and the corners 1 and 2 will come together.

No. 11. Stick corner 1 into opening 2 and the two shaded corners will fit into one another as in No. 12. If napkin is too soft, place a roll in it.

No. 12. The finished slipper.

Slipper

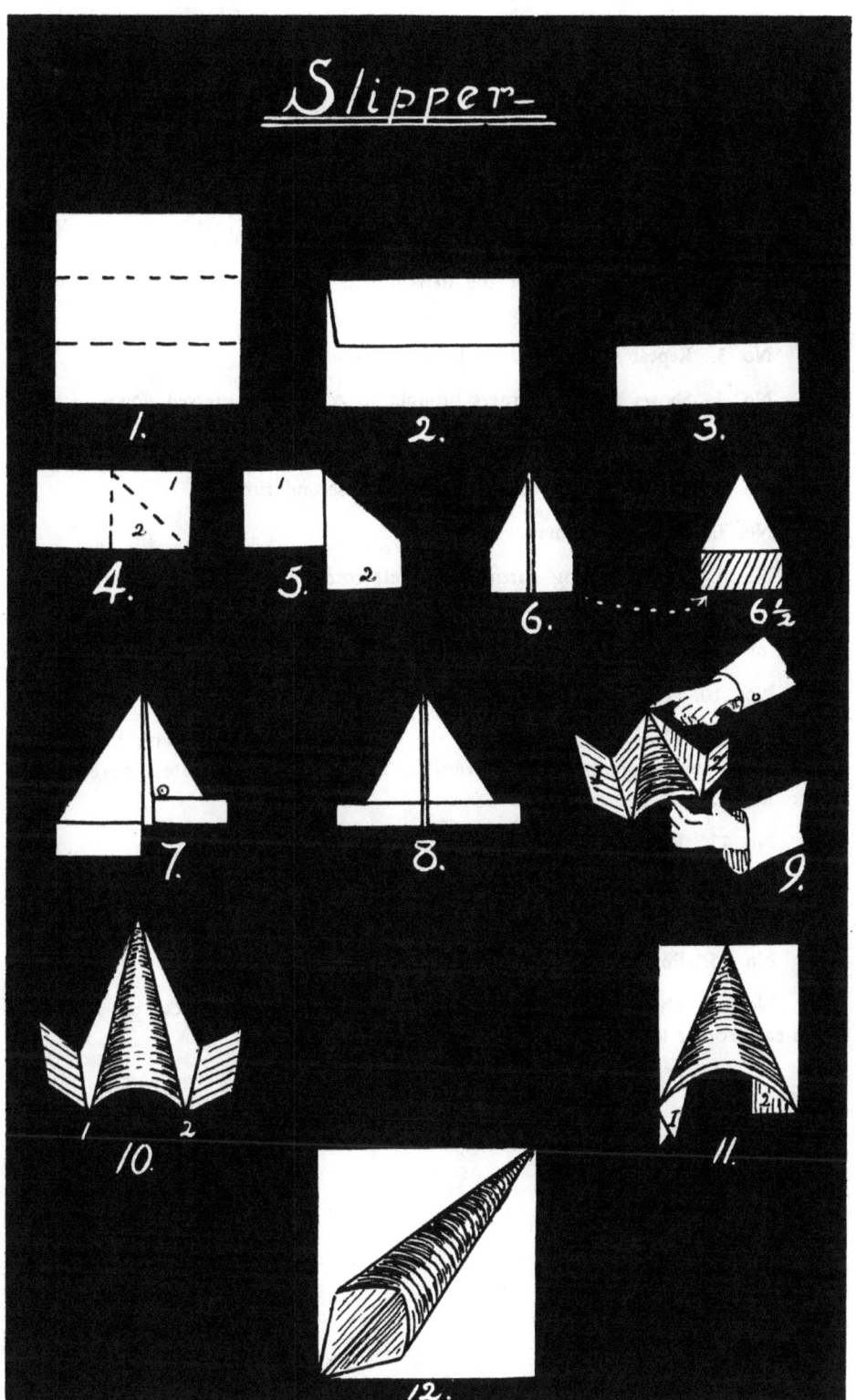

Rose Fold for Napkin

This is a European idea, and it is used a great deal for all services.

No. 1. Use a starched napkin, and spread out on table.

No. 2. Find the center of the napkin and fold left corner towards the center.

No. 3. Repeat same operation from opposite corner.

No. 4. Shows all four corners brought to center and pressed down.

No. 5. The same operation is repeated.

No. 6. Shows all four corners folded the second time.

No. 7. Turn napkin over.

No. 8. Repeat folding starting with left corner until all are turned.

No. 9. Shows all four corners turned, which, of course, greatly reduces the size of napkin.

Nos. 10, 11. All corners folded again.

No. 12. Place a round object in the middle. Hold tightly with the left hand and remove points from underneath. The dotted line indicates where the point was.

No. 13. Pull all corners out on four sides.

No. 14. Shows how to pull another set of leaves out on each corner as marked here.

No. 15. Pull all leaves toward your hand to form the rose.

No. 16. The finished rose. The napkin must be stiff, and you can put a roll in each corner to hold it up, if necessary.

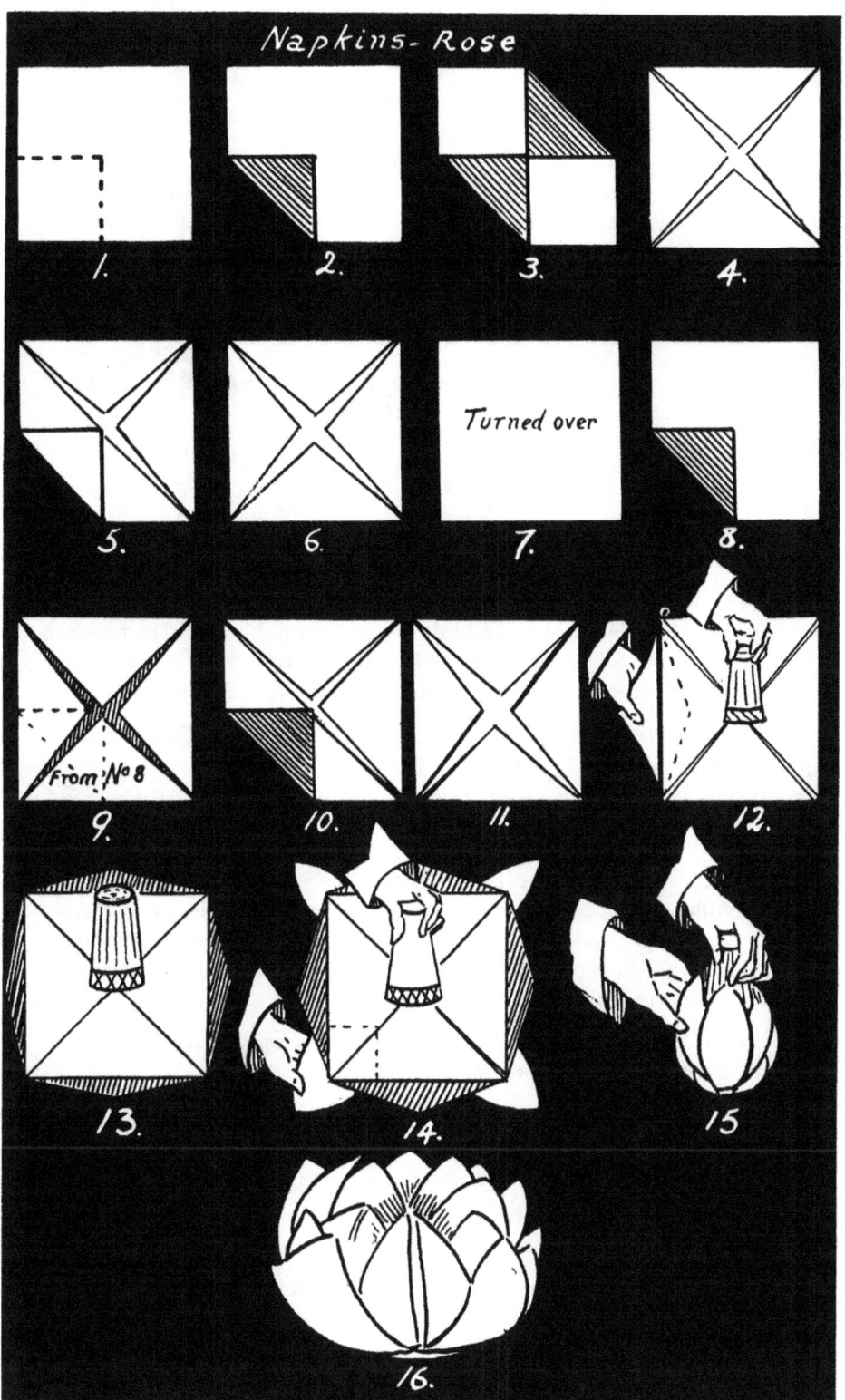

French Horn

This horn, sometimes called the horn of plenty, is made as a platter decoration. It is very attractive and helps to present the food in the best possible way.

Nos. 1, 2. Spread napkin on table. The dotted line shows a piece of wrapping paper placed on the napkin to fit.

Nos. 3, 4. Fold napkin at the center to make No. 4.

Nos. 5, 6. Find the center and turn upper right corner 1 down to meet 2. This gives you the shape shown in No. 6.

Nos. 7, 8. Repeat the same operation with the left corner to make No. 7. In No. 8, corner 1 is folded over again to meet line 2.

Nos. 9, 10. Shows corner 1 folded over to line 2. Do the same with the other side to form No. 10.

Nos. 11, 12, 13. Fold over right side again which makes napkin even narrower. The left side also is folded over again as in No. 12. The napkin is smaller now, but fold again to make No. 13. This is thick so it is put into a towel with the opening of the napkin in front as shown in No. 14.

No. 14. Place napkin in towel and sprinkle with water. Fold towel over napkin to make No. 15.

No. 15. The napkin is covered again and sprinkled with water over the towel.

No. 16. Set napkin on edge of table and place a heavy object on the top. We usually use a pot with a handle for convenience. Press down on the pot with the left hand, and pull the front of the towel with the right hand. Pulling slowly until the back part of the pot is reached, you can then release pressure and remove the napkin to make No. 17.

No. 17. Napkin is bent completely to resemble a horn. If not bent enough, place in towel again and repeat the operation.

No. 18. The finished napkin. If napkin is wet, place the horn point against a wall and place a heavy object on top to hold it in place until it dries. The horn, then, will not open.

No. 19. Shows how napkin is placed on a platter with another half-opened napkin in the middle to hold the two horns in position.

No. 20. Shows a platter with four horns which is very attractive for serving sandwiches, appetizers, or cold meats.

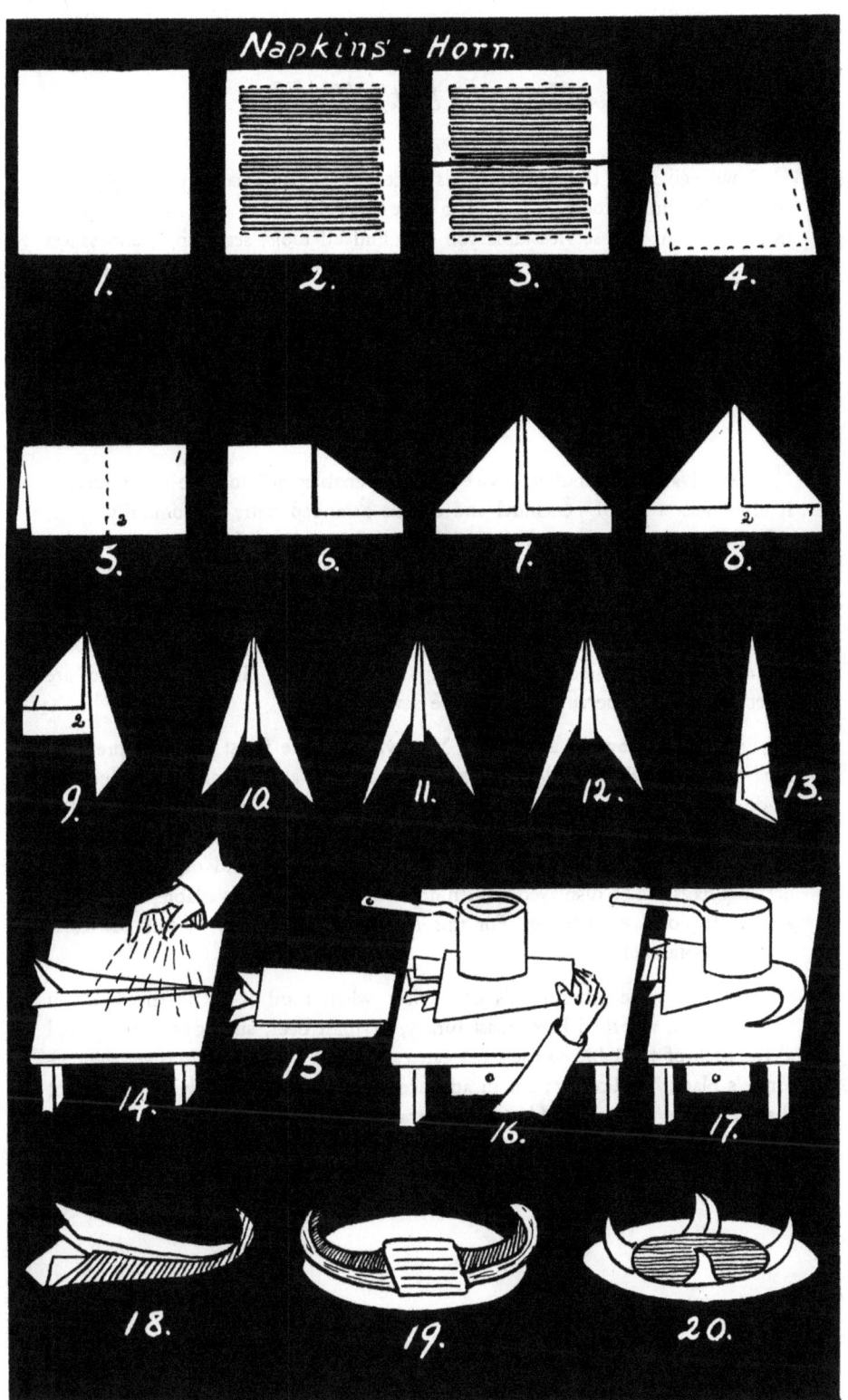

How to Set a Table

I will give you the fundamentals necessary to set a table properly. At a commercial dining room, it is well to have a service table. This is not required in a home. At this service table you will find all tools, seasonings, and sauces that may be needed by the customer. When a fork or knife falls on the floor, for example, you can replace with one from this table.

Setting a Buffet Table

One advantage of buffet service is that it enables one to have quick service. It eliminates a lot of personnel and can be arranged more economically. It is a flexible method, as you can arrange it for a few cents or for a high cost as for a banquet. The decision, of course, remains with the individual who pays for it.

Buffet service dates back to the Greeks. Many of their suppers lasted for days. Royal festivities always had buffet service. The smorgasbord, picnic tables, and cafeterias are copied from the original buffet service. The latter methods are especially popular because of the time saving feature.

Fine buffet banquets are costly. You will find the finest and best prepared food together with skillful art work to glamorize it at these affairs. Statues are made of important people from wax, tallow, sugar, or ice. The finest platter decorations are popular devices. A table of this kind should always have the finest table service, including a fine table cloth. Palms, and organization and national flags can be displayed. Much depends on the space available, the money, and professional knowledge. For this reason, Chefs trained in this particular field are obtainable.

Here are some other words of advice: when food is to be sliced or cut to order, such as baked ham, roast turkey, or roast beef, such dishes are placed at the back of the table so the Chef can carve it and place portions on the customer's plate. If slices are cut in advance, they can be placed with the rest of the meat. Ice pieces should stand on trays so that water can drip into them and prevent the table from getting wet. Make sure the silver is uniform in design. The entire buffet can be changed to suit the pocketbook or the occasion.

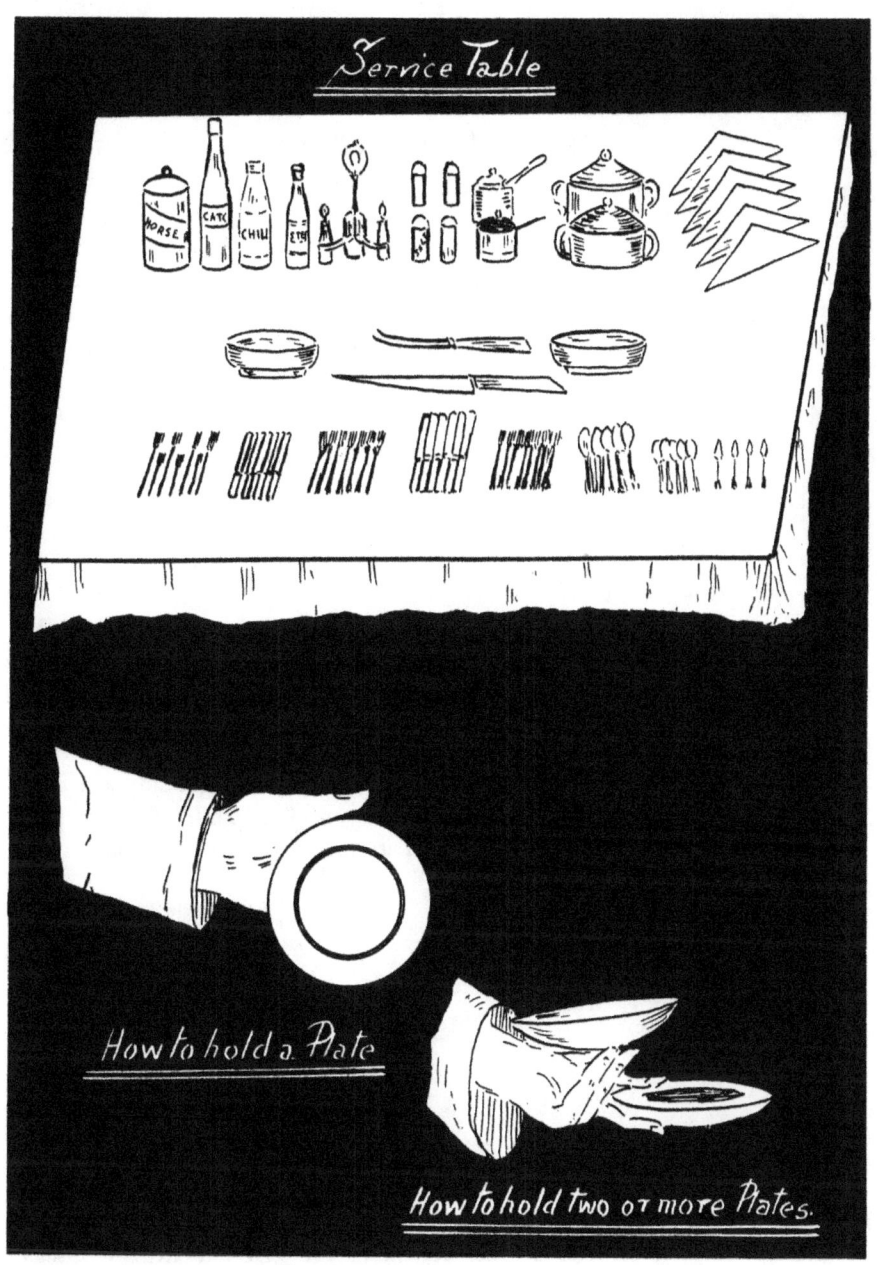

How to Hold a Plate

I have made two pictures showing the proper way to hold a plate. Never put your fingers into a plate, glass, or any container. Never try to hold more than you are able.

Breakfast Setting

A service plate contains a folded napkin. At the left is a fork, at the right, a knife, teaspoon, and a fruit spoon. At the top right is the coffee cup, and a glass of water which must be in direct line with the knife. Salt and pepper and the sugar bowl are placed in front. A butter and bread plate with a butter knife across it is at the left. A bouquet of fresh flowers will make the table especially pleasant.

Luncheon Setting

A service plate contains a folded napkin. A dinner fork and a salad fork, or two dinner forks, and a knife are on the left. On the right side is a soup spoon and a teaspoon. A glass of water is in front of the knife. Salt and pepper and bread plate with butter knife on it complete the service. Use fresh flowers again.

Dinner Setting

A service plate contains a fancy folded napkin. At left are two dinner forks and a salad fork. At right, three knives of which one is a steak knife, a soup spoon, and a teaspoon. An oyster or cocktail fork is placed across the rest of the tools so that the guest does not have to search for it. The water glass is placed directly in front of the knife nearest the plate. The wine glass is inside this and the cocktail glass a little to the right. Salt and pepper are in front with the bread and butter plate and knife. Fresh flowers.

Breakfast Setting

Luncheon Setting

Dinner Setting

Salad Course

A salad plate, a salad fork, a knife, a glass of water, a bread plate and butter knife are sufficient. Fresh flowers.

Dessert Course

A dessert plate with a dessert fork and a teaspoon on the plate, and a glass of water are sufficient.

Tea Setting

A dessert plate contains a fancy folded napkin. A dessert fork, a knife, a glass of water, a tea cup, and a sugar bowl on the left complete this setting. Decorate table with fresh flowers.

Fresh Flowers

Make it a rule to use fresh flowers. The kind is not too important. We usually use white ones for breakfast and varied colors for luncheon. Use dark colors for dinner and soft colors at tea.

Salad Course

Dessert Course

Tea Setting

General Rules for Buffet Table

Before we describe the table contents we must know whether or not we find any service on the table. Water, glasses, forks, knives, spoons, butter rolls, and napkins are placed on the tables with each customer's place designated. Fresh flowers also should be on each table. In this case, however, we would find only dinner plates on the buffet table and no other tools. Coffee and cream is served to guests later. If you must serve everything from the table, the picture will show you a good plan to follow.

1. Dinner plates
2. Napkins
3. Forks, knives, spoons
4. Rolls
5. Butter
6. Olives and celery
7. Butter and bread plates
8. Potato salad
9. Sliced tomato salad
10. Lobster Newburg
11. Smoked salmon
12. Sardines in oil
13. Herring in wine
14. Tuna fish salad or fish in oil
15. Hot roast prime rib of beef
16. Russian caviar imbedded in ice
17. Decorated Salmon
18. Spaghetti with meat balls
19. Breast of Chicken Supreme or sliced cold chicken
20. Marinated hearts of artichokes
21. Decorated beef tongue
22. Marinated celery hearts
23. Chicken a la king
24. Roast saddle of lamb (or crown roast)
25. Hot roast turkey
26. Shrimp salad decorated
27. Cold ham
28. Goose liver paste
29. Chicken galantine
30. Assorted sausage
31. Vegetable platter in aspic
32. Fresh Fruit platter
33. Assorted cheese platter
34. Vienna cheese cake
35. Strawberry torte
36. German coffee cake
37. Assorted French pastry
38. Apple strudel
39. Mocha torte
40. Marzipan cake
41. Spun sugar basket filled with dinner mints
42. Cream dispenser
43. Coffee cups
44. Coffee Urn
45. Pastry plates
46. Sugar
47. Floral leaves made by the gardener
48. Horn of plenty carved out of ice
49. Fresh flowers and palms
50. American Eagle carved out of ice with the American flag on each side

Cocoa or Chocolate Painting

I am going to show you the art of chocolate painting for cake decoration. This inexpensive art is not well known in America. It can be done for a few cents a day.

You can use cocoa butter and bitter chocolate, obtainable in any grocery store. The cocoa butter is in little squares. Break off a small square of cocoa butter and take the same amount of chocolate or cocoa powder. Place in a tin plate side by side. Put the plate over boiling water to melt these ingredients, but do not mix them.

Put the brush in some chocolate and thin with cocoa butter as you paint. As chocolate becomes thick, thin with butter. Follow your design. If you lack drawing ability, choose a picture which is appropriate for the cake. Put transparent paper over the picture and perforate the paper. Put the paper over the cake. Put cocoa powder on the paper and, as it falls through the perforations, it will leave outlines for you to follow in painting.

Commercial patterns are available. These are called "Schablonen," and have perforations ready to use. They are easy to use—children enjoy doing it. And, the decorations can be eaten, of course. They last, also, for they are not affected by weather conditions. There are many subjects, such as telegrams, buildings, birthday greetings, animals, birds, flowers, trains, boats, vacation scenes, music notes, footballs, and games of all sorts. There are many events during a year which can be put on cakes in this manner. So, practice this wonderful art and you will be surprised at what you can do.

If you are going to practice cocoa painting, I would advise you to practice on a porcelain dinner plate. You can draw on it, trace on it, paint on it, and wipe it all off when finished.

Cocoa is easier to apply than chocolate, and dark or bitter chocolate easier than other kinds of chocolate. Here are some ideas to follow in practicing. Notice the necessary tools. There is a pan of boiling water, another pan to put into the water with the cocoa butter and chocolate, a dinner plate, a ruler, pencil, and brush.

No. 1. Draw pencil lines one inch apart so they will be guide lines for letters of that height. Never make them smaller, as shown below on this plate, as it will not look as well. Practice the alphabet until it becomes perfect. Use just as little of the melted cocoa as possible, and when darker lines are needed, go over them again.

No. 2. When you have mastered the letters, begin with figures.

No. 3. This begins a step-by-step description of the designs in No. 9. With the ruler, mark off upper and lower points, then the horizontal points, and then points between. This will give you the right perspective.

No. 4. With the pencil, make a half-round line around each point.

No. 5. Make corrections now if necessary.

No. 6. Mark a second line around each point.

No. 7. Check again and make necessary corrections.

No. 8. Mark two straight guide lines.

No. 9. Write the word, "Mother." Make letters one inch high. Begin to paint with melted cocoa which brush can pick up easily. Apply slowly.

No. 10. Here is a simple design to practice. Be sure lines are straight.

No. 11. Apply your knowledge of number drawing here.

No. 12. Space letters properly.

No. 13. Shows a design good for border and lettering practice. This can also read, "Happy New Year," "Father," or the name of any other guest.

No. 14. A standard design.

No. 15. Shows a design for a card party.

No. 16. A design for a bowling party or tournament.

No. 17. This is especially appropriate for a spring party. The telephone wires hold a bird.

No. 18 Music notes, which can be used with any instrument.

No. 19. Shows the beginning of a scenic design. Begin with the tree.

No. 20. Add the mountains.

No. 21. Add birds, and a water line below the hills, to complete the design.

No. 22. This begins the design shown in No. 24. First make hills and water line.

No. 23. Draw the swan and the water.

No. 24. Make cattails, sun, and water.

No. 25. Shows beginning of design in No. 27. First draw the tree.

No. 26. Add shore line and the boat.

No. 27. The finished picture, ready for painting.

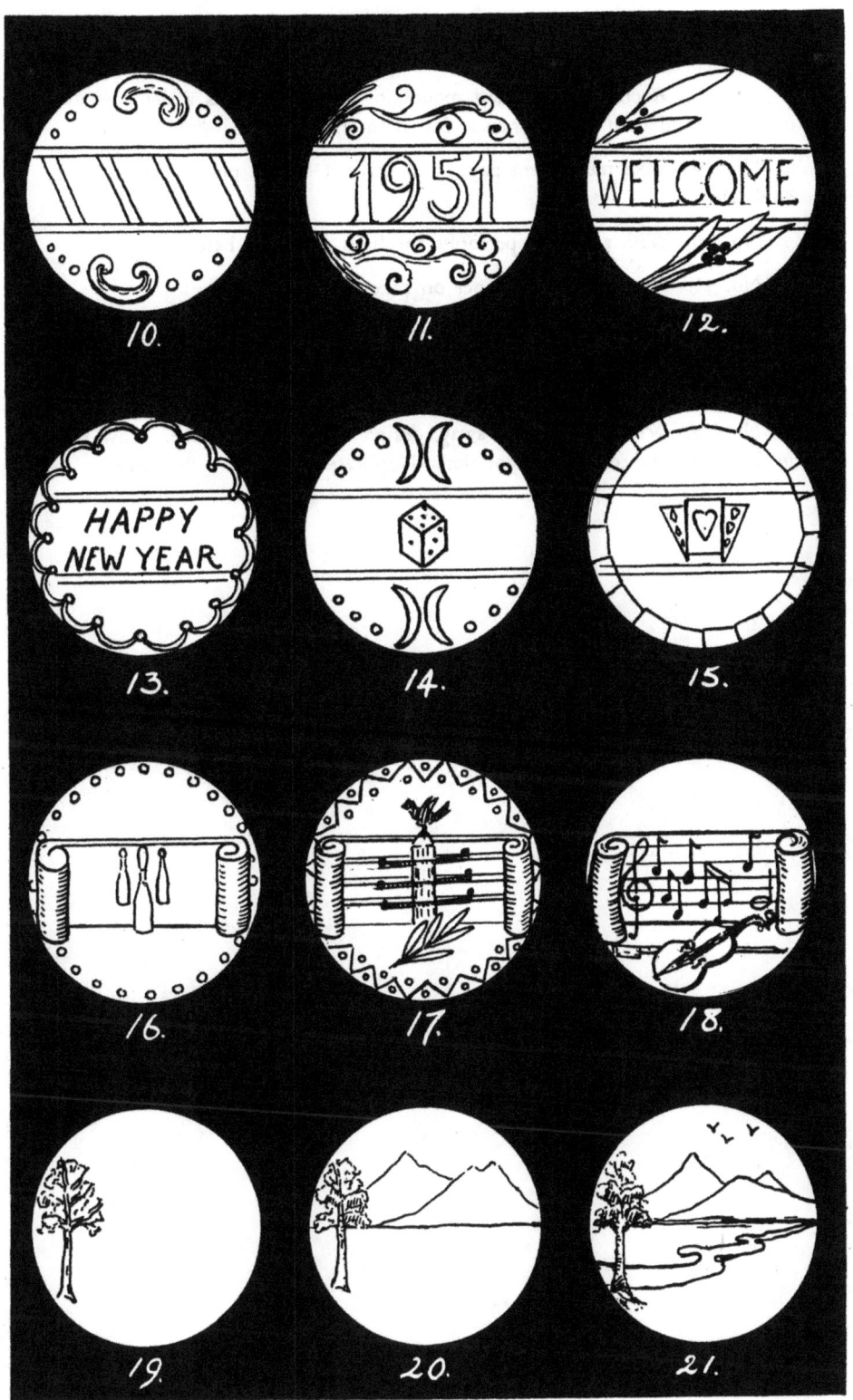

No. 28. A church, bird, and mountain design. Here is a demonstration of the method used to perforate a design to the cake.

No. 29. Take transparent paper and place it on the picture you desire to duplicate.

No. 30. With a needle, perforate the lines as shown here.

No. 31. Place perforated paper on cake.

No. 32. Hold with one hand, and with the other, put a piece of cotton dipped in cocoa powder all over the paper. Remove paper, being careful not to harm design.

No. 33. With paper lifted away, design shows on the cake. Now paint in the design to complete decoration. Duplicate any picture this way.

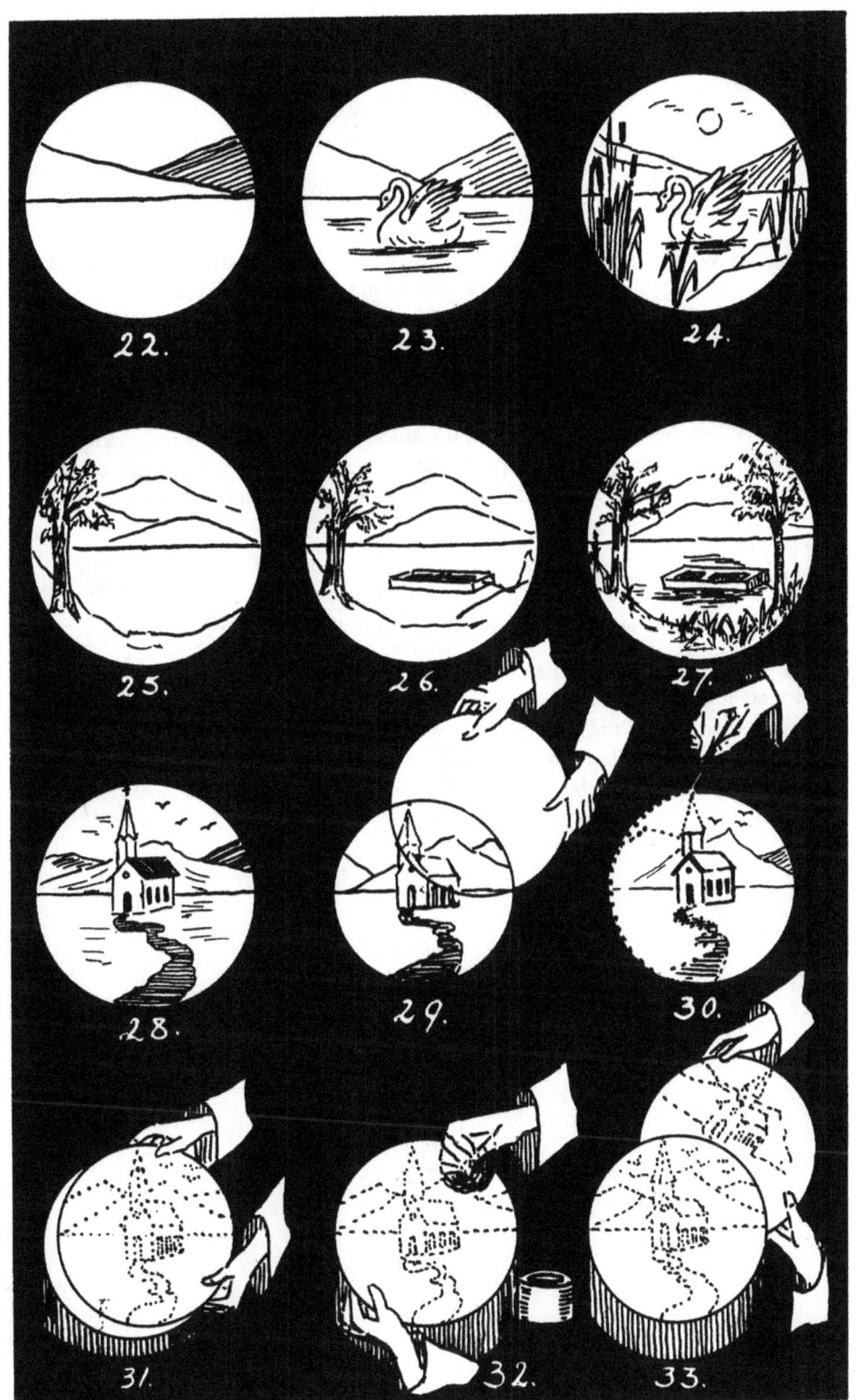

Bread Basket

Bread baskets are made for special occasions such as large banquets or buffets, window decorations or center displays.

The basket requires a frame of hard wood for the bottom. It should be about one inch thick, and either oblong, round, or square. Drill hole the size of meat picks, at a slight angle and of uneven number. The wooden picks for the holes can be obtained from a butcher. They are about five inches high, which can be the height of your basket. If a handle is desired, make it of sheet metal and no wider than one inch. Screw the metal handle to the wooden bottom. When the wooden pegs are in the holes, begin to weave the dough around the pegs until you reach the top. Finish with a thicker piece of dough on the last row. Brush it with egg yolks mixed with a little water, and then bake at 350 degrees.

How to make the Dough

Use either a heavy noodle dough, or the following:

Mix water and flour until it becomes a heavy dough. Work it hard for twenty minutes. Roll out in the thickness of lady fingers. Press onto a wooden peg so that it stays and then begin weaving. If it falls, remove and put in more flour and work again. No harm is done in doing this, for it must stand up, and this is not edible, but used for decoration only.

Tragacanth Gum Paste

2 egg whites
1 oz. of tragacanth
1½ cup of water
4 lbs. powdered sugar
1 lb. corn starch
Some bluing

This is the real tragacanth gum paste. Tragacanth is obtainable in any drug store. This method of preparation is quick, since the mixture is not boiled.

Soak the tragacanth in water in a large glass bowl. Cover overnight with a very wet towel. In the morning it will have swollen three times the original amount. Strain through a fine sieve on a marble table. Add two egg whites and just a very little blue coloring on the point of a knife. Place the powdered sugar, mixed with the corn starch all around the tragacanth and gradually work in by kneading. When all items are used up, and the sugar is nice and smooth, place in a stone crock with a damp cloth over it. After standing for 30 minutes, the sugar can be used as suggested above.

Tragacanth Gum Sugar

The recipe already prescribed is given here in picture form to insure freedom from mistakes.

No. 1. Shows material to be on hand, ready on the table, regardless of which reripe is followed.

No. 2. Shows a large bowl with one ounce of tragacanth allowed to dissolve overnight.

No. 3. The tragacanth is rubbed through a fine sieve on the next day.

No. 4. Powdered sugar and egg whites added in a ratio of three egg whites to five pounds of sugar are mixed. The bit of bluing is added.

No. 5. Mix together and work until it becomes a firm dough.

No. 6. Shows finished dough ready to be put into a jar for future use.

No. 7. Shows how to roll out sugar about 1/3 inch thick.

No. 8. Shows cardboard patterns placed on top of sugar to be cut with a sharp knife.

No. 9. The cut out pieces left to dry for two days, being turned every three hours.

No. 10. Paste together with heavy Royal Icing and dry overnight.

Gum Sugar

2½ oz. granulated gelatin
1 pt. cold water
2½ lbs. granulated sugar
1 cup glucose (or corn syrup)

2 cups cold water
10 lbs. powdered sugar
½ lb. corn starch

Dissolve gelatin in the pint of cold water in a clean bowl and let stand. Place 2½# sugar in cooking pot with glucose and 2 cups of water, and mix well. Cook slowly to 250°F. Remove and let mixture cool completely. When cold, add dissolved gelatin, and mix well. Keep stirring until it becomes a smooth dough. Place mixture on marble platter and work in sifted powdered sugar and corn starch. Work with hands until it is smooth. When it ceases to stick to marble, it is finished. Place this sugar in a stone jar and cover with a damp cloth on top of sugar and over jar. When not in use, place in ice box.

When using this dough, merely roll out required thickness and stamp out design. You also can model it by hand or cut with knives as the case may be. Houses like the Swiss chalet, require a blueprint. Or, cut needed pieces out of cardboard. Place these on sugar and follow design with knife. Place sugar on glass plate or wax paper to dry. Then make thick icing sugar and begin to build the house. Always begin at the bottom and allow to dry. Gum paste is used for making buildings, vases, statues, figures, animals, birds, cake designs, or any other subject in an economical way.

Cold Royal Icing

2 lbs. powdered sugar
8 egg whites

Juice of one-half lemon

Beat egg whites until half stiff. Then gradually add sugar. Keep beating until all sugar is gone. Add lemon juice, and keep beating until sugar is stiff enough to stand. Cover with a moist cloth over bowl to prevent hardening in open air.

Cooked Royal Icing

1 lb. granulated sugar
4 egg whites
Juice of 1/3 lemon
½ cup of water

Cook sugar and water to 270°. Beat egg whites with lemon juice in a separate bowl until stiff. Beat cooked hot sugar into the stiff egg whites, and keep beating until cold. Use a machine for this, although a small amount like this easily can be made by hand. Keep icing in a glass bowl or jar covered always with a damp cloth. Royal icing is used for decoration on cakes and baked goods as well as for sugar writing.

Pulled Sugar Work

This is the highest culinary art. It requires special training, a high degree of cleanliness, and proper tools.

All pots, pans, and tables must be spotlessly clean. The art requires a marble slab or table, a baker's scraper or spatula, a thermometer measuring to 400°F., and a small copper or stainless steel pot in which to cook the sugar.

Always use pure cane sugar. Dissolve sugar well before boiling it. Measure the sugar, water, and cream of tartar very exactly. You should also have an electric or gas sugar warmer to keep sugar warm while working with it. Often, the finished sugar is laid on a fine wire net close to the warmer, but a tray also will serve the purpose. For baskets, you will need a form made of wood or metal and sticks for weaving. Also have some coloring, which comes in glass jars, in paste form.

How to Cook Sugar

No. 1. Have all required tools, equipment, and material close at hand. This includes, water, sugar, cream of tartar, pot, wooden spoon, thermometer, coloring in paste form, scraper, brush, teaspoon, and towel. Have the marble table washed, dried, and slightly rubbed with oil. On the other table is the sugar warmer, Bunsen burner, and trays or wire netting. Do not attempt to make this sugar without the proper equipment.

No. 2. Add sugar to pot with water. Stir until completely dissolved.

No. 3. Stir sugar on stove until boiling. Remove any trace of dirt which accumulates on top of sugar with a spoon. Wash down the sides of the pot with a brush during the boiling.

No. 4. Cook 15 minutes and add cream of tartar already dissolved in little cold water. Insert the thermometer.

No. 5. Constantly wash down sides of pot with brush and cold water. Watch thermometer reading carefully. When it has reached the desired degree pour sugar as quickly as possible onto the marble table. This must be done quickly or sugar will rise in temperature and become worthless.

No. 6. Shows how to remove thermometer with one hand while pouring sugar on the table with the other.

No. 7. Shows how to fold sugar with scraper in order to allow all of sugar to cool evenly. The outside may harden while insides are still hot. So, repeat folding until all sugar is cooled. Add color paste by putting very little on the point of a knife.

No. 8. Shows how to pull sugar with hands as soon as it is cool enough to handle. Fold sugar over and over and keep pulling as far as you can stretch with your arms. It will then have a brilliant shine.

No. 9. After sugar is completely pulled, it is rolled up into a thick ball and placed on wire netting or on a tray in front of the warmer. The sugar is now ready to be used.

Recipe for Sugar Cooking

This will make a basket, a small ribbon, and a few flowers.

6 lbs. of granulated cane sugar
1 qt. of cold water
1 teaspoon, level, cream of tartar

How to Make Sugar Baskets

No. 1. Have wooden or metal form with required sticks in uneven number ready to use.

No. 2. Shows how it should look when sticks are inserted.

No. 3. The sugar, which has been on a wire netting before the warmer, is pulled out in rope-like length. The thickness of the little finger is about right. Fasten to one point and weave in and out of the posts until top is reached.

No. 4. Let cool for 15 minutes.

No. 5. Remove wooden or metal sticks and fasten hot sugar sticks on inside to hold weaving together.

No. 6. Remove whole basket from the form.

No. 7. Let basket become completely cold.

No. 8. Pull the same thickness of sugar and wind around until you have a bottom.

No. 9. Set basket on bottom and reinforce it with hot sugar so that it sticks well.

No. 10. Replace wooden sticks with sugar sticks and place them around. Pull sugar very thin so as to fill holes easily. Do not force any or basket will break.

No. 11. For the top of the basket, take two pieces of sugar the same length and twist together. Make this twist into a ring to fit the top of the basket.

No. 12. Put one on the top, and one on the bottom.

No. 13. For a basket with a cover, make a cover as you made the bottom.

No. 14. Two simple twisted handles are put on the basket. Hold ends over the Bunsen burner to heat enough to make them stick.

No. 15. A double basket with tops is shown here. For this you need a similar form, and they are made as outlined above.

No. 16. Make a variety of handles for your baskets with these methods. Take a wire with a green cotton covering of the type used by makers of artificial flowers. Never use plain wire as sugar will not stick. Raise sugar with one hand, and then pull wire through the sugar at mark below X. Keep raising sugar up every now and then.

No. 17. Shows how to pull a bent wire through the sugar. Give the wire the thickness desired for the handle by repeating the operation two or three times.

No. 18, 19, 20, 21, 22, 23. Show the various handles which can be selected. No. 22 shows a ribbon with two bows on each side.

No. 24. Show various basket forms which can be made.

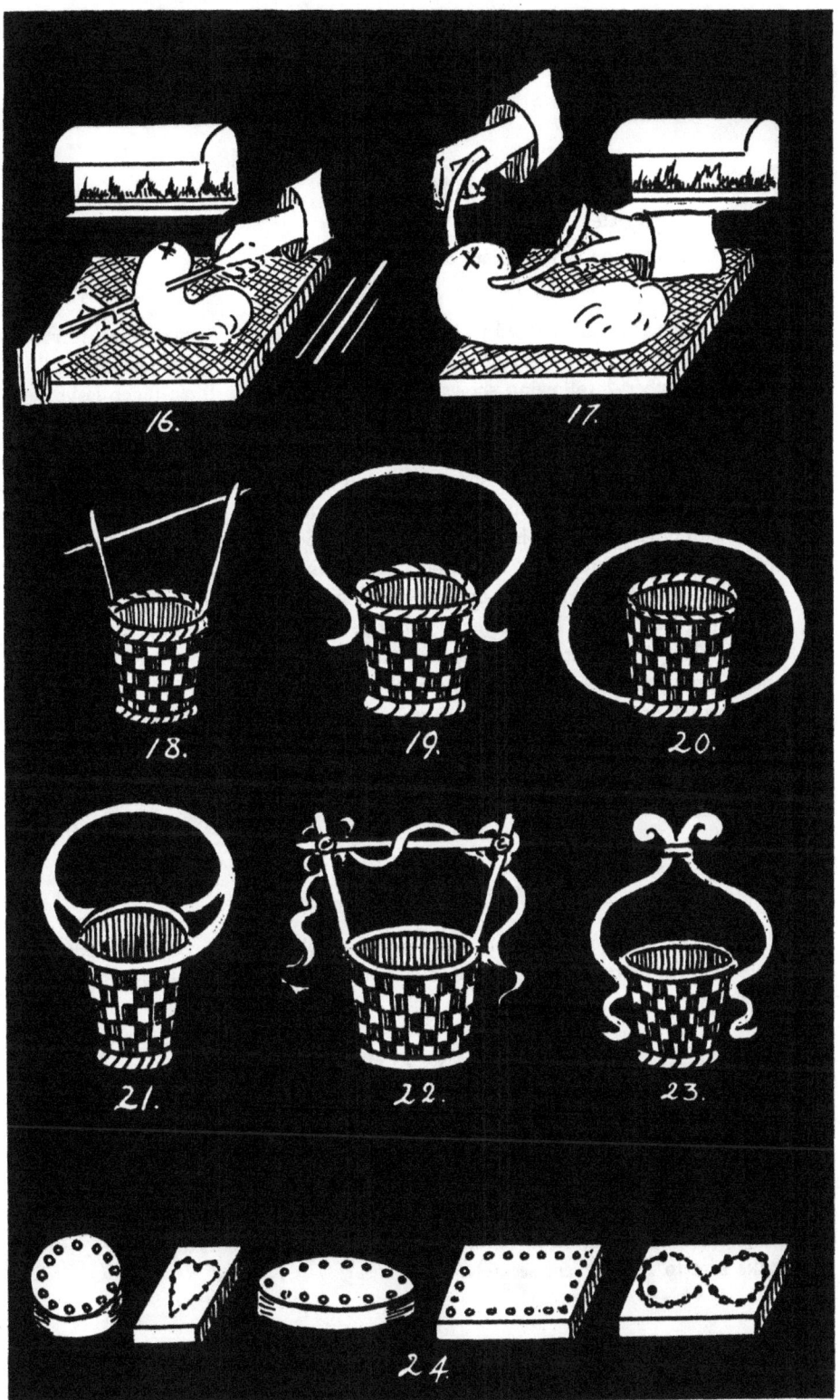

Sugar Roses

6 lbs. granulated cane sugar
1 qt. water
1 teaspoon, level, cream of tartar
cooked to 316°F.

The sugar is usually cooked to 316° in flower making. To make roses, form stem as shown in No. 1 following. It is made with a little sugar wound around a wire. Number 2 following shows just how to make the three inner leaves. Enough sugar is pulled from the ball to cover your thumb. Hollow this leaf by placing into your left palm. With the thumb of your right hand, hollow the sugar. Give it two or three turns and it will be hollow. Place on a tray away from the warmer. Now repeat the operation and make three larger leaves. Place with others until you have made 12 leaves. Set together by taking middle stem and placing three small leaves next to one another around the stem. The second leaves are always placed between the first. This is very important, so do not place leaves behind one another. Continue to place leaves until all are used. As you place them, heat each leaf on the flame of a Bunsen burner and they will stick to one another. Hold rose upside down while putting on leaves. This is much easier done in this way. Now make three small green leaves and stick them onto the rose bottom. They should be narrow and thin, and not over one inch long. The wire stem is placed into the rose by heating the wire and sticking it into the bottom of the rose and cutting at desired length.

Natural Flowers

You can make other flowers from sketches, photographs, or real models. This requires practice and patience, but, you can do it with determination.

Setting Up Flowers

When working with these, it is well not to wear cuffs or long sleeves. These can get in the way and destroy many hours of your work. Place left-over sugar into your basket. You can make it half or three-quarters full. Place flowers into this sugar which will hold them firmly. Start placing the flowers in the middle and work outwards. You can put flowers on the basket handles, but make sure to fasten them securely.

How to Make Sugar Roses

No. 1. Cook sugar for roses to 316°F.

    For baskets, 320°F.

    For ribbons, 318°F.

    For vases, 320°F.

The sugar is kept in front of the warmer, and it should be turned every time it gets too hot or every five minutes. Pull sufficient sugar to cover your thumb.

No. 2. Take this sugar in your left palm and with your right thumb, give it a hollow shape. Then lay it aside.

No. 3. Make three such small leaves with a center as shown here. Place them on a tray.

No. 4. Place leaves in order so that you can see at a glance how many you need to complete the rose. It will always be an uneven number, either 9, 13, or more.

No. 5. Shows how to set them together. Take the center, 3, and paste a small leaf on it by heating over the Bunsen burner. When hot, fasten to center.

No. 6. Do this with the second leaf, placing it next to the other.

No. 7. Continue with third small leaf, placing it next to the others. This gives you the center and three small leaves of the rose.

No. 8. Always hold rose upside down when adding leaves.

No. 9. When adding leaves, always place between other leaves, never on top or behind each other.

No. 10. Shows how to place leaves between others.

No. 11. Shows how to hold rose.

No. 12. The finished rose now gets three thin and narrow leaves which should be green.

No. 13. Bottom stem of wire and green sugar is now attached.

No. 14. Finished rose.

How to Make Sugar Ribbons

No. 1. Take three strips of sugar equal in size and length though they may be of different colors. Pull them the length of your arm, fold next to one another, and cut the folded side. Repeat this operation as many times as necessary until you have desired thinness of ribbon. Place them over a table edge as in No. 5.

No. 2. Cut ribbon with hot scissors or hot knife as shown in No. 3.

No. 4. Make bows by cutting ribbon in lengths of three to four inches. Bend together and assemble as a bow.

No. 5. Shows how ribbon should be kept until needed.

No. 6. A basket with a ribbon wound on handle.

How to Blow Sugar

No. 1. Take a ball of sugar the size of your fist. Round it well and begin to press into the ball, a round wooden object like a darning egg. Keep pressing this into the sugar, and at the same time, pull the sides of the sugar.

No. 2. Shows just how to press the wooden object down and how to pull sugar until it is about six inches long.

No. 3. Almost completed for blowing.

No. 4. Remove object.

No. 5. Begin to blow like this. Do not blow too hard or vase will burst.

No. 6. This is about the size the vase should be. If you want a long neck, just stretch the top.

No. 7. When the vase is completely blown, you must keep on blowing with a fan to cool the sugar. The sugar must be cold or vase will fall.

Nos. 8, 9, 10, 11. Shows the various vase designs. Decorate with flowers or paintings to your liking.

How to make Vases

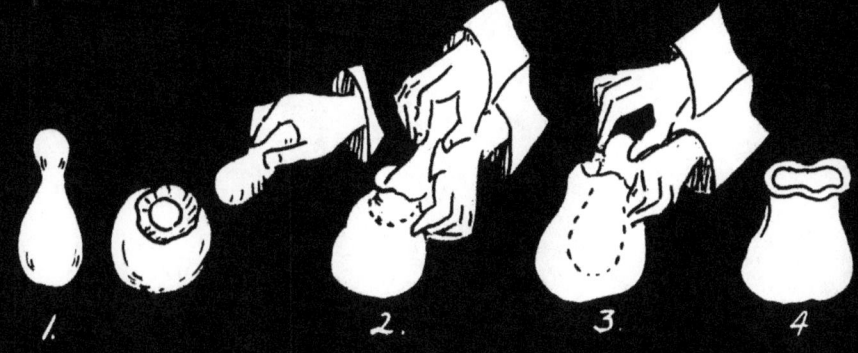

Blowing of Sugar

Wax and Tallow Work

This is an art in itself. The techniques used in sugar work and papier mache is also used in wax and tallow work. Wax is preferred over tallow as it is odorless. Also, it can be melted over and over and used for many years. Tallow, however, is less expensive and may be a product of the kitchen and no extra expense at all. Wax and tallow are used primarily for buffet tables, food shows, and important banquets. Wax work offers unlimited subjects and is adaptable to almost any occasion.

Wax Work

Wax work involves a lot of work and patience, and most of the time you are not compensated for it. However, if you like artistic work and are interested in it, you enjoy doing it, and, of course, it is appreciated by the public.

I have three classifications in my wax work; Flower wax, Molding wax, and Modeling wax.

The difference in these is the flexibility required in various jobs. Flower wax is the most flexible. Modeling wax is somewhat stiffer, and the molding wax is quite stiff. If trouble occurs in the form of breaking wax, it is too hard. Add more beeswax. If the wax is too soft, add more stearin.

Beeswax is found in two forms. The virgin wax is unrefined and a dark brown. The other is clarified beeswax which is white in color. Paraffin is a base, and stearin fills in as a base and stiffener. They are used in this recipe for an all-purpose wax:

¼ Stearin   ¼ Brown beeswax
¼ Paraffin   ¼ White beeswax.

Put this mixture in a stone crock and put in hot boiling water to slowly melt them. When melted, put on a marble plate to cool. Let cool enough to handle, knead it like dough, and it is ready for anything you wish to make. If it becomes too hard on your table, add a little turpentine in cream form and work the wax.

Here are recipes for various purposes:

Flower wax: ¼ Stearin, ¼ Paraffin, ½ Brown beeswax.
Molding wax: ¼ White beeswax, ¼ Paraffin, ½ Stearin.
Modeling wax: ¼ White beeswax, ¼ Paraffin, ¼ Stearin, ¼ Brown beeswax as with all-purpose wax.

Modeling Wax Flowers and Baskets

No. 1. Use preparation of wax described as flower wax. Melt wax, but prevent from letting it become too hot. Pour wax on metal or marble table.

No. 2. Let wax stand until almost cool, then knead by hand until it is smooth as bread dough.

No. 3. It can be rolled or pulled in any way until it becomes hard.

No. 4. Shows a heater used for sugar work. It also can be used for wax work and keeps the wax at a proper temperature for a longer time. The wax is put into trays to keep warm, ready for easy handling.

No. 5. Roll out some wax to use for basket weaving. Make bottom first, winding wax in spiral form.

No. 6. Shows how to weave a basket with wax. Make basket frame of wood or metal. Wood or metal sticks are placed in holes in the bottom. The holes are one inch apart, and there are an uneven number. Keep wax near flame when weaving. When finished, remove sticks and metal bottom and replace with wax.

No. 7. The sticks and the bottom are removed from the basket. The woven basket is placed on the wax bottom. Fasten it by adding liquid wax. The sticks are replaced with wax sticks to complete the basket.

No. 8. Shows how to make rose petals. Place a nut-sized piece of wax in the left palm. Press with the right thumb to form a leaf. In making a rose, make the center first, shown here by 1. This is a bit of wax with a point. Then make three small rose leaves in the shape of hearts as shown here by 2. Place these next to each other to learn how many leaves are needed. 3 indicates the large rose leaves which must be of an uneven number. You can make 13 to 15 leaves effectively.

No. 9. Put rose petals together. Notice that the inner part is held upside down as it is heated. Quickly place on center stem. The three small leaves are taken first as shown beginning with No. 10.

No. 10. Shows how first small leaf should look when held in upright position.

No. 11. Add the next leaf, but never overlap or place on top of the previous leaf. Place them alongside of the other.

No. 12. The three small leaves attached to the center stem.

No. 13. Place leaves in between each open space on the rose. The bottom should be round as indicated here.

No. 14. This shows an incorrectly-made rose with a pointed bottom. It should be cut off before attaching more leaves.

No. 15. The finished rose placed on a wire stem.

No. 16. The finished rose and leaves of green wax are attached to green wire and placed on a wax basket. The basket has two wax handles. The basket can be used over and over, as only a very hot climate will affect it. You can make it any color you wish. Merely color the wax with oil coloring when working it on a marble table.

Wax Basket

Here is an especially effective wax basket, with a spliced handle. The handle has wire inside the wax. Merely put the wire into hot wax and then into cold water. Repeat the operation until you have the proper thickness. The handle is decorated with roses, leaves, grape clusters, grapevines, and a butterfly. It can be painted and shellacked.

Classic Wax Art Piece

This piece was made of white wax and was designed as a centerpiece. There is a border made out of braided wax. Below, we see a dog and a wild boar. There are birds on top, together with various animals. The display is made in three sections. On the very top is a tree trunk with a mountain lion looking down. There are rabbits, partridges, and pheasants among the lower figures. This piece won first prize at the 1940 National Food Exposition in Chicago.

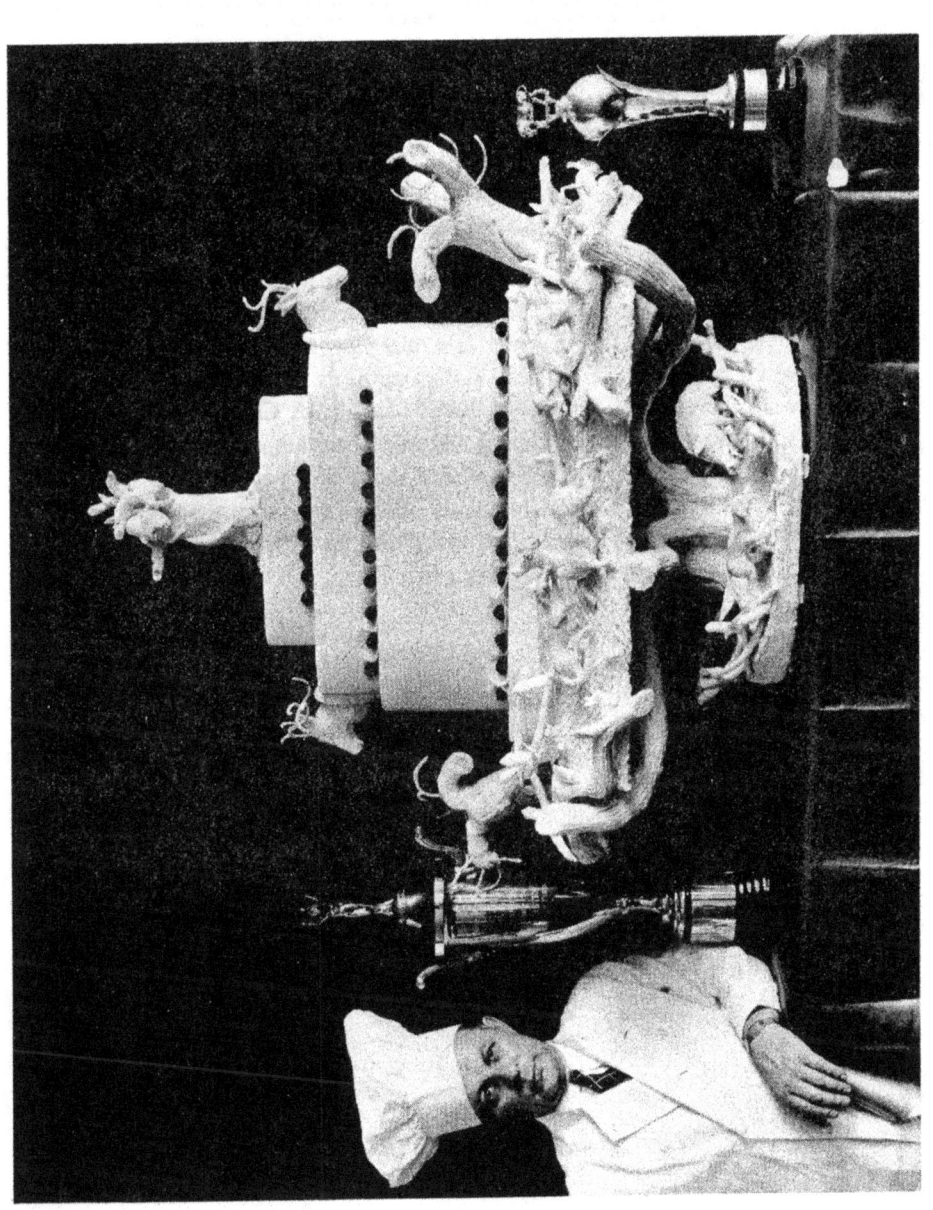

Classic Sculpture Work

This classic piece represents the Gods of Food from one end of the world to the other. It is 15½ feet high and weighs 1½ tons. Made out of wax, it took 363 days to complete. It earned for the author a grand prize in 1941 at the National Food Cookery and Allied Trades Exposition and Salon of Culinary Art at the Stevens Hotel in Chicago.

I will attempt a description of it. At the top is a suckling pig with three silver spears with limes. There are symbols of Gods at each side. Below are two Chinese pheasants. In the center is a mirror with a heavy vine all around it. There are grapes at the top, fish and game birds on the sides. Below is a vase of wild flowers, and opposite, a basket of fruit. A Chinese pagoda stands on one side, and on the other side is a church. There are apples, oranges, peas, and wheat shown. On top of the bowl is a statue of a boy carrying a child on his back while a goose bites at his pants. Below are carrots, potatoes, green onions, celery, artichokes, a deer head, and a wild boar. Lobster and frogs, turtles and fish, are caught in the fishing net.

Plaster of Paris

It is very important that you should be able to make a plaster of Paris mold. There often are requests for certain designs which we are not able to find in a book and, therefore, must make with a mold. Few persons have the knowledge required to make molds, and I do not think that there are many books on this subject. However, I shall try to present some advice on this art.

Many persons in the hotel and restaurant fields think that art in cooking does not pay—but they are mistaken. I have found that attractive show windows, attractive table decorations and attractive ways of presenting food has brought bigger and better business to the dining room. I have often been asked to go a thousand miles to do some special art work in the culinary field, so the American people are ready and anxious to see these things, and want to learn it.

Remember it is the competition which says art does not pay. Yet the very same people often call you the next day. Art always pays whether it is in music, clothes or food.

Making Half-Plaster Mold

No. 1. It is essential to have all items ready when making molds. Here is a table fully prepared, ready to make a mold. The plaster may be dental plaster or a quick-drying plaster. Also have a bowl of water, artist's clay, a can of melted lard, the design to be made, a roller, wax paper, a spoon, and a brush with which to brush on the lard.

No. 2. Work the clay, kneading it by hand until it is soft. Roll it into a strip 1½ inches high and ½ inch thick.

No. 3. Place wax paper on the table. Stand the clay strip on the paper and press both ends of the strip together. Reinforce the clay strip on the outside to prevent plaster from running out. Lay the design in the middle of this strip, leaving ½ inch space on all sides. Now brush the design, the wax paper, and the clay strip with oil or melted lard.

No. 4. The mold is now ready to be filled with plaster of Paris. When making the plaster, add plaster powder to the water and never the reverse. Use as much water as you expect the mold can hold. Select a round-bottomed bowl, fill with the cold water needed, and sift the powder into the water until the water will not absorb any more. At this stage stir with a spoon. Add powder until the mixture becomes heavy. Pour it at once over the design, filling the mold to the top.

No. 5. Let the mold set until it is hot, which will take about fifteen minutes. If mold is hard, remove the clay band. Then remove design from the plaster mold.

No. 6. Keep molds dry for a day or so, and shellac them with white shellac. Let this dry for a day. This mold can be used for marzipan, gum paste, and wax work. For gum paste or marzipan work, brush the inside with corn starch. For wax work, the mold must be oiled.

No. 7. This shows a finished cake with a marzipan design on top, made from this mold in a few seconds.

How to Make a Clay Design

Clay designs are usually made by more experienced artists. Occasionally, we get an order to make a design which is not obtainable from a book, and then we must use our own creative ideas. First draw the idea on paper. Gradually mold the clay by hand and form the desired mold. This type of work requires extreme exactness, and is, therefore, a slow procedure. It takes many weeks to make some designs, so we use ready-made models whenever possible. In this case we are making our own model out of clay, and when the clay is properly molded it should look like No. 1. I will explain the necessary steps required.

No. 1. This is a picture we intend to form out of clay.

No. 2. Take seven or eight pounds of Artist Clay and work it with your hands until it becomes soft and flexible. Then shape it into a log as exact as possible. It should be like the picture in every respect. Plaster molds can only be made out of perfect clay models. This takes many days, but when perfection is reached the model is ready for casting.

No. 3. The finished clay design is now greased with warm lard, which is applied with a fine brush.

No. 4. Shows the clay band rolled out to proper size for the height of the log. This band is reinforced on the outside with additional clay so that the plaster of Paris cannot run out.

No. 5. Pour the liquid plaster into the mold, usually about half full.

No. 6. Let plaster set until it shows signs of thickening.

No. 7. Watch the plaster carefully so that it will not get too hard, and then place the log half way into the plaster.

No. 8. Let the clay log remain in the plaster until the plaster is hard, usually in about twenty five minutes. Then remove the clay band.

No. 9. With the aid of a chisel, smooth the plaster. At each corner, make a hole with a table knife, round on the bottom and about $\frac{1}{2}$ inch deep.

No. 10. Now make the second half of the plaster mold, to fit the top of the design. Merely repeat the same operation for this. Place clay band around the mold, brush the clay and the plaster mold with lard or oil.

No. 11. This form is ready to be filled with plaster to the top of the band.

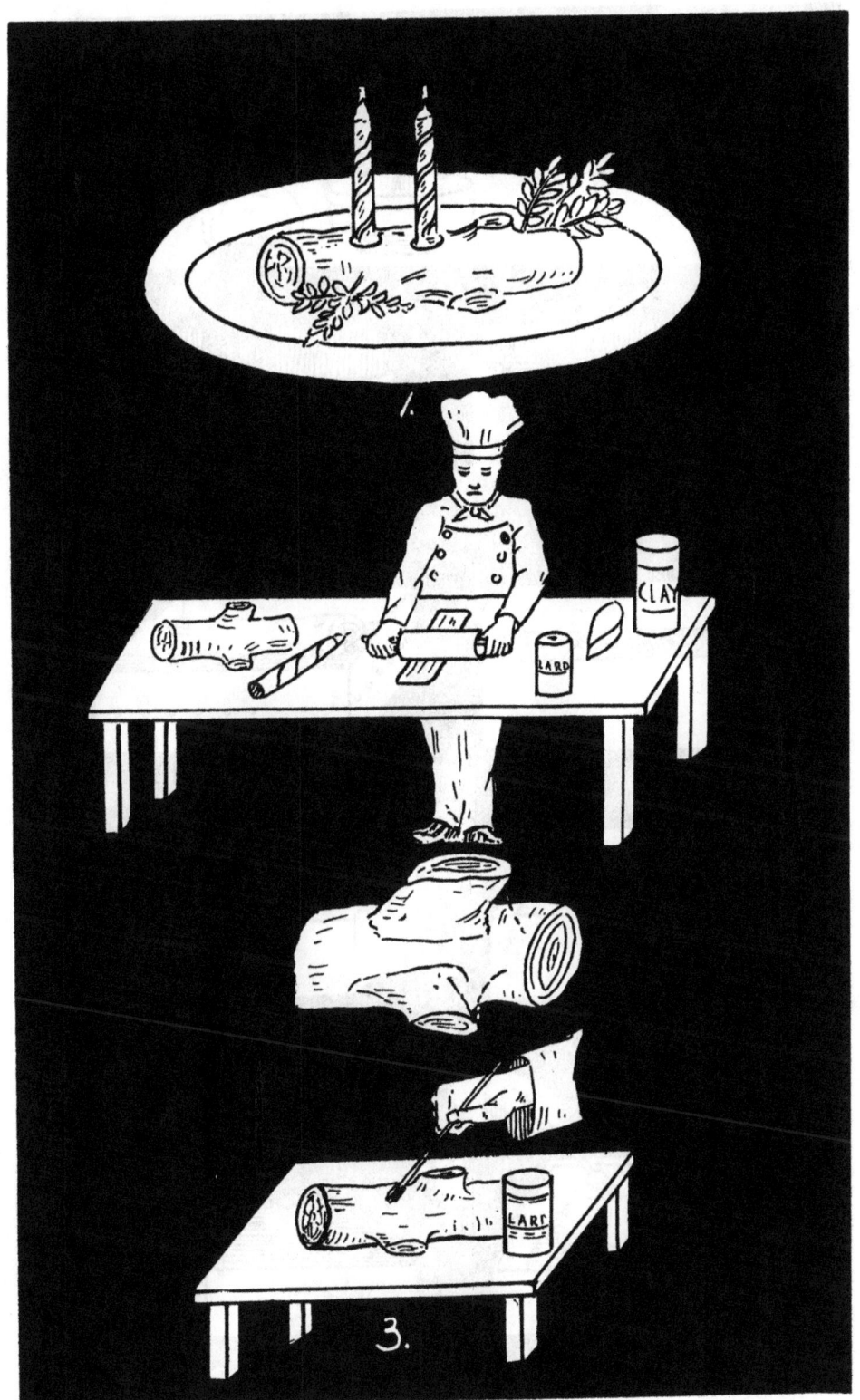

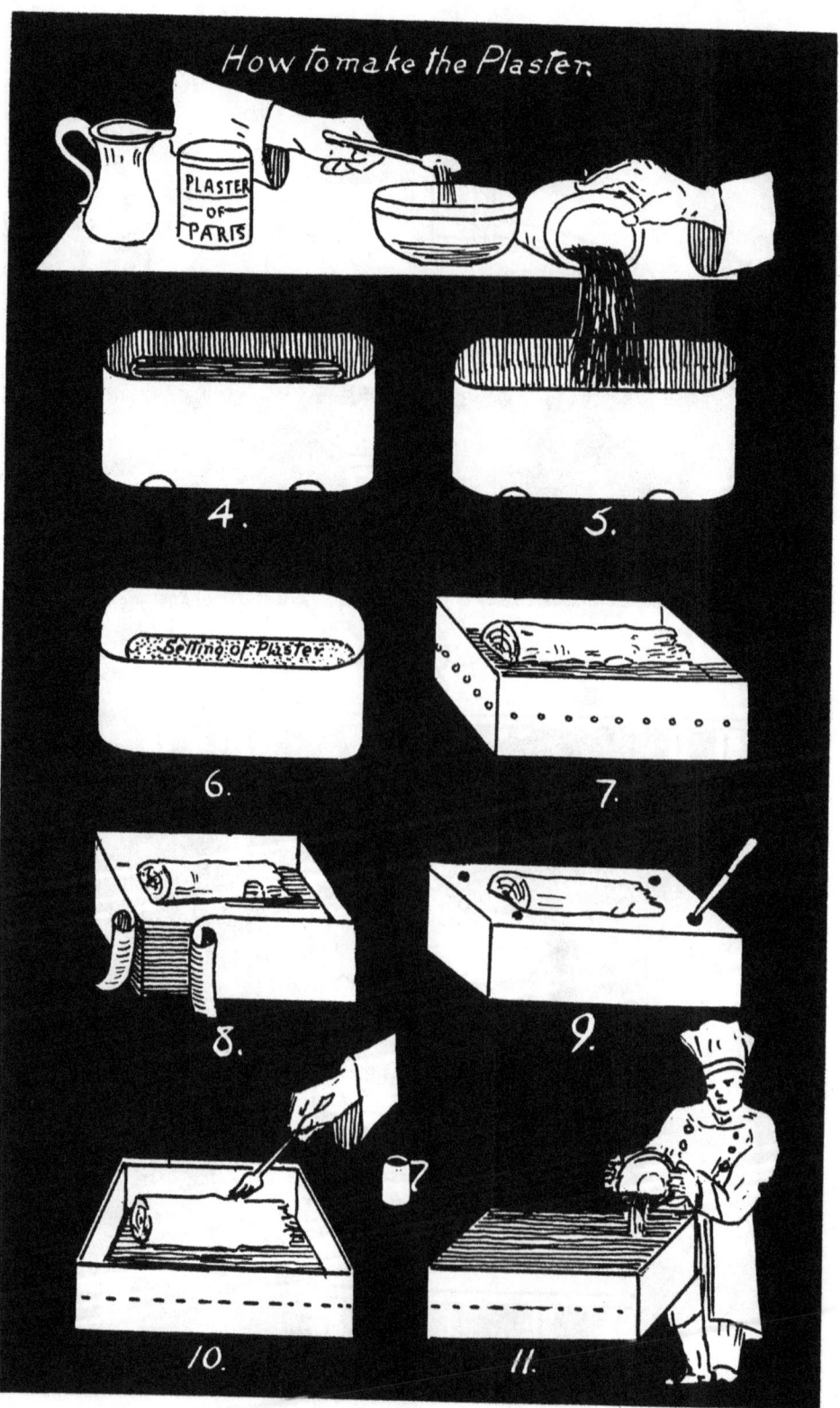

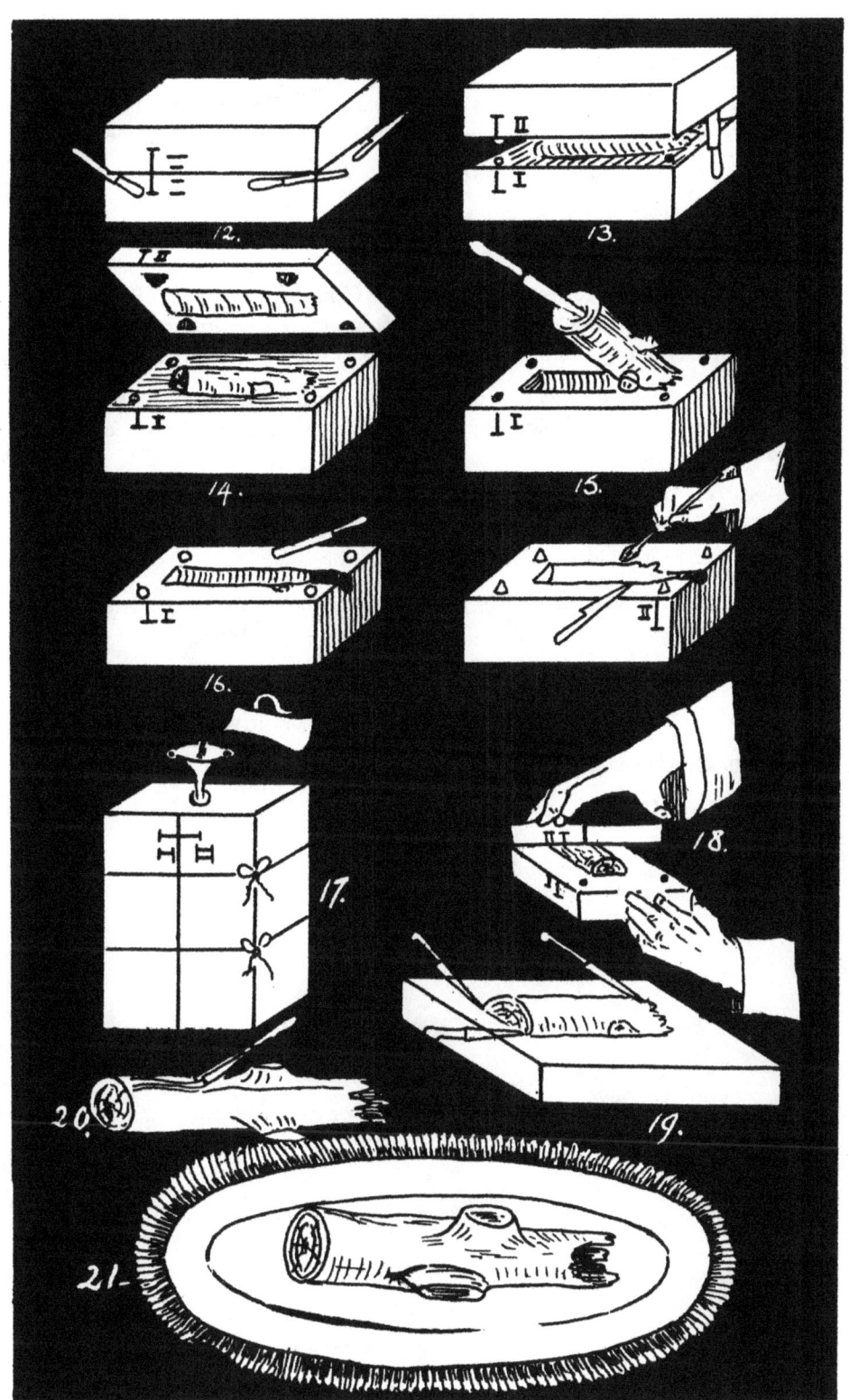

No. 12. After the clay band is removed, and the plaster becomes hard, separate the upper mold from the lower with a knife inserted in each corner.

No. 13. Shows how the molds separate.

No. 14. The clay model will be in the top or bottom.

No. 15. Shows how clay log is removed, using a knife to lift it out. This now has given us the correct model in plaster from that clay model. From now on the clay becomes obsolete and we work now with these plaster molds, which will be filled with wax to obtain the exact model from the former clay model.

No. 16. Shows the two half plaster molds. Drill a hole on top so that wax can be poured into the mold. Dry for a day in a warm oven, shellac, and dry again.

No. 17. Fit mold together and tie with string. Set upright. Insert funnel in the hole and pour luke warm wax into it until it is filled. The wax will cool and shrink, so it is necessary to refill once or twice.

No. 18. The wax remains in the mold until cool, then the molds may be separated.

No. 19. If wax is hard to remove, use a knife.

No. 20. Fine details are carved into the log. Paint it white or brown.

No. 21. The finished wax log. Make holes for candles if you wish.

How to Make a Candle Mold

If you wish, you can make your own clay design, and a plaster mold from it. We shall make a candle, and we begin by rolling the clay out onto the table until the correct perspective is obtained.

No. 1. Clay is rolled out in a band the length of candle. The ends are closed and the bottom reinforced. Plaster is poured in and the band half filled.

No. 2. When plaster is partially set, place the candle into the plaster and press down at both ends. Let plaster harden completely which will take about 15 minutes.

No. 3. When plaster is hard, remove the clay band. Use a chisel to make lines in the candle.

No. 4. With the aid of a chisel, make the locks on the sides of the mold. These can be made round or oblong. Smooth the top of the mold with a chisel, and, when clean, brush well all over with oil or lard.

No. 5. Put the clay band around the mold again, and this time raise it so it will be one inch higher than the candle's highest part. Grease half-mold well and fill to the top with plaster of paris. I often place wax paper in the first mold, greasing it well on both sides, and then pour the plaster over it.

No. 6. Let mold stand until it gets hot. This means the plaster is hardening.

No. 7. Remove clayband and clean mold with a chisel.

No. 8. To separate the molds, use a table knife. Insert it at one end very carefully. Make a hole at one end with a round chisel, to use in pouring wax into the mold later.

No. 9. Remove the candle, and clean the mold of undesirable plaster.

No. 10. This finished mold, made from a clay design, follows principles used in making all designs. This shows how the inside looks. Notice that locks must fit perfectly. This is now ready to be filled with wax.

No. 11. Grease mold well, put together, and tie with string. Place a small funnel in the hole and pour in wax. Wax should only be warm, not hot.

No. 12. Put string into the wax to form the wick.

No. 13. Now separate molds and remove the candle.

No. 14. Shows the finished wax candle. It can be shaved to fit any candle stick or holder.

No. 15. The candles are placed in a birch log, also made of wax.

No. 16. You can paint the log and the candle.

No. 17. The finished centerpiece out of wax as it was seen in the start out of clay.

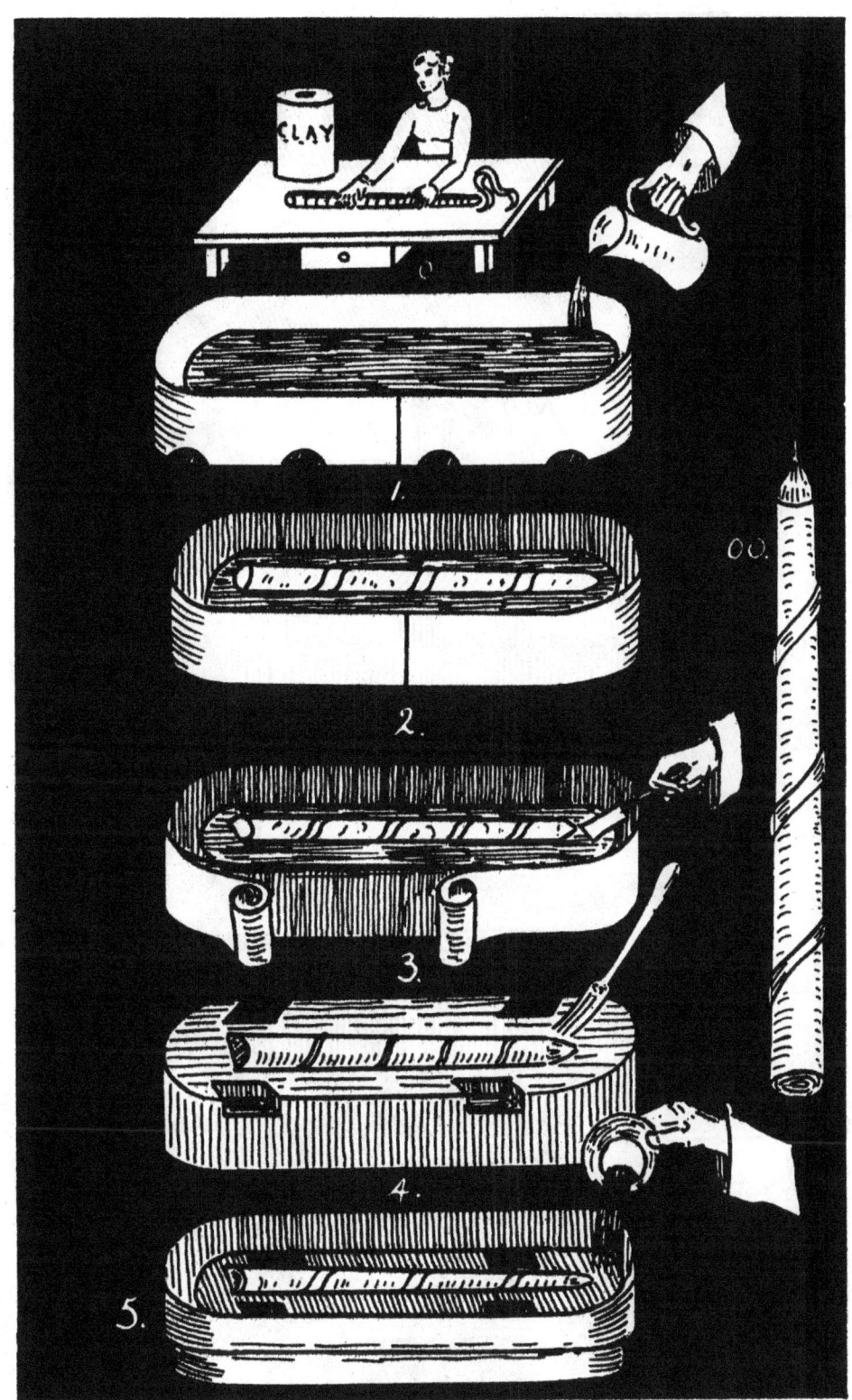

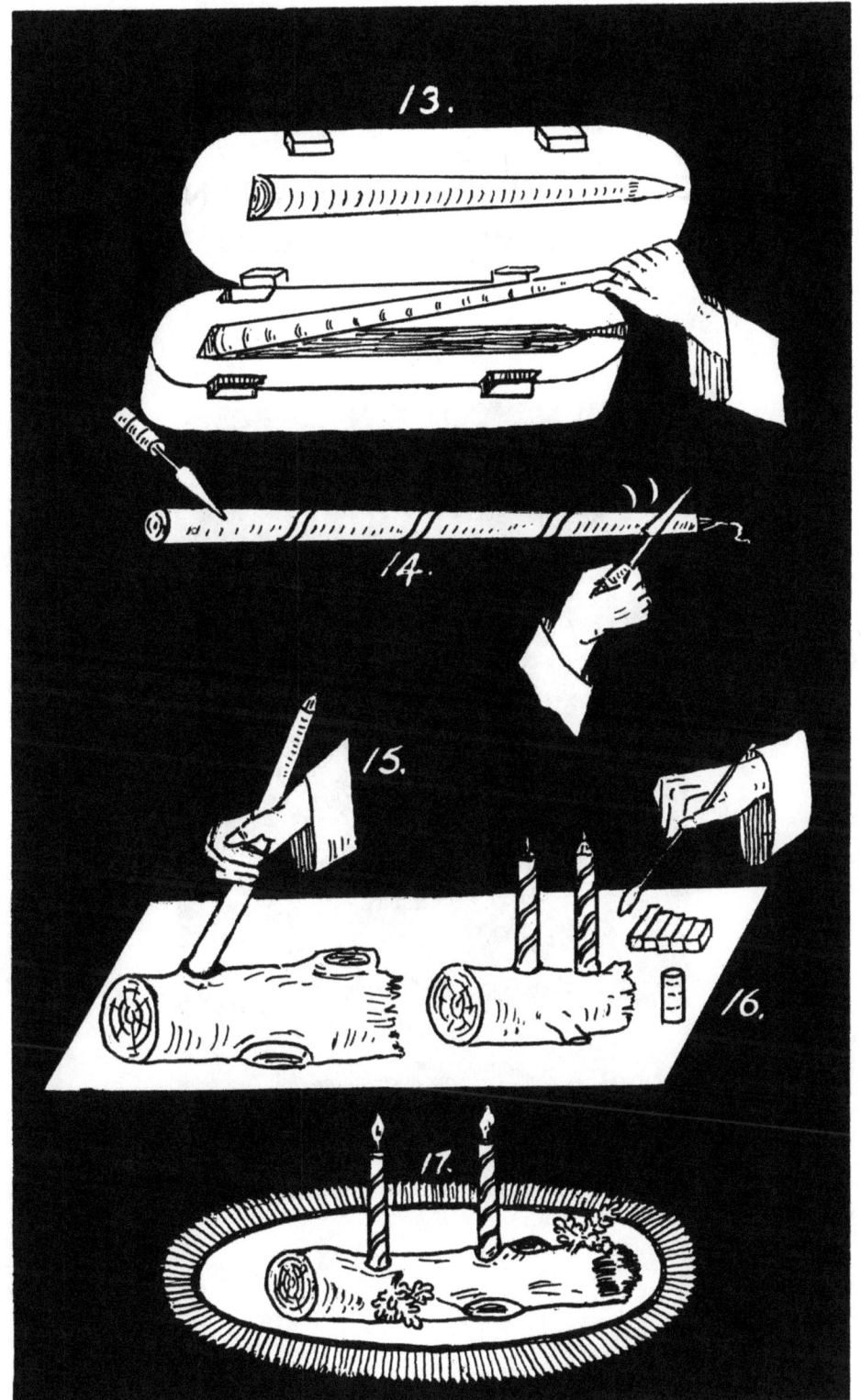

COACHWHIP PUBLICATIONS
CoachwhipBooks.com

COACHWHIP PUBLICATIONS
CoachwhipBooks.com

COACHWHIP PUBLICATIONS
CoachwhipBooks.com

How to Cook Sugar

No. 1. Have all required tools, equipment, and material close at hand. This includes, water, sugar, cream of tartar, pot, wooden spoon, thermometer, coloring in paste form, scraper, brush, teaspoon, and towel. Have the marble table washed, dried, and slightly rubbed with oil. On the other table is the sugar warmer, Bunsen burner, and trays or wire netting. Do not attempt to make this sugar without the proper equipment.

No. 2. Add sugar to pot with water. Stir until completely dissolved.

No. 3. Stir sugar on stove until boiling. Remove any trace of dirt which accumulates on top of sugar with a spoon. Wash down the sides of the pot with a brush during the boiling.

No. 4. Cook 15 minutes and add cream of tartar already dissolved in little cold water. Insert the thermometer.

No. 5. Constantly wash down sides of pot with brush and cold water. Watch thermometer reading carefully. When it has reached the desired degree pour sugar as quickly as possible onto the marble table. This must be done quickly or sugar will rise in temperature and become worthless.

No. 6. Shows how to remove thermometer with one hand while pouring sugar on the table with the other.

No. 7. Shows how to fold sugar with scraper in order to allow all of sugar to cool evenly. The outside may harden while insides are still hot. So, repeat folding until all sugar is cooled. Add color paste by putting very little on the point of a knife.

No. 8. Shows how to pull sugar with hands as soon as it is cool enough to handle. Fold sugar over and over and keep pulling as far as you can stretch with your arms. It will then have a brilliant shine.

No. 9. After sugar is completely pulled, it is rolled up into a thick ball and placed on wire netting or on a tray in front of the warmer. The sugar is now ready to be used.

Recipe for Sugar Cooking

This will make a basket, a small ribbon, and a few flowers.

  6 lbs. of granulated cane sugar
  1 qt. of cold water
  1 teaspoon, level, cream of tartar

Cooked Royal Icing

1 lb. granulated sugar
4 egg whites
Juice of 1/3 lemon
½ cup of water

Cook sugar and water to 270°. Beat egg whites with lemon juice in a separate bowl until stiff. Beat cooked hot sugar into the stiff egg whites, and keep beating until cold. Use a machine for this, although a small amount like this easily can be made by hand. Keep icing in a glass bowl or jar covered always with a damp cloth. Royal icing is used for decoration on cakes and baked goods as well as for sugar writing.

Pulled Sugar Work

This is the highest culinary art. It requires special training, a high degree of cleanliness, and proper tools.

All pots, pans, and tables must be spotlessly clean. The art requires a marble slab or table, a baker's scraper or spatula, a thermometer measuring to 400°F., and a small copper or stainless steel pot in which to cook the sugar.

Always use pure cane sugar. Dissolve sugar well before boiling it. Measure the sugar, water, and cream of tartar very exactly. You should also have an electric or gas sugar warmer to keep sugar warm while working with it. Often, the finished sugar is laid on a fine wire net close to the warmer, but a tray also will serve the purpose. For baskets, you will need a form made of wood or metal and sticks for weaving. Also have some coloring, which comes in glass jars, in paste form.

COACHWHIP PUBLICATIONS
CoachwhipBooks.com

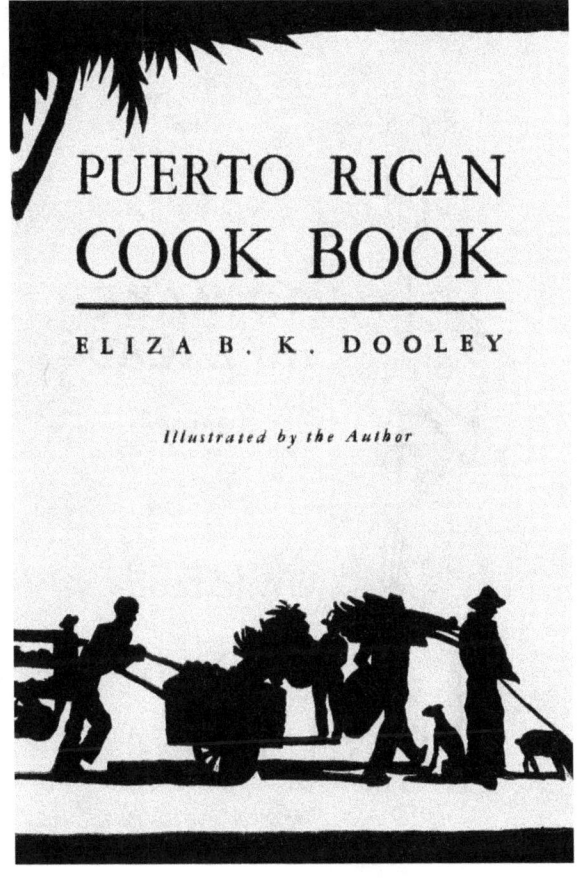

PUERTO RICAN COOK BOOK

ELIZA B. K. DOOLEY

Illustrated by the Author

COACHWHIP PUBLICATIONS
CoachwhipBooks.com

COACHWHIP PUBLICATIONS
CoachwhipBooks.com

COACHWHIP PUBLICATIONS
CoachwhipBooks.com

COACHWHIP PUBLICATIONS
CoachwhipBooks.com

www.ingramcontent.com/pod-product-compliance
Lightning Source LLC
Chambersburg PA
CBHW081920180426
43200CB00032B/2865